CW00524848

THE LEGEND

GRIZZ

THE LEGEND
by PHIL GIFFORD

rugby press limited
Auckland

The author and publishers wish to thank all those photographers and organisations who have contributed to this book, in particular Peter Bush, of Wellington, and the Christchurch Star which so willingly made its extensive photographic files available.

© 1991 Margin Release Ltd.
First published in 1991 by Rugby Press Ltd
67-73 View Road, Glenfield, Auckland 10, New Zealand.

Layout/design by Sportz Graphics Ltd, Glenfield, Auckland.
Typeset by Sportz Graphics Ltd.
Cover art by Grant Hanna, Auckland.
Printed by GP Print Ltd, Wellington.

Rugby Press Ltd is a member of the Medialine Group
of companies. P.O. Box 100-243, North Shore Mail Centre,
Auckland 10, New Zealand.

ISBN 0-908630-36-0

All rights reserved. No part of the publication may
be reproduced or transmitted in any form or by any
means electronic or mechanical, including photocopy,
recording or any information storage retrieval system,
without permission in writing from the publisher.

Contents

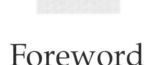

Foreword

You'll sometimes hear people talk about the sacrifices made for their sport.

With rugby, I've been lucky. I've enjoyed it, and still do, and I've been rewarded with the game giving me at least as much as I've put into it. My thanks to a great game, and to everyone, players, officials, and followers, associated with it.

I'd like to thank the people who have made the sacrifices so I could be involved in the game. My parents, and my sisters, so often covered for me on the farm when I was away with rugby. I was helped too, by people in the Omihi district, and by the Glenmark club.

With Canterbury, and now with the All Blacks, there have been letters, phone calls, and messages of support that have certainly been appreciated. Travelling in New Zealand, the feeling of support has always been strong. If there's been resentment about selections, or anything else, people have never made it apparent.

To my family, Keryn and our children, thank you for your support at times when we didn't have a summer holiday together, because farmwork left over from winter had to be made up. My thanks goes beyond words.

Alex Wyllie
September, 1991

1

Behind the Grizzmask

Nobody in New Zealand is lukewarm about Alex Wyllie.
He is either the epitome of everything that's good and
robust in the game, a living, breathing example of the tough pioneer
spirit, or one of the dark forces, a man preoccupied with rugby as
it was played in the past, when the fist ruled the forwards, and the
boot of the first-five ruled the rest.

But there's more to the feelings about Wyllie than his approach
to rugby. Just as the great motor racing driver, Stirling Moss, says
he would be forgotten today if his parents had named him William,
so Wyllie might not be such an icon of the game if he was a slightly
built former centre.

As several of his former teammates comment, Wyllie looked
tough when he began as a player, and that hasn't really changed.

People overstate the size of men they admire, but it is a fact that
Wyllie is a very strongly built man. Well, massive actually. At one
stage during the research for his book I wanted to talk to Wyllie after
he'd finished harvesting a field of oats at the North Canterbury farm
his son now runs. It was a hot South Island summer's day, with heat
haze above the tarsealed road at the front gate. Wyllie was working
in a pair of football shorts, and when he jumped down from the
harvester, it was easy to see why he was such a nightmare for
opponents to tackle. In his youth they didn't do gymnasium work,
and if they'd heard of steroids they probably thought they were
something you dosed sheep with. The extraordinary size of the
shoulders, arms, and torso, was built on nothing more exotic than
plenty of farm-killed lamb, and was fine tuned picking up bags of
grain.

With the size goes a boyish liking for physical contact. His All
Black manager, John Sturgeon, says that the pair often spar with
open hands, slapping each other in a game you'll see on a thousand
school playgrounds. "I did a bit of boxing in my youth," says the

Christchurch Star

Alex Wyllie...an icon of the game in New Zealand.

tall, lean Sturgeon, "and that helps when you spend a lot of time with Alex."

People have to be prepared to be a little bruised once they get to know Wyllie. In 1990, I was sitting in the back row of the media section in the No 3 stand at Lancaster Park. A hand suddenly smacked into the back of my head. The effect was very similar to a softball batter taking a swing while he warmed up. I hardly needed to hear the guffaw from behind me to know that Wyllie was making it known he was there.

Lyn Davis, a wiry little halfback who played nearly 200 games, snapping at Wyllie's heels for Canterbury, reckons you should be flattered at being hit by Wyllie. "Alex isn't a bully, he only thumps people he gets on with."

It would be wrong though, for the people who rubbish him, (many of whom do so without the benefit of an actual meeting), to consider that because Wyllie is so robust, he's a brash, boastful, person. Quite the reverse.

He comes from a background in which to talk about yourself, to brag, is almost the ultimate sin. We'll get to what the ultimate sin actually is later.

Wyllie grew up in a farming community, a real community, where the links were forged before good roads and cheaper cars made slipping into the city for a night out as easy as turning on a television set.

In the Omihi Valley entertainment had to be homemade. The young, and the not so young, men played rugby, and worked together at hay-making time. For a dance at the local hall nobody hired a band. One of the farmers played the violin, one of the farmers' wives played the piano. Sprinkle some talcum powder on the floor, and they danced all night.

They played their rugby as hard as they could, but if anyone had put on airs because they'd had a good game, or scored a try, they wouldn't have done it for long. This was, and, to a degree, remains, a place where, as John Clarke, in his days as Fred Dagg, observed: "Nobody wins a race, the other joker just happens to finish behind him."

The young Alex Wyllie didn't need lectures on what loyalty to your team meant in rugby. He saw examples of it every weekend in winter. Players well past their prime turning out to make up the numbers. As former All Black fullback Robbie Deans says, of his efforts to retire from club play, perhaps next year: "It's very hard to turn down a request to help out your club in the country."

As a small, boy Alex watched his father, Joe, coaching the local Glenmark team, not, as several of Joe's players recall, with any sophisticated methods, but with a belief, that continues to this day, that team spirit is the key to winning rugby matches. You can see that attitude in so much of what Wyllie did as a Canterbury coach, and continues to work at with the All Blacks.

With the Canterbury side in 1982-86 he may have drilled the team mercilessly, but he also nurtured the party side of the group. That was the way in the country. Wyllie's wife, Keryn, recalls how, with the Glenmark team on rugby Saturdays, there was a pattern of watching husbands play rugby, arranging a communal babysitter, then, after the men had been to the pub, joining them for a party at someone's home. "With hindsight it was pretty chauvinistic, but that was just how it was then," says Keryn.

Shared hardships draw a group together, and the release after those hard times is all the more intense for the wait. Sundays at Lancaster Park with the Canterbury team leaned to the boys' day out, and there were often very big days, with some wild moments. Once, a heavily intoxicated player even followed Wyllie into the toilet, intent on fostering an argument, and ended on his rear. Talk to the man today, and, while he doesn't want specific details revealed ("it's all a bit of a haze to me"), he carries no grudge. "In a team, you have a few, ah, unusual things happen, but they're over the next day." The stories, which get better with time, become part of the bonding process.

Even in 1988, when the All Blacks almost lost the drawn second test with Australia, Wyllie would, instead of a blistering training run, organise a private party for the team, which left those who drank in tatters, envying a teetotaller like Michael Jones. The Wyllie critics might call it a sign of his rough-edged approach. Lips purse at the idea of alcohol consumption being used as a tactic by a coach. But keep in mind that a man the media worship, league coach Graham Lowe, did something almost identical, as recorded in his star player Mark Graham's book, when Lowe's Brisbane club team were floundering in the late 1970s.

Which brings us to the Wyllie media image. It almost splits in two. On the one hand there is how he is seen in Canterbury, where they have the benefit of hearing him on 3ZB every Saturday morning, talking with a frankness that shows how relaxed he is with people he fully trusts, and, perhaps unconsciously, how relaxed he is about the hearing he will get from his local audience.

On the other hand, there is how he is seen in the rest of the country, especially in Auckland. Even there, the picture isn't as simple as it might seem.

For a start, Wyllie is not unhelpful to reporters he hasn't been badly treated by. On the Australian tour in '88, the first chance a group of journalists from outside Christchurch had to travel with Wyllie the coach for any length of time, he surprised many. Lindsay Knight, a highly experienced writer, says Wyllie was easy to deal with. "You got a straight answer, and he was prepared to make

Christchurch Star

Wyllie...he doesn't lavish praise or make extravagant criticisms.

himself available," says Knight.

What Wyllie doesn't enjoy is talking about his personal feelings. He'll explain a selection, he won't explain how he feels during a game. He'll give some background on a player, he won't say if he feels elated when that player performs above expectations.

The Glenmark in the man rebels against statements that glorify himself. Ask how he feels after a test win, and the reply is "quite good." He doesn't lavish praise, and he doesn't make extravagant criticisms.

He doesn't go for trial by media either. When his coaching abilities were being savaged on television, Wyllie didn't enter the fray. His knowledge of how the media operates is certainly not inconsiderable. He knows that nothing kills a controversy faster than no response. Journalists can feed off an argument for weeks by carrying bad news from one combatant to the other. When Wyllie refuses to spat publicly with an Andy Haden, he leaves Haden shadow-boxing, which eventually becomes not only pointless, but boring.

Journalists who do displease Wyllie tend to live in fear. Not of actually being knocked around, but of the enormous force that Wyllie musters in an argument.

When he's unhappy, and in full public flight, to say people edge away is understating the case. Fleeing the area would describe it a lot better. In a disagreement, he's a verbal battleship, firing lasers from the eyes, the glare shielded by eyebrows that quiver in indignation, the heavy artillery of his words booming out in lethal clusters. He can be kidding, and All Black manager John Sturgeon and he sometimes stage mock verbal battles. But I don't actually know any journalist who's happy to take the chance that Wyllie might be joking when he seems very displeased.

The nickname Grizz comes from how prickly he was as a young player, and Wyllie's progress to the highest levels of the game in New Zealand is quite remarkable when you consider how many tall poppies are lopped off in rugby here.

Take the career of Fred Allen as a terrible warning to men who don't toe the twists and turns the New Zealand rugby party line can take. Allen was, without question, the outstanding coach in New Zealand in the 1960s. He was also blunt, and suffered fools, or foolish suggestions, about as well as Wyllie does.

Allen became the All Black coach in 1966, cleanswept the series against the Lions that year, took an unbeaten team to Great Britain in 1967, and, to the end of the 1968 season, had a test record as a coach of 16 test matches for 16 victories.

Before the tour of South Africa in 1970, Allen heard whispers, from people he believed, that he would be dropped as coach for that tour. Let's just repeat that. There were plans to fire him. So, to avoid giving an anonymous committeeman in Wellington the pleasure of sacking him, Allen quit as coach.

That's at the level of rugby administration in New Zealand that, in theory, should always lead the way for the rest of the country.

Now if that's what happened to Allen, the miracle is that Wyllie ever survived past the club stage as coach.

Russ Thomas was the leading national administrator during Wyllie's climb to his position as All Black coach. Thomas would be deposed as chairman of the New Zealand Rugby Union in 1990, after four years in the job, apparently because he was perceived as clinging to old-fashioned attitudes about the game. Thomas can give the impression of fussiness, which makes the warmth of his attitude to Wyllie a slight surprise.

"To those of us close to Alex he could be a very aggressive personality," says Thomas. "Some people had great difficulty living with that. To some he used bullying tactics to get his own way, but I think every good administrator in rugby should be able to understand the strengths and weaknesses of the people he's dealing with. You could say some don't like Alex because of his aggressiveness, but that's the man and his nature. That's what's lifted him to the top. You can't have it both ways. A passive person gets passive results."

It would be unfair, and untrue, to suggest that All Black coaches

Peter Bush

Russ Thomas... "Alex could be a very aggressive personality."

in the past have won their position from the patronage of one or two key officials. But it would be fair, and true, to say that the best posture for a potential All Black coach is head down, and mouth shut. By and large the coaches since Allen have been well respected, and easy going, with Brian Lochore the prime example, or likeable, but without the spark that the great coaches in any sport have. Jack Gleeson had a steely edge to him, but he didn't often display it in public, and JJ Stewart, a strong personality, turned away some wrath with his keen sense of humour.

Let nobody be under the impression that all great coaches have a soft, loveable side to them. Arthur Lydiard, on his record perhaps the greatest coach of any sport this country has ever seen, could be brutal with athletes he felt had disobeyed his instructions. "The most precious thing we have in this world," says Lydiard, "is time. People can waste my time once, they never waste it twice. Life's too short to bother with people who won't apply themselves."

That's basically Wyllie's approach too. He brooks no interference with his team, because the team is what's vitally important to him in rugby.

It's a recurring theme in conversation with him. It's why he will never approach a provincial player directly, if there's an aspect of play he wants that player to demonstrate. Wyllie will only operate through the player's coach. To do otherwise would be unfair to the man's team. No use having a first-five running to prove a point to national selectors, when the provincial team's pattern might be to kick to keep the ball ahead of a powerful forward pack.

It's the reason he doesn't spend a lot of time on the telephone to his All Black players. Some very good coaches spend enormous amounts of time talking with their star performers. Wyllie can go for weeks without chatting to some of his key men.

It's the reason he worried about the introduction of All Blacks Ltd, the company that should provide generous payouts every year to All Blacks from promotional work and advertising. With the cash might come divisions in the team.

It's the reason he could be so tough on provincial players who

The team is what's vitally important to him in rugby.

turned up late for training. The team had to be kept waiting if one man wasn't there, and that just wasn't on.

It's the reason he had no sympathy for Vic Simpson's argument that Simpson wouldn't best serve Canterbury on the wing. If you're asked to play for your province, you pull on the jersey, and only then do you worry about what number is on the back.

But the unswerving dedication to the team he's involved with does not fully explain his huge success, first with Canterbury, and then with the All Blacks.

As players will explain in this book, it is a big mistake to dismiss Wyllie as a blood and guts coach, who understands nothing more technical in the game than thudding up the middle of the paddock with the ball controlled by the forwards.

Wyllie himself might never express it this way, but he is a true student of the game. As the universal game for so many years in New Zealand, rugby has drawn from all walks of life. A Rhodes scholar can be passed the ball by a freezing worker, a farmer can cover defend to help out a doctor. So All Black teams have been blessed over the years with the solid common sense of the non-academic, who has gathered his views from bitter, practical experience.

Reading is not one of Wyllie's favourite pastimes. But he has stored volumes of rugby knowledge in his memory, to be drawn on at will when confronted with a problem.

Because he brings his theories down to the very basics, it's easy to underestimate their depth. In France in 1990 he established that the problem with the All Black forwards was that too much time had been spent by too many of the All Black tight five in the powerful Auckland and Waikato packs, where it was possible to have the luxury of engine room men running with the ball, and actively seeking the chance to do so. Two losses in build-up games proved the point. By the time of the first test the thankless, but essential tasks of mauling and rucking were being performed by all the tight forwards. The results? Two emphatic test wins.

If the test of somebody in full control of a subject is how they can reduce it to its basic elements, then Wyllie is an A student of rugby. Canterbury coaching coordinator Wayne Smith, universally admired among current rugby players as an astute and articulate judge of the game, remembers how impressed he was with Wyllie's grasp of the needs of back play. Wyllie's Canterbury captain, Don Hayes, was spellbound by Wyllie's explanations of the mechanics of back row play. "He just made it so simple to follow," says Hayes.

Then there is Wyllie the bush psychologist. A former schoolmate, Wal Scott, remembers being asked by Wyllie to help out with a North Canterbury sub-unions side that was travelling to Nelson for a game. Scott, who had virtually stopped playing club football, was reluctant to turn out, but Wyllie told him the alternative was to play a teenager at prop, who might well suffer serious injury against the experienced opposition front row.

So Scott found himself in a dressing room, wearily slapping on liniment, wondering a little why he'd let himself be talked into the nonsense that was about to take place. "There were some new guys in the team, and Alex couldn't have been more helpful to them. Then he came to me. Christ, he just gave me heaps. What was a short, fat, unfit bloke like me doing with players who had trained hard, and were ready to play a proper game of football? What the hell did I think I was doing? I was furious. Here I was helping him out, and all he could do was be nasty to me. Of course I went out and played in a rage, which was exactly what Alex had wanted."

With his natural reserve, Wyllie never reveals too much about what he's really thinking. Not many would ever compare him to former All Black captain, Graham Mourie, but in one aspect there are similarities.

Mourie, from a farming family in Taranaki, keeps a lot of his opinions to himself. Mourie commanded an enormous respect from his fellow All Blacks not only because he was a very good footballer, with a great ability to endure pain, but also because, in a team of compulsive chatterers, like Stu Wilson and Andy Haden, Mourie was happy to listen, rather than talk. When he did speak, his fellow players listened. And when he spoke he'd had time to decide exactly what it was he wanted to say. One of his favourite answers to a question was: "What do you think about it?" He rarely revealed what he thought, which quickly developed what amounted to a mystique about him.

Wyllie doesn't even bother to answer a question with a question. He'll issue a laugh, that's a lot like a snort, or just look at the person speaking to him, and raise an eyebrow. He absorbs information, and will sometimes act on it, but he doesn't join in idle gossip. Wyllie will pass brief, pungent comments on people he doesn't respect, but he doesn't waste his time with loose talk. You won't hear lurid details of rugby scandals from Wyllie.

That all helps when he comes to coach a side. He always draws back from being scathing about a footballer he's been watching, just in case that should get back to the player. Such natural reserve grows increasingly valuable as an All Black coach. Opinions he might have voiced as Wyllie the former All Black carry a lot more weight, and have the potential to cause a lot more resentment, when they come from Wyllie the All Black coach.

The fact he does have concerns about doing the right thing by the game and its players is a hint to another side of Wyllie the rugby man. He is genuinely concerned that the game in general should prosper. His dislike of the over use of the rolling maul in provincial football in New Zealand isn't for selfish reasons. Carrying it into international rugby in the All Blacks doesn't work as successfully as it does in local play, but the hiccups caused there are not as important to him as the dreariness that the tactic causes for the spectators. For the same reasons, even as the kicking of Grant Fox generally acts as a safety net against All Black defeats, he actively dislikes games that are dominated by goalkicking.

He's protective of the legacy of rugby, and was furious in 1985 when it seemed the Ranfurly Shield might take on the name of a sponsor. But he's forward thinking about many areas of the sport, from player payment to televising of games, to changing the rules to enliven the game.

He was the first coach in New Zealand to embrace the fitness methods of Jim Blair, the former Scottish soccer player, who tossed out the endless running and soul destroying repetition of traditional rugby practices. They were replaced by gym work, shorter, sharper, running, and gridwork with footballs that some coaches still see as play, not work. As Blair himself says, if Wyllie was really the Grizz image personified, then he would have been the last man to take on the new methods.

Above all, Wyllie loves the game. Once again, it's not a phrase that comes easily to his lips, but how else do you explain a man who roams the country more than an Automobile Association signpainter, watching rugby games, talking rugby, and then returning home to watch videos of the game. In private he doesn't hammer the sport in conversation, but he isn't wearied of rugby discussions, the way most players are. At a club prizegiving he will corner the senior coach, and discuss motivation for a championship game the club team is about to face.

To survive the endless rugby round, he carries a keen sense of humour. Some of it is typical rugby club stuff...a man walking by with a delicately balanced set of beer jugs is an almost constant temptation to the Wyllie elbow. But he can also be drily amusing, with a liking for extended tests of patience.

The first time Kevin Schuler, the All Black loose forward replacement on the 1989 tour to Wales and Ireland, met Wyllie it was as a young No 8 being coached in the '87 New Zealand Colts team.

Wyllie asked Schuler to try a move from the back of the scrum. Schuler did. Wyllie told him it was wrong. "Watch me," said Wyllie, "and do it this way." He demonstrated.

Schuler copied Wyllie's moves. No, it was still wrong. Do it again.

Still wrong. Do it again. Schuler follows the instructions even closer.

Still wrong. Schuler throws the ball down in disgust. "I give up, what do you bloody want me to do? What's going wrong?"

Wyllie almost smiles, and says quietly to Schuler: "Perhaps your sweatband's too tight."

His loyalty to players is well known, almost to the point where some have questioned if he sometimes lets their past services be rewarded well beyond a fair cutoff date.

It's true that Wyllie doesn't chop and change a team very easily. But he will do it, even with players who have given him superb services, like Warwick Taylor, Bruce Deans, and, in the biggest selection shock of modern All Black rugby, Buck Shelford. In the end his total belief that the team must come first overrules everything else. Oddly enough, for such a hard-nosed player, who on the field never seemed to mind what damage he caused to his opposition, he agonises more than a lot of coaches over dropping an experienced man. People who doubt that he loses sleep over having to make axings should try to remember how Wyllie looked on television when he was being interviewed the morning Shelford was dropped. And remember also, that unlike many, many coaches in the past, Wyllie spoke personally to Shelford before the team was publicly announced. It may not have appeased the more fanatical Shelford supporters, but it was a genuine gesture of goodwill.

In Grizzspeak the long night hours pondering the decision on Shelford are described as something that's "hard to do". Once again, the Glenmark attitude prevents any whining about it. You do the job, and you don't bleat when the flak flies.

Unlike many coaches, who bloom in the spotlight, Wyllie, described too often by close friends as shy to not be, doesn't give any sign of enjoying being the centre of attention. He's gracious in a casual sort of way to people who recognise him (a group that includes anyone who owns a television set in New Zealand to Japanese tourists, who, in the wake of All Black promotions in Japan pushing New Zealand primary produce, quickly form queues to have their picture take with Mr Wy-rie). In hotel bars he will even be friendly enough to lurching strangers who offer beery greetings. His ability to make a level look as threatening as a raised fist means that he very rarely has to tell someone to get away from him.

The rugby lifestyle involves, in many cases, a lot of drinking. It isn't universal, with current All Black manager Sturgeon virtually a non-drinker, and the religious convictions of Michael Jones and Va'aiga Tuigamala ensuring they don't drink alcohol at all. But there are also casualties from drink in the sport, and Sturgeon is one who tries to dissuade the men around him, including Wyllie, from drinking too much. He isn't always successful, but rumours of alcohol affecting Wyllie's ability to coach the side in France in 1990, for example, are demonstrably untrue.

With so much of her husband's time taken up by rugby, Keryn Wyllie still remains a loyal supporter of his sport.

On the lawn at Omihi in 1972, Alex and Keryn, as Jacqueline kicks off while Alex directs Kristin.

Keryn's father owned the Waipara Hotel, so Keryn grew up not far from where Alex's parents farmed. She has no clear memory of Wyllie the schoolboy, but Wyllie the young man about the district, driving cars very fast, and making his mark as a rugby player, would soon be Wyllie the husband.

The couple lived in the cottage on the Wyllie farm, and Keryn, who had been working as a hairdresser in nearby Amberley, was soon settled to farm life. The children, Craig (25), Jacqueline (23), Kirstin (21) and Amanda (18) spent their primary school years on the farm, heading to Christchurch for their secondary schooling.

If Alex is a man who has learned to live with fame, even if he doesn't enjoy it, Keryn shies away from publicity. Some early experiences with published stories horrified her. The assistance she had on the farm from Alex's father and farm workers when Alex was away on tour was somehow almost forgotten in one story, which implied that the gallant rugby widow was basically running the farm, and bringing up a toddler, single-handed.

"I'm what I would call a real home-loving person," says Keryn. "When the children were young we had so much help from Alex's parents, and my parents, with babysitting, that I was able to keep up with the Canterbury games. But touring wasn't something I wanted to do. I was quite happy to be at home."

Like their mother, the younger Wyllies are quite content to stay well away from any shadow cast by their father's public profile. Jacqueline, now back in Christchurch after living in Europe, and Kirstin, back in Christchurch from Massey University, are independent young women, while Amanda, a seventh former, shows quiet strength when she casually remarks that while she enjoys visits to the family farm, "if I'm doing some work there and it gets too tedious, I just stop."

Craig, who enjoys talking about himself as much as most people enjoy a visit to the dentist, is a talented rugby player. Dark, like his mother, he is about as tall as his father, but much more lightly built.

He usually plays loose forward, where one very experienced teammate says the only thing handicapping his chances of provincial honours (he is a North Canterbury squad member) is searing pace. "Everything else, the skills, the anticipation, and certainly the guts and tackling, are all there."

Glenmark clubmen love to talk about the match in 1990, when Glenmark played University in a Town-Country champion of champions clash.

Playing centre for Varsity was Victor Simpson. Moved to centre for Glenmark was Craig Wyllie.

The first time Simpson got the ball he charged straight at Wyllie. There was a smack as Simpson was crashed to the ground. Simpson's reaction was exactly as the shrewd heads in the Glenmark club had hoped. The Varsity wingers didn't see the ball for the rest of the afternoon. Again and again Simpson raced at Wyllie. Again and again Wyllie flattened him with fierce tackles. Robbie Deans, the Glenmark fullback that day, can hardly stop laughing at the memory. "Vic was pretty bow-legged when he came off the field."

Craig, working the family farm, enjoys his rugby, but says, without any noticeable regret, that he may not have put in enough effort at a young age to get a lot more back out of the sport now. "I feel that I'm still learning things."

What the whole Wyllie family have in common is a quality that in the big city frenzy of the pre-stockmarket crash days was considered hardly worth bothering about. You can trust them. From Alex's father Joe sealing stock sales with a handshake, to Craig refusing to let a vastly more experienced player intimidate him, there's an unshakeable integrity.

In Alex Wyllie it's reflected in many ways. It can be in a refusal to make promises to players that he can't keep, in a lengthy drive to an obscure rugby club that he promised to speak at, in a set of rules for a team that he makes sure all players live by. Because the ultimate sin in the Wyllie ethic, as mentioned earlier, is to be someone you can't trust. It's not something anyone who knows him well would even mention in the same breath as his name.

2

Flat out and
fully loaded

Watch a group of small boys at play. They'll rough and tumble, but most of it is pretty mild. On a football field, the majority don't want to tackle, and, if they get a bump in the nose, screech to a tearful halt.

Then there are the boys like Alex Wyllie.

Scraped, bumped, bruised, bleeding, grazed, cut, Elastoplastered from head to toe.

This is a kid who, with the traditional pedal car, sets out a course for it at home. Alex's track runs down a steep bank, until the car's going as fast as its little wheels will turn. There's still time to bail out, but not for this kid. The good part's just arriving. Fling the wheel over, roll the car, and smash into the tree at the bottom of the bank. By the end of summer the car looks like it's been in a motorway pile-up.

This is a kid who in the space of a few months just after he'd started school fell off a chair and cut his chin open, patted a horse on the rump and needed stitches in his head when the horse lashed out, and fell out of a tree on to a poplar stake, driving it under his kneecap so hard his father couldn't pull it out. That took a trip to the doctor at Waikare to remove.

And this is a kid who almost met his match, quite innocently, by looking around a corner of a shed at his uncle's farm, when a Bulldog tractor was being started. The handle flew off like a mortar round, and a glancing blow on the side of Alex's head was enough to knock him cold. A full blow would almost certainly have killed him.

Dave Wyllie, a first cousin, four years older than Alex, still looks a little amazed 40 years later when he talks about his schooldays' playmate. "I don't think anything ever scared him, from the time he could run around."

Alexander John Wyllie was born in Christchurch on August 31,

1944, the fifth in a family of six children. The only other boy died as an infant before Alex was born, so he grew up with four sisters, three older, Beverley, Barbara, and Pam, and one younger, Rose.

The Wyllies had farmed in the Omihi Valley, about an hour's drive north of Christchurch on State Highway One today, since 1908, and the first Wyllie to emigrate to New Zealand, from Scotland, Alex's great grandfather, had established a homestead at Sefton in 1863.

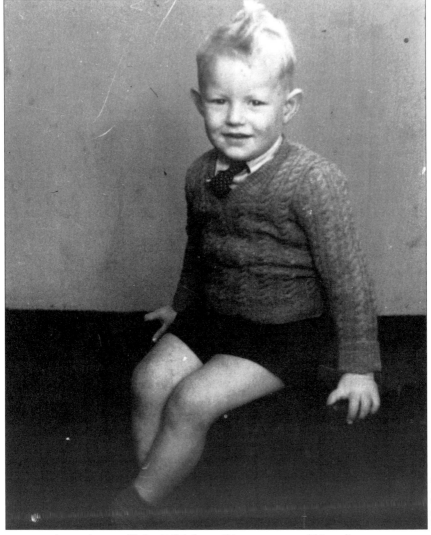

A cousin says "I don't think anything ever scared him..."

Wyllie Collection

The country rolls away over broad river plains, fertile enough to be cropped for oats and wheat and barley, as well as to support beef cattle and sheep.

It's a place where family ties are strong. All Black Richard Loe being Alex Wyllie's nephew sometimes bemuses people in the rest of New Zealand, but in areas like Omihi, to disqualify good rugby players because they're related to the coach or captain or club chairman would leave you without a team.

Alex (which all his family and Omihi friends pronounce to rhyme with relic, not telex) spent a lot of spare time at his cousins' place, a mile or so down the railway line towards Christchurch. Down there he had four boys to play with, and rugby was always first choice.

Omihi primary school in the early 1950s must have been one of the very few in the whole of rural New Zealand where rugby wasn't the staple recreation. Nobody can remember exact details, but the general belief is that the ex-serviceman in charge didn't like the boys playing rough games.

The Wyllie boys grew to believe that he had a special set against them. On the days when they went home for lunch, they'd return to find, too late, that rugby had been planned for that specific break. In the first period after lunch they'd be grumbling through yet another session of orchestral music, beseeched to imagine the birds coming off the water as the strings swelled in "Swan Lake."

So the big front lawn of Uncle Archie's place was a paradise to Alex and his cousins. They'd press gang a couple of boys whose father worked for the Railways, and then it was look out rose bushes, as they smashed their way up and down the lawn. Sometimes Uncle Archie called a halt. He'd grab the football off them, growl "for God's sake go and do something else," and march inside. As soon as he was gone a schoolcap would be produced, and the game continued.

Football was always a big interest, but not the only one, at Alex's home. His parents have both, in their own ways, been immersed in rugby. His mother, Jean, is the daughter of Jack Sloss, who started the Omihi-Scargill rugby club in 1923, which a couple of years later would become Glenmark. Alex's father, Joe, was a teenage wing forward for Glenmark in the days of the 2-3-2 scrum.

Joe was in the team when Jack Sloss would wheel out his big V8 Buick, and as many as 10 players would pile in the car for a trip up to Oxford. There was so much room in the back seat a couple of stools could be put on the floor, and the players took turns nursing each other. Jean and her brothers and sisters went to the games sometimes, "but if there was only room for the footballers, we had to stop at home."

In 1948 Joe, then 41, was coaching the Glenmark team, although in North Canterbury then rugby was still getting back to normal after World War II. "We were playing friendly games," he says, "just to keep the young fellows interested, to keep the game going. We went to play at the Sefton Domain, and we were short of reserves, so I came in to play fullback. I'd kicked the ball, and the fellow who came in to try and tackle me tried to get out of the way. But we got our legs crossed and I fell over him. It just went 'bang'. They reckon it echoed around the trees round the ground like a bullet."

Neighbours rallied round and helped on the farm, which was just as well, because the recovery time was ridiculously long. "I knew from the time they put the leg in plaster that something was wrong. My foot started to go a different colour a few days later, and they had to take the whole plaster off, put me in traction to straighten it out, and put a plate in my leg. I've still got the plate."

(His doubts about his treatment were confirmed 18 months later when his other leg was broken after a bull charged him when he was on a hack cutting out some cattle. Back at the Christchurch Hospital the same nurse suggested he had bones that didn't knit easily, and would need another operation. This time he transferred to a private hospital where a specialist set his leg, which quickly healed.)

But while he would later play an important role in the revival of the Glenmark club, Joe Wyllie was a man whose pastimes were never confined to rugby. He's bred and trained animals for most of his adult life. He ran a team of magnificent Clydesdale horses until 1941, and, as the girls started growing up, turned his attention to breeding ponies. That led to trips throughout New Zealand to select breeding stock for a national saddle pony stud list.

After 40 years on the Canterbury Clydesdale council he began breeding shorthorn cattle, serving several years as president of the Canterbury shorthorn committee. An association with the Amberley Agricultural and Pastoral Show began in 1945, and he still serves as patron. "Joe Wyllie is a superb judge of animals," says a local stock agent. "He knows what to look for, and can sum up stock very quickly."

The affinity with animals never really rubbed off on Alex. Take the ponies for example.

All his sisters were keen on riding, and competed in gymkhanas all over North Canterbury. The only impression Alex ever made was in the car once, waiting for his sisters. Bored, he hacked off all the front of his hair with the scissors they used to trim the horses' tails and manes.

He competed just once. Says his father: "He was about eight years old, and he had a little black Shetland pony. He wasn't very fussed about riding it, but he went into the ring."

The judge stopped him after the round and offered some friendly advice. If Alex was a little more careful with his hands, if he'd approached one of the barriers at less of an angle, he could have been the winner. The small boy glowered at the judge. "This is the first time I've been in the ring, and it's going to be the last." It was.

His sisters say the only time they can ever recall him getting real enjoyment from riding a horse was when one of their classmates from their boarding school in Christchurch, Rangi Ruru, was gingerly riding a pony in the paddock by the house. Howling down the paddock came Alex, yelling and whooping, and startling the visitor's pony so much it bolted, bouncing her on to the ground.

He wasn't big on milking the house cow. To this day his sisters don't believe his claims that milking gave him eczema of the hands. He has never, in his father's memory, slaughtered an animal. Workers recall the Wyllie genius for remembering he had to check the back paddock just as any killing was about to start. The checking always seemed to take about the time it did to kill, dress and hang the beasts. The woolshed wasn't a favourite place either. "He's never changed," says his father. "He'll tell you it isn't busy, go out and cut some hay, and leave you up to your ears in wool for lack of men. What he likes are tractors and trucks, something he can push to the limit. Machinery's no good to him unless it's flat out, and fully loaded."

With his sisters he developed his love of argument. "Stubborn?" says one. "Stubborn? He'd argue black was white." His parents suggest that Alex wasn't the only strong-minded one in the family. "They're all reasonably strong-willed," says Joe Wyllie, "not that that is a fault. If you're confident enough to express an opinion, I think the main thing is to have a reason for why you've done something. If you have, then you should stick to it."

Alex Wyllie as a small boy being physically fearless, and mentally aggressive, may be no surprise to those who know him as an adult. In the area of rugby alone though his choice of idol may not have been so predictable. The great winger, Ron Jarden was the player who captured the primary schoolboy's attention.

"He was going to be an All Black like Ron Jarden, that was his aim," says Jean Wyllie. Jarden, who would die at a tragically early age of heart failure, was an All Black between 1951 and 1956, a quicksilver wing, who relied on speed and skill much more than muscle power.

Even at an early age, Alex Wyllie was showing that he had skills and athletic abilities himself.

He always had an excellent sense of balance, an attribute almost every talented sports person shares. His trike, it may come as no surprise to learn, lost a rear wheel early in its life. The preschooler quickly learned to ride it on two wheels. He could walk along the top of a paling fence before he'd turned five.

Wyllie Collection

At Lancaster Park to play for the first time, Alex Wyllie (second from right in the back row) wasn't the only boy in big shorts!

For his first taste of bigtime rugby he had to combine balance, a love of contact, and speed that would shortly be confirmed at boarding school in the city.

He was selected, as a 10-year-old, at second-five for a Hurunui-North Canterbury team that travelled to Lancaster Park to take on a Christchurch team. At that stage Alex, the only primary schoolboy in his team, was still of only average size for his age. A pair of white pants had to be bought for him on the way to the game, and they were so big they almost had to be tied under his armpits.

As the youngest boy in the team he was due to play only one half of the match. Funny pants and all, he tackled the townies the way he would in Town-Country matches years later. Says his father, with some pride: "He was the last one they would have put off at halftime."

Like most children in the district, boarding school in Christchurch was next on the list.

He showed some reluctance to go to St Andrew's College. His parents recall he would have preferred Boys' High, probably, they remember, because at the time Boys' High was performing better at rugby.

Wyllie arrived at St Andrew's in 1958 in the second form as a 12-year-old. By now he was no longer a wiry, strong boy, but a very big strong boy. In some of the photographs from his days in the preparatory section of the school, he's as big as some of the masters.

He certainly swept through the lower schools' athletics championships, winning the 100, 220, 440 and 880 yards, plus the high jump, long jump and cricket ball throw.

On the rugby side, he was too big and strong to play against other second formers, so he went into the third XV, as a centre. With his pace, and size, he could hold his own without any real problems.

But the next year came a change that didn't please everyone. His coach in the second XV, Frank Finnegan, moved him into the forwards. "He was very strong and fearless, and there was no way he was going to be dealt to by anyone, but I thought he could do with a bit more discipline. I thought he'd score just as many tries from there. I remember that his father was most unhappy about the change, and came down to the school to complain, but Alex just went from strength to strength. If he had a weakness it was that when he took umbrage at something, he settled it there and then, usually right out in the open."

A couple of times during his third form year Alex played for the first XV, against Scots College, in Wellington, and Xavier College, and the first XV coach, Ian Clark, knew he had a potential star in the making. "He was a remarkable forward, very strong, very fast, quick to the ball, and with good hands."

His march through rugby at St Andrew's then was relentless. In the fourth and fifth forms he was in the first XV, as a 16-year-old earning selection in the Canterbury under-20 team. By the time of his last season he was being reviewed in the school magazine in superlatives. "Outstanding forward, the best for many years. He was of inestimable value to his team. Tireless worker." But there's

Wyllie Collection

Only a third former, but already Alex Wyllie, at left in the back row, was turning out on occasions for the St Andrew's 1st XV.

a hint that his knack of taking command wasn't something school-teachers totally approved of. "Inclined sometimes to do too much on his own."

His style of play as a forward was very direct. His nickname was "The Tank" and Ian Clark recalls a try against Boys' High in which Wyllie dragged several tacklers over the line with him, then marched back to the 25 to kick the conversion that won the match, 5-3, for St Andrew's. Wyllie was, and would be throughout his rugby career, a long, powerful place kicker. He favoured the torpedo style, never adopting the round the corner kick. In fact the nearest his sisters came to sharing his rugby training with him was when the young-est, Rose, seven years his junior, was ordered to help him with his goal kicking. "I had to go every night and chase the ball for him," says Rose. "I got drafted into it, and abused if I was too slow."

The academic life didn't have much appeal. "I think rugby was his main reason for being at school," says Finnegan. Clark remem-bers Wyllie as a boy with "both feet on the ground, not somebody who threw his weight around, not really rowdy. He wasn't a fool, and he didn't tolerate them either."

Wally Scott, a veteran of the first XV when Wyllie played his first couple of games, thinks the young man may have been more aggressive on the field than the coaches remember. "After his first game we were all amazed at how well he'd played. But what really sticks in my mind is that before the game the coach (Ian Clark) told him there was to be no hitting other players, or swearing at them. He wasn't loud, or a braggart in the dressing room, in some ways he was quite shy. But when he got on the paddock, by God, it was all guns blazing. He just loved dropping his shoulder and making physical contact."

What did emerge at St Andrew's, even though it was not something he pursued once he'd left school, was that Wyllie was a talented athlete. In 1961 Wyllie won four events in the senior athletics competition, throwing the discus 124ft, the shot 38ft 4in, long jumping 18ft 7 and a half inches and winning the 100 yards in 11.1s.

The sprint and long jumping titles are probably the most note-worthy. For many years Wyllie set up over-confident backs for embarrassing losses on tour by challenging them to sprint races, negotiating a small start for himself, and holding them off over the length of a football field. A time of 11.1s is not Olympic material, but on a damp grass track (bad weather had delayed the athletics), with no special training, it's more than could be expected from the majority of 13 stone schoolboy forwards.

When he wasn't playing rugby, boxing, competing in athletics, or killing time in class, there was cricket. While very keen on the game he didn't have the same success that he did in other sports. He

St Andrew's Collection

Wyllie the promising athlete (top, on right of back row) and Wyllie the tidy dresser (below, second from left in the back row) at St Andrew's.

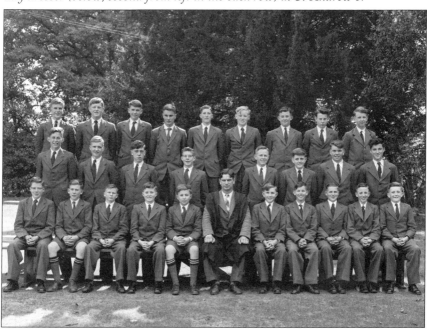

Wyllie Collection

St Andrew's Collection

In his last year at St Andrew's, 1961, they called Alex Wyllie (second from left, front row), the tank, and said he was "the best forward for many years."

never gained a permanent place in the first XI, although he did have two seasons in the second XI.

Today Wyllie says that he probably should have concentrated more on the academic work at St Andrew's. But at the time the agricultural course he took was strictly a task to be completed, not much more. The regulations and disciplines of St Andrew's he does look back on with approval. People like Doug Bruce, who often roomed with him, remark on how organised and tidy the adult Wyllie is compared with many footballers, almost certainly a result of boarding school life.

When his fifth form year was over there was never any real question of what Wyllie would do. "I was happy enough to be out of school," he says. He went back to the family farm, and he would soon demonstrate that, given the right challenge, he could take a keen interest in stock.

"We had an 18-month-old shorthorn heifer," says his father. "I said to Alex that if we could handle her, she could do well at the (Amberley) show. She wasn't a dirty beast, she was quite good tempered, but she was determined to have her own way, and she had a bit of size too.

"Well, Alex took her out into the paddock, and he wrestled her to the ground, then he held her there. There were two determined personalities in that paddock, but from then on he was the boss. We took her to the show as a two-year-old, and she won supreme champion."

THE LEGEND: *In his first season as Canterbury coach, Alex Wyllie once held such a tough training run that the wife of one of the forwards thought her husband had been drinking when he staggered through the door two hours late.*

THE REAL STORY: *The player was lock Kerry Mitchell. "We played very badly in a game on the Saturday, and Alex made us train for hours at Rugby Park. I was completely stuffed. My wife had cooked a nice meal at home, and she was really unimpressed when I got home. She thought I'd got boozed after training." Was he too exhausted to offer a full explanation? "Yes. I was gone. Alex had his ways of making a point."*

CREDIBILITY RATING (OUT OF 10): *10.*

Legend

3

No friendly games

The Glenmark Rugby Club doesn't have the fanciest clubrooms in New Zealand, and in summer, when the grass gets knee high, the ground at the Omihi Domain doesn't look too flash.

But in the winter, with a southerly nipping at the town end of the paddock, and the supporters lined up on the eastern bank in swandris and oilskin jackets, the intensity of the football would light up the southern electrical grid.

In Canterbury, when they think of Glenmark, they think of Alex Wyllie.

In the Waipara pub, it's a bit the same. With a fire blazing in a huge open grate, a bunch of Wyllie's old clubmates are yarning about his playing and coaching days with Glenmark.

Jock Croft remembers the time he and Alex went to a clearance sale on a Friday. At the time there was a rule, originally set by Joe Wyllie, that nobody was to be seen in a hotel after they'd finished training on Wednesday night.

The sale was a long way from Omihi, and so was the local pub. So at about midnight they set out for home.

Next afternoon Wyllie was circling the Glenmark changing room, laying down the law to each player.

He arrived at Croft. "As for YOU, I've got it on bloody good authority that you were in a pub until midnight last night. By God, you'd better make a bloody good effort today after letting your mates down like that!"

Croft was stunned. He was damned whichever way he turned. Wyllie, on the other hand, had scored twice. The sort of joke he loves had been pulled on Croft, and Croft had to sweat twice as hard on the field to win back the goodwill of the rest of the team.

Then there was the time they were playing United, on a bleak, cold day when, with about 10 minutes to go, Wyllie dislocated his thumb.

"You'd better go off and get it strapped," said his fellow players. "No, it'll be alright, I'll just tuck it in under my hand," said Wyllie, who played on until the end of the game.

Going off injured while playing for Glenmark was something nobody can ever remember Wyllie doing, and it was something he hated to see others do.

He did have to leave the field a couple of times at the invitation of referees.

Warren Eaglesome, a retired shoes salesman, has the distinction of being the first referee to order Wyllie off.

He refereed in glasses, which was meat and drink to the crowds at the Omihi Domain. Waiting for the ball to be thrown into a lineout once, he heard a clear voice call from the crowd: "Look at that, the bugger's got four eyes, and he still can't see."

But it was in Rangiora that Wyllie got his marching orders. "They were two very keen rivals," says Eaglesome, "and the crowd used to give the players hell. There'd been a bit of scrapping going on, and I issued a general warning. Alex and another young chap from Rangiora had a poke at each other right in front of the grandstand. It left me no option. They both went off. I wouldn't say it was the worst instance I've ever seen on a football field. But sometimes we have to decide as referees that the limit has been reached."

In 1970 Wyllie was ordered off again, playing for Glenmark against Kaiapoi, at the Omihi Domain.

The referee, Mike Hargreaves, said in his report that Wyllie had "viciously elbow jolted the Kaiapoi No 4 player, felling him and splitting his lip."

Wyllie told the North Canterbury sub-union committee that his jersey had been held by the Kaiapoi player. "I had my back to him, and all I did was...(indicating a backward swing of the arm). Any human being would do that. It wasn't an intentional movement. If that was called a vicious blow, I'd hate to see what some blows on a rugby field would be called." The Kaiapoi player, Wyllie and his teammates still believe, was auditioning for a role in Hollywood.

In Omihi they were outraged. The referee worked for a tractor company in Amberley. It was a long time before they saw any of that brand in the Omihi Valley again.

As it happened, North Canterbury officials decided that, as Wyllie had missed a match at Lancaster Park between the Cantabrians and the Barbarians next day because his case hadn't been heard, that was sufficient penalty.

Nobody mentioned that Wyllie had a hamstring pull that would have prevented him playing in that game anyway.

Not that two orderings off in 20 seasons of club rugby indicates that Wyllie was a dirty player. All Black captain Ian Kirkpatrick

Christchurch Star

Alistair Hopkinson (with ball) and Ian Kirkpatrick were teammates of Wyllie for Canterbury and the All Blacks.

played against him several times in North Canterbury club competition in 1967. Kirkpatrick, and his schoolmate from King's College, Hamish Macdonald, were working on farms, and playing for Rangiora. "Grizz didn't know me from a bar of soap," says Kirkpatrick. "I found him hard and uncompromising, but he wasn't dirty. I'm bloody sure if you mucked him around you would have got it." What does "got it" mean, a punch or a boot? "A punch. He never kicked anyone."

As time went by Wyllie reached a stage where he could play referees like a piano.

He learned some of those skills from Alistair Hopkinson, a man whose toughness on a rugby field was matched by his sense of humour.

When Hopkinson was playing for Amberley he knew how to niggle Wyllie. In one game, as a ruck broke up in some heat, Hopkinson, at the referee's shoulder, said to Wyllie: "Look here sonny, just watch your step." Wyllie instantly replied: "Who the bloody hell are you calling sonny?" Hopkinson shrugged a long suffering shoulder at the ref.

By the time he was coaching Glenmark, nobody needed to give Wyllie any hints about how he should deal with referees. Warren Eaglesome describes him as "a talkative player. If he wasn't happy about a decision, he'd question it and demand an answer."

Clubmates say that before a match Wyllie would run through the strengths and weaknesses of the ref of the day. "He says: 'This guy flogs us in the lineouts, so leave them alone.' By the end of a game he'd just about be controlling the ref. He'd point... 'for Christ's sake ref, have a look here.' He knew their weaknesses, and he knew how to exploit them."

He also knew how to unsettle opposing teams.

Publican Dave Morris remembers when he was running the Amberley hotel, and coaching the Amberley club team.

"If you played at Glenmark it was like playing for the Ranfurly Shield, it was a big day up there, or when they came to Amberley. Glenmark were the champions, but we had some good footballers too. The trouble was Alex'd come down to the pub on the Friday night, the cunning bastard, and by the time he'd finished talking to them about what he was going to do the next day, I'd have half a team. They were never the same.

"Then, when we got to the game, we'd never know where he was going to play. He was likely to turn up in the backline, anywhere he thought we had a player that was danger to them."

On the field Wyllie quickly made his mark. The first year he was out of school he was played on the wing in a game, and insisted that he run one of Glenmark club's signature moves, called "Fast", in which Alex would run in from the blindside to take the pass from the halfback. The halfback, Brian Peters, had been in the team for a decade, but Wyllie's confidence on a rugby field, and his ability to call the right shots, was already fully developed.

Alistair Hopkinson, a close observer of Wyllie in club play, and a teammate for Canterbury and the All Blacks, has enormous admiration for how Wyllie approached games for Glenmark.

"If an All Black goes back and plays club rugby, sometimes they just fill in. But Alex's attitude never altered. He gave his absolute best for Glenmark, as he did for the All Blacks. His attitude was far better than mine. I'd go back and think, 'This isn't such a hard game,' and just lope along, but not Alex. He didn't know how to play a friendly game, it was a hundred miles an hour every time."

Loyalty to his club was something Alex Wyllie didn't need to be lectured about. Just living at home was enough to pick it up.

In the Omihi Valley they had started their football club without the benefit of a permanent ground.

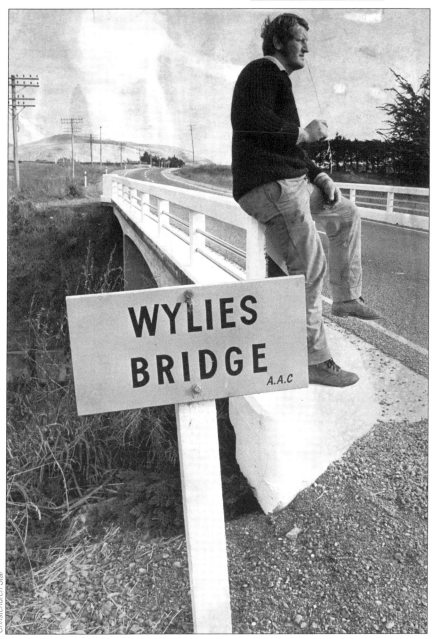

Christchurch Star

They've spelt the name wrong on the sign for years, but when footballers reach this spot, they know the Glenmark ground is just up the road.

The name Glenmark was chosen to replace Omihi-Scargill. The original Glenmark Station, a huge local holding, was so big that it was said from the highest point the original owner, George Moore, could look in any direction, and all the land he could see was part of the station. Glenmark's rugby colours, of blue and gold, were originally carried by the horses raced by Moore's.

Local farmers took turns to offer a paddock to the rugby club for the winter, and the working bee at the start of each season was to move the goalposts to whoever's farm was home to the club that year.

Not that the grounds were too rough. "We had the pick of the paddocks," says Alex's father, Joe. "The one my father offered was quite flat, and had a big plantation of trees at one end, which gave shelter, and made it an ideal spot. After the game we'd go to the Railways siding grain shed, and have afternoon tea there."

In 1929 Glenmark won their first championship, but by the early 1950s the club was struggling. A group of players came to Joe Wyllie, who had coached them to championships some years before, and asked him to coach again.

So in 1954 he took over the job. By 1956 the team placed second in the competition, and in 1959 Glenmark were champions again. A member of the team in those years says that Joe Wyllie had a good knowledge of the game, a keen eye for a player, and, most of all, he had an unshakeable belief that if Glenmark played the game properly, they would win.

"There wasn't much coaching as we know it today. Joe tore into us at halftime, and just prior to the game. There was nothing too sophisticated about the methods being used, but we developed tremendous team spirit. Night after night we'd end up at Joe Wyllie's place after the game."

Watching and listening was young Alex. "When he was a schoolboy he asked a lot of questions," says his father. "He asked less and less as he got older. In rugby he always had that, I suppose you'd call it vision, the ability to see what was going to happen, and why it would. It was something that came naturally to him."

Coaching Glenmark came to an end for Joe when he knew Alex was about to leave school, at the end of 1961, and start playing senior football. "I thought I'd be better out of it when my own boy was involved."

It was no more than people in the Glenmark club would have expected from Joe Wyllie. "He gave Alex all the encouragement a father could," says an old teammate of Alex's, "but he was never one to skite about how well Alex was doing. Mind you, if anybody started rubbishing Alex he was quick to stand up and be counted."

Wyllie played just one season in the under-21 team for Glenmark, and was then asked to turn out for the seniors in 1963. He knew

Christchurch Star

Farming and football, at the heart of life in Glenmark.

what to expect. "From the time my father had been coaching this was a team that at times could only rake up thirteen or fourteen men, yet they won because they set their own standards and disciplines. It was an unwritten law that nobody was in the pub from Wednesday onwards. They stuck together, and they set standards. That was something I tried to achieve when I started coaching Canterbury."

The teenage Wyllie's first game for Glenmark, against Kaiapoi, had an unusual prelude. He had been in the city with some friends, and parked his car near the Square to buy some takeaways. A van driver apparently objected to where the car was parked, and punched Wyllie in the face through the car window. As Wyllie opened the door his attacker put the boot in. By the time a policeman arrived the pair were wrestling in the gutter. Wyllie ran on the field against Kaiapoi sporting a brand new black eye.

(Years later he would run into the van driver in a hotel in Rotorua. The man walked up and said: "I'm the bloke who put the boot into you in the Square that time." Wyllie didn't chat with him. "Nice to meet you, now piss off.")

Wyllie took his place in a hugely successful team. In his first senior year, 1963, Glenmark were three seasons into what would become a nine year term as North Canterbury club champions. In those nine years the senior team, often with Wyllie and his three cousins from the front lawn days, Dave, Donald and Stuart, would play 128 games for 117 victories.

The golden era didn't finish then. In 1974 North Canterbury combined with Hurunui, and, in the new competition, Glenmark were champions from 1976 to 1982, and have yet to finish worse than third in the competition. In 1991 Glenmark were again champions, with Robbie Deans in the backs, and Craig Wyllie (Alex and Keryn's son) on the side of the scrum.

In case the city boys thought Glenmark were only big fish in their own small pond, in 1978, as the Canterbury sub-unions' champion team, they came to town and beat the Christchurch champions, New Brighton, 32-9, under lights at Denton Park. It was the first time a town champion had agreed to play the top country team.

Wyllie scored a try, and set up another with a burst from the back of the scrum. It was, Wyllie says now, quite a big night. "The country hicks came to town and proved they could play rugby as well." Without prompting he dismisses the suggestions made at the time that New Brighton were under strength for the game. "They might have had a hard game a few days before, but that's not really the point. They knew they were going to be playing us."

If the rugby club's successes and Alex Wyllie went together in many people's mind, so too did Wyllie and the social life of the district. Take, for example, the annual cricket match between

Rugby Press

An unorthodox tackle doesn't stop Alex Wyllie getting the try for Canterbury sub-unions.

Glenmark and the Railways.

Ron Bartlett was in the opposition team. "We'd end up playing in the dark, and Alex would still be rocketing them down. There was an endless supply of grog and tucker, and the game would always end up in an argument. There was never a clearcut winner.

"Someone would be marking the book, and Alex would be looking over their shoulder, and he'd say we were five runs short, or say they should be given five more runs, so it never got properly settled. By the time it was all finished and we got back to the pub, it'd be pitch dark, and I mean pitch dark."

Only once did the whole cricket aftermatch grind to a halt. The beer ran out. Publican Morris set out to get some more, but in the meantime Canterbury rugby team manager, Les McFadden, produced a bulk cask of wine. "Thirty litres," says Morris, "and they were drinking it out of pint glasses. They were bloody hopeless the next day."

Then there were the Glenmark balls. A big marquee would go up outside the Domain hall, which has now become the Glenmark clubrooms.

The marquee attracted the attention of Robbie Deans, who knew Alex from the days when Robbie and brother Bruce were Glenmark juniors. "I was on the way back home to swot for Varsity exams, and I thought, "This looks interesting,' so I shot in. Alex was there, and he said I could have a ticket to the ball if I swept the hall out afterwards. I didn't realise I'd have to do the sweeping for four years to pay for one ticket."

Bruce Deans, and some of the other younger members, took a shine to climbing up the side of the marquee, then running over the canvas top. It was a dangerous game for the marquee, and also for the tent runners, because Wyllie was the security man who ran around the marquee trying to catch them.

Amberley clubmen acted as barmen, and late at night when supplies of spirits were running low Wyllie was also bar manager. Serving doubles instead of singles was likely to result in a very swift cuff over the ear.

But no matter what the function, there was always enough energy for some football.

One of the Glenmark players was having a stag party, and in the early hours of the morning, sides were picked up and "The Singlets" played "The Underpants". Floodlights went on and the teams risked frostbite in unusual places. Travellers on the highway possibly thought they were hallucinating. Dave Wyllie remembers having to make a head-on tackle of cousin Alex. The horror of the moment has apparently obliterated which side each was playing for.

On a more serious note, the Glenmark Rugby Club, says Joe Wyllie, has done more to build community spirit than any other organisation in the district. "Miles above everything else really, the whole district gets behind it. In the old days there wasn't much else, but even today a good crowd of young people still come along to the football."

And for Alex Wyllie there are warm memories of how everyone in the Glenmark team stuck together. He recalls one man, a Dutch soccer player, who had never handled a rugby ball until he was roped into the blue and yellow jersey. The Glenmark approach is summed up by Alex in three words: "They stuck together."

THE LEGEND: *When he was still a teenager, Alex Wyllie, driving an Austin-Healey that had once been raced by Bruce McLaren, drove it across a T-junction, and the car landed halfway up a macrocapa hedge.*

THE FAMILY'S STORY: *"The car was white, with blue stripes, low slung with no top. Alex came out from Rangiora by the Woodend store, went straight across the main road, and into the hedge.*

THE WYLLIE VERSION: *"I didn't go through the hedge. I might have, if the car coming the other way hadn't hit me. I was coming out the back road from Rangiora, it was a bit late, and I might have been going a wee bit quick. What didn't help was some loose shingle. I suddenly started to run out of road, and seemed to go straight on out. Another car was coming down the main road towards Christchurch, and hit the passenger's side of my car. We all got out reasonably well, considering. A mate of mine from town was going to come out to home with me, and if he hadn't changed his mind he mightn't be here today. The seat he would have been sitting on ended up right beside me. He would have been fairly squashed. Nobody in the other car was hurt. My car? We had to sell it as a wreck."*

CREDIBILITY RATING (OUT OF 10): *5. Half the legend is true.*

Legend

4

Not a happy man to meet in the other side

Alex Wyllie impressed Fergie McCormick in only his third provincial game for Canterbury.

They were playing against Auckland, at Eden Park.

Wyllie was 19, marking Aucklander Lew Fell at the end of the lineout.

Fell, a man no bigger than a middleweight boxer, worked during the evenings as a printer in the New Zealand Herald's newsroom.

On Saturday afternoons the mild mannered newspaperman turned into a blood chilling footballer, leaping on to inside backs in a single bound, and ripping them to shreds.

Early in the game with Canterbury, Fell tried to make a blindside run. He was heavily tackled by Wyllie. Fell got up and started swinging. He went down again.

At this point McCormick, no stranger to physical contact himself, came running in from fullback, as referee John Pring called up Fell and Wyllie. Says McCormick: "I thought, Christ, we can't have this young fellow sent off already." McCormick was ready with helpful advice for the referee, but there was no need. "He told Alex to get back into position, and he told Fell that if he couldn't take it to go and have a shower."

Wyllie was a tearaway flanker and his first Canterbury coach, Bob Duff, says "his appearance in those days was a wee bit frightening to some backs. He was physically hard, and very aggressive, and he had the ability to really give it a go, to break tackles."

In 1962 Duff had Wyllie urged on him for the Canterbury Country team, when Wyllie was still playing under-21 football for Glenmark. "A chap by the name of Charlie Watson was the Country selector. I was coaching. He said to me, 'I have a young fellow I want to play, he's just out of college, 17 years of age, and he's very good.' In those days the Town side was virtually the Canterbury team, and I thought it was a bit tough for a young fellow. I said another year wouldn't do him any harm."

When Duff picked Wyllie for Canterbury in 1964 he was joining a powerful team, led by All Black loose forward John Graham.

Graham, now the headmaster of Auckland Grammar School but in those days a teacher at Christchurch Boys' High, knew who the new boy from Glenmark in the Canterbury team was.

"I was coaching a Boys' High second XV that played St Andrew's," says Graham, "and in those days Alex was really the terror of secondary school rugby. He dominated the game. He was so hard physically, and a lot of the kids genuinely feared him.

"When he began for Canterbury he was rawboned, largely untutored in the finer points of the game, but he had all the skills needed to be a top loose forward. He was quick and strong, with extremely good hands, and the natural sense of how play would develop, that lifts naturals like Michael Jones and Graham Mourie from being good players to being outstanding."

Wyllie was soon a popular member of the team, says Graham. "He had that South Island country person's way of being at ease with people. He enjoyed company and revelled in it. It seems a little strange, when so much farming work is so lonely, but perhaps that's the reason they're keen to get on with people."

Duff says that the young Wyllie was aggressive in a game, but, "like most people when they first come into a team, he kept his mouth shut off the field, listened a lot, and proved himself out on the paddock, not by talking."

By 1965 Wyllie had cemented a place in the Canterbury team, playing in the match against the touring Springboks that was just lost, 6-5. He would go on to play 214 games for Canterbury, captaining the team for the last eight seasons.

A group of those Canterbury veterans, Wyllie, McCormick, Tane Norton, Alistair Hopkinson, and Lyn Davis, still often meet in McCormick's hotel, the Cantabrian, to joke about the times they've all had together, to discuss the way rugby's going now, and to revive some of the better stories.

Like the Ranfurly Shield victory over Hawkes Bay in 1969. Canterbury had shaped as the top challengers all season, although they were rocked a little when Otago, for the first time in many years, beat them 20-17 at Lancaster Park.

Despite bad weather closing the Napier airport, and the Canterbury team having to fly to Palmerston North, then trek three hours by bus to Napier, precluding a Thursday training run, Canterbury fired from the start, and won 18-11.

On the Sunday morning at the Canterbury team's hotel, Derek Arnold, in those days playing in, not helping to coach, the side, found some sparkling wine in a fridge at the hotel. That didn't last long.

Peter Bush

Alex Wyllie (left) and another Canterbury stalwart, Ian Penrose join the battle against Otago in 1971.

By now starting to hum along, the players then moved to Hawkes Bay captain Kel Tremain's home. All the Hawkes Bay players were already there, at their end of season party.

Somehow the entire Canterbury squad caught the plane to Wellington, where a stopover of about an hour was needed. Just enough time, figured a group including Hopkinson, Ian Kirkpatrick, Hamish Macdonald, Jake Burns, Kerry Tanner and Wyllie, to slip into town for a few beers at the Grand Hotel. In 1969 there was no bar at the airport, and certainly no Koru Club.

Time slipped by, until, says Wyllie, "we arrived back at the airport just in time to say 'hooray' to the plane taking off. We were able to get on to the next plane. I think they were quite pleased to see us leave Wellington."

In Christchurch a huge crowd, estimated at 10,000 people, was there to greet the conquering heroes as they left the NAC aircraft. Some were a little bemused at not being able to spot some of the familiar faces, but most didn't notice, in the excitement of the day.

Finally the Grand Hotel boys arrived, with a handful of family, two men and a dog there to welcome them.

Defending the Shield in 1970 wasn't something that Wyllie was able to play a major role in. He was in South Africa, with Hopkinson, McCormick, Burns and Wayne Cottrell.

The return from South Africa didn't bring instant selection either. The Canterbury coaches, Professor Jim Stewart and Morrie Dixon, were in a quandary about what to do for the last three challenges, from Southland, Otago and Wellington.

Stewart, now Sir James, says that Hopkinson and Wyllie were not in good condition, after what had obviously been a lot of drowning of sorrows after being left out of the All Black team for the fourth test in South Africa. "I didn't put them in the game (against Southland, won 20-9). That night Alex was up against a bar, going on about how 'bloody Stewart' had dropped him. My wife is a very quiet, christian lady, who I had never heard swear before. She wheeled around on Alex and said: 'Just shut your bloody mouth!' Alex was lost for words. His jaw just dropped. From that moment I think he always respected her."

Canterbury lost the Shield to Auckland in 1971, and won it back, with Wyllie as captain, in 1972, at Eden Park. It didn't become the golden memory for him you might have expected.

"The Auckland game was a midweek one," says Wyllie. "The previous Saturday there had been a test against the Aussies in Christchurch. Canterbury had played Taranaki. The All Blacks in the Canterbury team flew to Auckland to meet up with the side. We had been going to challenge North Auckland on the next Saturday, but Auckland had already won the shield. We had a Tuesday game with Auckland that suddenly became a Ranfurly Shield match. It wasn't a big crowd, and it wasn't really a great game. We were defending desperately at the end, but we won, 12-6."

Once again, Wyllie wouldn't get to enjoy anything like the era the team he coached would have in the 1980s.

In the very first challenge of the 1973 season Marlborough would bowl over Canterbury.

There's a tradition with early season Ranfurly Shield games. In a nutshell - they're easy. You line up a union that hasn't beaten your

Wyllie charges into Marlborough's Jim Thompson, but Canterbury lost the Ranfurly Shield in the first challenge of 1973.

side for about 30 years, say, with a straight face, that you're taking them seriously as a challenger, and then your team never gets out of second gear while beating them by 30 points.

Oops. "I don't think our officials at the time had looked very closely at our programme," says Wyllie. "I guess they just thought that if we couldn't beat Marlborough there was something very wrong with us. But our preparation had been hopeless. You don't lose on purpose, but I can't remember any Canterbury officials coming into the dressing room afterwards to say 'bad luck.' In fact, some of them were pretty upset with us over the fact we'd lost it. Perhaps they should have looked to themselves, and the preparation they'd given us. Marlborough were a good team."

Very early in the game, after the powerful Marlborough prop, Jim Joseph, had smacked into Wyllie with a shoulder charge, Wyllie muttered to Norton: "This is going to be a battle."

It was only four minutes from the end of the game that winger Brian Ford scored from a 70 metre run that took Marlborough from 9-6 to 13-6, and out of any danger. But, as Wyllie said then, and says now, "There were no excuses, they won well on the day."

On the way home Marlborough supporters draped ribbons, scarves, and rosettes on Wylie Bridge (which has been spelt incorrectly by the Automobile Association for as long as everyone can remember). The mailbox toppled too. In later years Wyllie took to wrapping his mailbox in barbed wire, which discouraged pranksters. He never quite adjusted to visiting his parents-in-law in Kaikoura, and having to drive past signs saying: "You are now entering Marlborough - Ranfurly Shield Country."

Sir James Stewart, who had started coaching the Canterbury team in 1967 (and would do so until 1973) knew of Wyllie's abrasive

Peter Bush

Fergie McCormick was pained here when he missed a penalty. Without Wyllie's help he might have been in more pain in his last game for Canterbury in 1975.

reputation when he took on the Canterbury team, and he knew that Wyllie particularly didn't have much time for university men.

Says Sir James: "He did have a jaundiced view of students, and he gave some a pretty rough time. We had our moments, but we did establish a productive relationship. Alex always had extraordinary commitment, almost unbelievable. We trained three nights a week, and on a Sunday morning. I can't remember him being late for practice, let alone missing one. I've never seen such commitment in anyone in rugby."

Alistair Hopkinson compares Wyllie's approach to the game with that of Fergie McCormick. "They were the same, tremendous enthusiasm, they'd play any position they were asked to. You could build a team around them."

McCormick, who played 220 games for Canterbury, sometimes as vice-captain when Wyllie was captain, says: "When Alex was on your side, you just couldn't meet a nicer bloke. But he was not a happy man to meet when he was in the other team."

There are many outstanding Wyllie performances that spring to McCormick's mind, the successful challenge against Hawkes Bay, the Otago challenge in 1972, and a Sunday festival game, played in Christchurch the day after the drawn 1971 fourth test between the All Blacks and the Lions.

Says McCormick: "Any All Blacks in the game you could forget about. I told Alex to get off his arse and get into it. He mouthed off at me, and Lyn Davis joined in. From that moment on Alex took their whole pack on, he virtually played them by himself. The day after a test, and all because someone niggled at him."

On another occasion, McCormick recalls he found out how protective Wyllie could be.

Canterbury were playing against North Auckland in 1975, in what would prove to be McCormick's last game for his province.

"I'd had a pretty hard time," says McCormick. "I'd hurt my knee and Alex was doing everything he could to look after me. I jumped on Hamish Macdonald's brother, Rod, and all hell broke loose. I shouldn't have done it, and if I'd been spotted I could have been ordered off. Then they kicked an up and under, and I reckon Alex took three of them out before they got me. He looked after his teammates."

Probably the worst media attack ever on a provincial team came in 1971 when the Lions beat Canterbury 14-3.

Canterbury players were labelled "thugs" after Ray McLaughlin was invalided out of the tour with a broken thumb, and Sandy Carmichael was photographed with both eyes closed with bruising.

It's worth pointing out that the broken thumb came when McLoughlin miscued a punch on the top of Wyllie's head. Twenty years on Hopkinson, who propped the Canterbury scrum that day, chuckles at the memory. "There was a flare-up, but Alex wasn't involved at all. He came in to have a look at what was going on. McLoughlin threw a punch, and he broke his thumb. Alex was the unlucky bystander in that one."

Coach Stewart says he objects strongly to the suggestion made that Canterbury launched a premeditated onslaught. "We thought we had the chance to beat them, and the tension was very high. It was clear in the previous games the Lions were doing a lot of damage in the front rows. Hoppy said to me, 'What am I going to do about it?' I said, 'It's in your hands, but I'm not going to have the whole game ruined by the front row', and that was where it started getting out of control."

Hopkinson says that from the first scrum Carmichael started

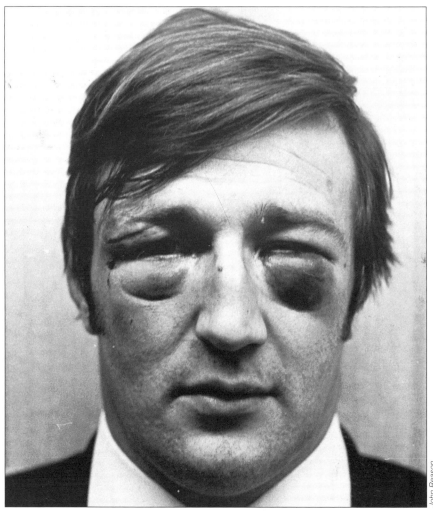

John Reason

The photograph that outraged Britain. Lions' prop Sandy Carmichael after the 1971 game with Canterbury. Wyllie's head broke the other prop, Ray McLoughlin's thumb.

boring in on Canterbury hooker Norton. "There were a few fists flying, and it didn't look too good on TV, but there was no kicking. It's one of those things that when I was coaching Canterbury Country I always said, 'If you get sent off for kicking, don't come to me for sympathy.'"

So why did the Canterbury team get savaged so badly by the British media?

Wyllie and Hopkinson firmly believe that the key to the media assault lies with the shrewd Lions manager, Dr Douglas Smith.

Along with coach Carwyn James, Dr Smith provided probably the most intelligent management team to ever bring a touring side to New Zealand.

Wyllie says: "After the game it was going to be reported as a hard game, typical of a top New Zealand provincial side. Then Smith and James got hold of their own media and said, 'No, this is what you'll write it up as, it was dirty rugby. And if it doesn't stop all hell will break loose.'" At the aftermatch function Hopkinson can remember the BBC's Cliff Morgan saying that it had been a "good hard game".

Why was it so important to paint Canterbury in such a bad light? Says Hopkinson: "They'd been using illegal tactics in the front row, and lying on the ball and killing it. That wasn't on when they played Canterbury, and they almost got beaten." Wyllie believes that Hopkinson is one player the Lions were determined to make sure wasn't selected in the All Black front row.

Sir James Stewart says he had no knowledge of the conspiracy theory, "but sometimes the players are closer to that sort of thing than I would have been." He does say that at the time the scrumming technique of the Lions was in advance of any team in New Zealand. "We actually learned from the methods the Lions were using."

Wyllie says bluntly that the whole game wasn't as bad as it was portrayed. "I think we were silly enough to go along with what they were saying."

The trust fellow players had in Wyllie didn't stop some fierce rows breaking out on, and off, the field.

McCormick remembers how a missed touchfinder would see the Wyllie head raised from the scrum, and a furious inquiry as to what game the back thought he was playing.

In fact, Wyllie the player sometimes conducted a running verbal battle with his backline.

Halfback Davis, most often Canterbury vice-captain to Wyllie, says: "We argued on the field about how much ball he let the backs have. Basically he wanted the ball to stop at Doug Bruce, because Alex reckoned it was 'no use giving it to those dumb pricks out wide.'

"To get the ball from Alex at a scrum was something you had to mark on the wall."

Davis was appointed captain in 1972 when Ian Penrose retired. Halfway through the season Davis handed over the captaincy to Wyllie, and Davis would remain a backline general until he retired at the end of 1977.

The two, Wyllie big and powerful, and Davis small but tough, were good friends, although an observer would never have thought so, says Davis. "He loved taking the mickey out of you, trying to make it hard for you. I did the same to him. He used to belt the crap out of me. He'd slap you across the back of the head. I never used my hands, I used to boot him. I'm talking about being in the back of the bus, having a few. I know he got back just as much from me as he dished out.

"That's the point about Alex, he's not actually a bully. He would never inflict pain on someone who can't hit back."

Hamish Macdonald, a rock hard lock forward, who had travelled to Canterbury with his schoolmate Ian Kirkpatrick in '67, was more than big and tough enough to battle with.

Doug Bruce says that at halftime in one match Wyllie and Macdonald started arguing. "Jim Stewart came on at halftime, and started talking about ball that was being missed in the lineout. Alex told Hamish that he'd missed a few, and Hamish said Alex had missed some too, and they were away. Jim had to stop them arguing to finish the team talk. It went on into the evening. Jim had to sit between them all night to keep them apart."

It would be wrong to suggest that Wyllie wasn't prepared to try something totally new and bizarre on a rugby field. Once.

In 1975 the Canterbury team travelled to Blenheim for the first game with Marlborough since the Ranfurly Shield had been lost to them in the '73 upset.

So there was a certain amount of needle when Canterbury set out for the match in '75. Derek Arnold, the slight, but quick and aggressive All Black midfielder from the successful Hawkes Bay challenge of '69, was co-coach for Canterbury with Tiny Hill.

Arnold decided that a new style of play would be used against Marlborough. It would be dizzying, French-style football, the ball spun from all parts of the field, running the opposing team off their feet.

Part of the revolution was that Wyllie could throw the ball into the lineout. Sixteen years later Tane Norton can't tell the story without starting to laugh. "It was a brilliant idea, but it ignored the fact that there were fifteen other people out there trying to stop what we were doing. We got a real hiding (41-17). I was thinking, 'Jeez, I hope they don't score fifty points.' I always remember Alex on the trip home. God, was he sour. He just said: 'Well, that's the bloody end of that!'"

There are some mixed feelings among his former teammates as to how Wyllie's style at No 8 affected the Canterbury pattern. McCormick says there would be brutally honest discussions at training about the backline not getting the ball until Wyllie and his forwards had "two or three goes with it."

Even a fellow forward, Norton, says the enjoyment Wyllie got from good scrummaging could lead to excesses. "His application to the scrum was unbelievable. Some loose forwards are leaners in a scrum. Not Alex. But we were playing Bay of Plenty in Rotorua

Peter Bush

Wyllie the goalkicker, observed by Tane Norton, who once had to call off an attempt at a 50 metre pushover try.

once, in mud up to our ankles, and Alex wanted us to push them half the length of the paddock. There was no way we were going to be able to do it. They were buried in the mud as well. We just told him to get stuffed."

Sir James Stewart says, with a hint of hesitation, that if he had a criticism of Wyllie as a player it was in the way his first instinct was frequently to charge into the middle of the opposing ranks.

"Alex's response was often to go down the guts, and knock someone over. It was very much grind them down, and get stuck up front, rather than think a little bit laterally and move it wide. The nature of the game in general was different in the '60s, but I think we might have blossomed a bit earlier if Alex hadn't been so preoccupied with knocking them over. He'd take off from No 8, create space and then line the fullbacks up for a charge. That used to worry me a bit. Apart from that he had a very mature attitude to the game."

Lyn Davis suggests that in his last couple of seasons for Canterbury Wyllie slowed the game down to suit his own pace, rolling the ball forward yard by yard, echoing the methods sometimes adopted by the current Auckland team.

On the other hand, Wyllie's ability to deliver ball from No 8 to his halfback, or to set up blindside moves, from which Canterbury would score try after try, was unquestioned. In fact, when he did slip the ball directly to the first-five, it was usually so well done that Tane Norton and Kerry Tanner would take delight in seeing a pass that wasn't so accurate fumbled by the first-five. They'd run behind Wyllie and call, "Nothing wrong with the pass, Alex!"

As a runner from No 8, Wyllie could be absolutely devastating. Davis, who at halfback was in the perfect place to observe such runs, says: "Alex was able to stay on his feet with the ball in his hand, and keep making progress. He had a very hard upper body. He was a bruising bugger."

For such a rugged player, says Davis, Wyllie's ability to stay on his feet meant his back was rarely criss-crossed with sprig marks after a match. "Alex never seemed to be on the bottom of a ruck."

Norton, captain of the All Blacks for the 1977 test series against the Lions, says Wyllie as a captain "never wasted words, but what he said had the stamp of authority about it. He led by example."

He was also, says Norton, very blunt. There was a game in 1974 when Davis had, for the first time in his career, to leave the field injured. Wyllie, says Norton, obviously thought that Davis would return to the field after treatment. When the replacement halfback, Steve Scott, suddenly popped up at Wyllie's elbow, he was greeted with the words: "What the hell are you doing here?" Norton laughs. "It was a great welcome for the bloke's first game."

The dressing room before a game when Wyllie was skipper was a good place to be, says Norton. "He was strong, and you felt good about going out on the field. He never had any other thought than going out to win."

THE LEGEND: *Alex Wyllie put one of Alistair Hopkinson's stock firm's cars off the road, into a fence, and couldn't get it out.*

THE WYLLIE VERSION: *"We'd played Otago in Christchurch in the days before the motorway had been put in. Hoppy and I were going home. He was driving. We were laughing about something that had happened in South Africa, and going round a corner, we hit the shingle. Hoppy straightened up just in time to go straight along a good, new fence. All you could see were batons going 'ping, ping, ping' right over the bonnet and over the top of the car. I got out to see if I could pull the barbed wire off the car, but it was so tight, we couldn't get it off. In the end a neighbour came down and pulled the car out.*

"I was at a clearing sale not long afterwards, and one of the heads of Hoppy's firm said to me: 'You'd be a bright driver wouldn't you? Pranging one of our cars the other night.' I said, 'It wasn't me.' He just laughed and walked away. To this day I think he's convinced I was driving. That Hoppy's a pretty good tale spinner."

THE HOPKINSON VERSION: *A laugh. "Alex was a wild driver when he was young. Lucky to be alive."*

CREDIBILITY RATING (OUT OF 10): *1 (for who was driving). 10 (for who owned the car, and for how hard it was to get it out of the fence).*

5

Scaring Visagie

T he after-match function at Carisbrook in Dunedin in 1964 is fizzing along for the Otago team. They've just beaten Canterbury 11-3, and there's an Otago forward, Don Clark, just named to play his first test against the Wallabies at the ground the following Saturday.

Alex Wyllie has marked Clark off the end of the lineout.

As the jugs of Speights go down, the noise level of the conversation goes up. In his school somebody asks Wyllie how he'd got on against the new All Black.

It's not a very serious question, and Wyllie doesn't give a very serious answer. "I think it'd be harder marking Morrison (Hugh Morrison, a solid lock from Cromwell who often played No 8 for Otago when Clark wasn't available)."

Later in the night Wyllie is occupied at a urinal when he hears a sharp voice behind him.

"You want to learn to keep your bloody mouth shut about things, Snow." It's the All Black selector, Fred Allen, the man who had taken his Auckland side to a record number of Ranfurly Shield defences, and who would shortly take over the coaching of the All Blacks. Allen's reputation precedes him. He's called The Needle, a man who himself once called Pinetree Meads a "doddering old bugger" in an All Black team talk, a man who once made All Black wing Malcolm Dick stand in an Auckland lineout at training as punishment for sloppy throwing in.

Now he's firing a few rockets at a 20-year-old Wyllie, who has the good sense to keep his mouth shut. "I don't think Fred took very kindly to what he thought was a criticism of his selecting."

The memory of that dressing down is still clear to Wyllie today. As anyone would, he wonders whether it ever had any influence on his progress to the All Blacks, a step he wouldn't make until after Allen had stepped down from the New Zealand panel.

Allen too can remember the incident. At 71, he's still a straight shooter, with strong views on games and players. If he'd been the coach in Argentina and the props hadn't been up to scratch he wouldn't have bracketed them, they'd be out of the side for a test. "It brings them to heel very quickly," Allen laughs.

So did Wyllie go on Allen's blacklist?

"No, not at all. I had a word with him, in Dunedin, as I would with anyone with ability, to try and steer him right. But you can never let personal feelings get in the way of your selections. If you did that you'd get nowhere in the game.

"There were some handy young footballers that were keeping him out, like (Graham) Williams and (Ian) Kirkpatrick. Alex was a good, fiery player but he didn't get the nod. I certainly never held a grudge against him, and these days I've often supported him when his coaching is criticised."

Wyllie would play All Black trials in 1967, 1968 and 1969, without winning the All Black jersey. He was encouraged to keep trying by the chairman of the New Zealand union, Tom Morrison, who told Wyllie that in his own case there had been three trials before he finally became an All Black in 1938. "He (Morrison) came to me and said, 'Don't chuck it in.'"

At the end of 1969 Wyllie trained harder over the summer than he ever had before. "After Canterbury won the Ranfurly Shield (from Hawkes Bay) I was told I had a fair chance of getting away next year to South Africa. I knew that 1970 was probably going to be it. If I didn't make it then, I probably never would."

Twenty-two years ago, work on the farm itself provided its share of physical conditioning. "There wasn't so much mechanical gear used them," says Wyllie. "So things like carting hay, handling grain, was a sort of fitness programme, without you knowing you were actually doing it. I did some running as well, but never long distance stuff. I'm talking about going out for ten or fifteen or twenty minutes as hard as you can, then coming back, and seeing how your times compared, so you could look at your recovery rate.

"Players who run too many miles in the off-season can keep going at one pace through a match, and at the end of a game could probably turn around and play another. That's no use. When you see players who have trained until they're skin and bone, they get knocked around more than a man who's in good nick, someone who has lasted the game well, but certainly couldn't play another. It's the old story, a good big man will always beat a good little man."

Under the stand at Athletic Park in 1970 they announced the team for South Africa. At long last Wyllie was an All Black. His first match wouldn't turn out to be much fun

The All Blacks played two games on a Sunday afternoon in Perth, with Wyllie on the side of the scrum in the main match,

Christchurch Star

Alex Wyllie crosses the line in the match with Eastern Transvaal, but the referee called him back for a knock on.

against Western Australia, won 50-3. "I wore a pair of boots, for the first and last time, that were too small for me, and they were so uncomfortable that I didn't have a good game at all. Others remarked on it. So it was a bad start."

Once the team arrived in South Africa, where 4000 people crammed Jan Smuts Airport in Johannesburg, things started to perk up for Wyllie.

"I like playing on hard grounds," says Wyllie, "and that's what we had there. I was happy with my form." On the other hand, like most of the players on the 1970 tour, he wasn't crazy about the training sessions being run by coach Ivan Vodanovich. It wasn't the intensity of the training that was the problem, Wyllie believes, but the type of training, "typical of those days, when you ran round and round a damned field, then turned around to run the other way, to unwind, so you wouldn't get giddy."

In the games before the first test the All Blacks ran the ball through the backs whenever possible, and it seemed to be working. It was the fifth game, with Transvaal, before there was a try scored against them.

But it wasn't all going as smoothly as it looked on paper. For a start Colin Meads, the senior forward, suffered a broken arm in the match with Eastern Transvaal when he was booted in a ruck. Captain Brian Lochore had broken his thumb in Perth, and, ironic-

Colin Meads was only using a camera because of his broken arm when the All Blacks cruised the Zambesi. Later he'd return to the team with the arm protected by a plastic frame.

ally, would make his comeback, after missing seven games, in the same match Meads' arm was broken.

And, perhaps even more importantly, the men behind the Springboks were looking and learning.

The South African coach was Johan Claassen, later to be the manager of the 1981 Springboks tour of New Zealand.

Says Wyllie: "Claassen had a hand in coaching some of the teams we played against before the first test, so they tried different tactics against us to see what worked best. They had everything filmed, so they could study us, and our tactics never really changed, so when they came to the first test they'd had ten games to see how we played. They had big men in the forwards for the tests, good loose forwards, and strong tacklers in the midfield. We virtually played into their hands. We should have taken the ball up to them, and got into them a bit. If we'd got stuck into them we might have had a chance."

As it was, the Springboks rolled the All Blacks 17-6 in the first test in Pretoria, the first loss for the All Blacks on tour.

"They knew exactly what we were about. Mind you, I'd hate to have ten games before a test now, as a coach. It's a hell of a lot.

"My feeling is always that when the All Blacks meet the Springboks, it's Greek meeting Greek. This time they'd done all their planning before they went on the field, and we'd shown our hand.

"They were also out there to die for their country. They had flags on the wall, pictures of (John) Vorster (the South African Prime Minister) in the dressing room, they were hyped up.

"On the field all they did was to knock us over, and score from our mistakes."

The reaction back in New Zealand to the first test loss was absolute horror. On tour with the team, veteran broadcaster Winston McCarthy whipped up the heat in his column in *Truth* with a call for the "meanies" to be brought in for the second test in Cape Town.

Wyllie was named as one of "the meanies", along with Alan Sutherland (who, like Wyllie, had not played in the first test) and Alistair Hopkinson and Bruce McLeod (who had).

These were men, raged McCarthy, who hated losing, and did something about it. They knew that the Springboks were cleverly getting offside around the mauls and rucks. But on the tour so far, the All Blacks weren't allowed to take things into their own hands. "There have been a number of flare-ups," wrote McCarthy, "but should any New Zealander retaliate, he has been severely admonished after the match, and sometimes even during the game itself. I know some players think this is unfair on them, and they feel that when they are obstructed, they should be allowed to retaliate.

"In other words, they feel it is time the velvet glove was tossed away, and they became men again, instead of girls."

McCarthy and his followers would have their wish come true, when all four so-called meanies would turn up in the All Black pack in the second test.

The All Blacks won, 9-8, but Wyllie, looking back on his first test match, says he would hate to ever see a game like it again.

"We came out on top, but the game was on the verge of being bloody dirty. There were guys who were raked, and kicked, and punched. It wasn't good for the game."

Something Wyllie did manage was to intimidate the South African first-five, Piet Visagie.

Ian Kirkpatrick says "Grizz was in bloody good form off the back of the lineout. He certainly put a bit of fear into Visagie." Even Wyllie, who shies away from anything that sounds like self praise, says "some of the South Africans admitted that he didn't like facing me."

After the second test Fergie McCormick would be vilified for what the South Africans at first claimed was a stiffarm tackle on Sid Nomis, who lost his front teeth. Later, film would show that McCormick actually had his back to the South African winger. McCormick threw his arms up, after the ball had been kicked past him, in an illegal attempt to obstruct Nomis. The point of

Wessel Oosthuizen

Piet Visagie...who, says Ian Kirkpatrick, had a bit of fear put into him by Wyllie.

McCormick's elbow struck the Springbok in the mouth. McCormick says it was an accident. Wyllie, who was hard on Nomis' heels, agrees.

A group who didn't were the Springboks. Everyone knew that McCormick's life would be made miserable if they could get their hands on him.

The third test, in Port Elizabeth, saw the All Blacks, in Wyllie's mind, make several crucial errors.

For a start the All Blacks were reshuffled, despite having won the previous test. Four changes were made to the team, including the return of Meads, with a protective casing on his left arm, which had not fully healed. "The whole team selection was hard to understand. I believe it was muddled. I'm not saying that the players who were there shouldn't have been there, just that the selections weren't consistent, so the players didn't have a chance to settle down and be consistent."

The Springboks were a lot shrewder in their selections. "The only changes they made were to get a bit more height into the lineouts," says Wyllie. "They'd gone into what was needed in depth. I guess it was summed up when Danie Craven said to us late in the tour, 'Perhaps we should pick your team for you.' At times the South Africans couldn't believe our selections."

Knowing that McCormick was on the Springbok hit list, Wyllie believes the fullback should have been kept out of the backline for the first twenty minutes or so. "We should have told Fergie to keep out of it, to stay in the background until they'd started to forget about him. After twenty minutes the hype starts to go, and they're concentrating on playing rugby, not the man. As it was, they got to him early in the game, got hold of him, and almost crippled him."

McCormick has a very clear memory of the third test.

"I wanted to go off, but they wouldn't let me. I wasn't good. I didn't have any pace left, and I couldn't tackle. Alex came back and helped me on numerous occasions. I admire him for that, that's the sort of man he is. I told him to leave me, but he wouldn't, and I

Things got fiery in the fourth test with the Springboks, but Wyllie wasn't involved. Like all the Canterbury players, he was watching from the stand.

believe that's why he lost his position for the fourth test. I'm not the only one who thinks that."

How does Wyllie remember his covering that day? "You always go where you think the ball is going to go. If you think it'll be kicked behind the backline, you go to cover that. I still feel that I was putting pressure on Visagie."

Certainly, Wyllie was never told which area of his play in the third test wasn't up to scratch. In fact, he wasn't given any reasons at all. With a fourth test that would see the Springboks win, or the All Blacks draw, the series, there are some who note that of McCarthy's "meanies", just one, Alan Sutherland, would play at Ellis Park in Johannesburg.

Could that tag have proven a problem for Wyllie, Hopkinson and McLeod? "It shouldn't," says Wyllie, "but in a selection I suppose you'd have to consider it. Others could say, 'Well, this is the direction the All Blacks are taking. If they pick (these players) then all hell could break loose.' Then, in the game, you only need something to blow up, and you're in the gun. So it possibly could affect the selection of a team."

A South African critic, Neville Leck, would describe the dropping of Wyllie, for Tom Lister, as "probably the hardest decision the All Black selectors had to make. Wyllie was the All Blacks' best forward at Port Elizabeth (in the third test)."

After the fourth test team was announced Hopkinson, never one to miss the chance to use humour to make a point, was on the team bus, called for silence, and asked all the Canterbury players in the test team to stand up. Nobody moved - because nobody from Canterbury would play in the test.

While the '70 tour may not have had a happy ending for the team, or for Wyllie, he has remained a staunch supporter of official rugby contact with South Africa. When men in white coats picked tacks off Lancaster Park before the first test with the Springboks in 1981 one of them, little noticed by the media at the time, was Wyllie.

So it was an odd twist that many confused his position on the Cavaliers in 1986. "It was apparently said in South Africa that I was against the Cavaliers going, possibly because I was anti-South Africa. That's never been the case. To my mind touring South Africa is the biggest, the best, challenge a New Zealand player can face.

"The thing I thought was that the Cavaliers made a mistake in the way they went, in some of the deceptions that had to go on here in New Zealand. At the time I also made the point, and I believe it's been proven, that the South Africans cannot have any more teams going there unofficially. I've run into Eastern Province players in Argentina, at a ski resort, and a Natal team in Cardiff, and they say they realise now that the Cavaliers actually set back how quickly South Africa could get back into international rugby.

"All I was saying at the time was that, while the cancellation of the All Black tour there was obviously very disappointing, for the sake of the game, and not for some individuals' own ego, I don't believe they should have gone."

What if there was an official All Black tour in 1992? How would New Zealand go? "The set pieces would be vital. If we held our scrums, and won fifty per cent of the ball in the lineouts, I think we could beat them. We'd certainly have to use all the ball we did win.

"It is very hard to judge. As big and tall as they are, how long could you withstand that sort of pressure when you're up against them? And, on the other hand, how good would their mobility be around the field?

"There are so many things to consider. You don't know how much the set pieces would drag out of the All Blacks. It's hard to judge what would happen in the last ten to twenty minutes when the heat's really on."

For Wyllie the player, 1971 would see him play three tests for the All Blacks at No 8 against the Lions, after Alan Sutherland, back row in the first test, broke his leg in a charity game.

The '71 Lions won the first test (9-3) and lost the second (12-22), before winning the third (13-3). A 14-all draw in the fourth test made them the first, and, to date, the only, Lions to win a test series in New Zealand.

In '72 Wyllie was a reserve to Sutherland as the All Blacks swept aside the team the headline writers called the "Awful Aussies" in a three test series. The fateful tour of Great Britain and France would follow.

After the tour to Britain, the All Black coaching job will be filled by JJ Stewart, formerly the head of Flock House at Bulls, an agricultural college for young men who had left secondary school.

Stewart is an unusual man to have reached the top of our national rugby tree. He has a very keen sense of humour, not always a high priority with the New Zealand union, and he's often been very outspoken. At times, as an administrator, he tried to prod the union into forward thinking, when that was basically considered a crime in Wellington.

A man who enjoyed a drink, he could be blunt, even gruff, and he was given a job in '73 that nobody would envy.

The previous year the All Blacks had toured New Zealand, a trip that involved nine matches, one against the New Zealand Juniors, and eight against provinces.

In '73, with a tour by the Springboks cancelled by the Labour Government of Norman Kirk, the New Zealand union, in what many of the players, including Wyllie, saw as hawking the silver fern as a purely commercial proposition. quickly set up a four match tour.

Peter Bush

JJ Stewart...given a job in 1973 that nobody would enjoy.

"It made a mockery of the All Black jersey," says Wyllie. The tour began with a loss to the New Zealand Juniors in Dunedin, 10-14. Future All Black Bruce Gemmell captained the Juniors from half-back, and at flank forward was Graham Mourie. Wyllie was not in the All Blacks, North Aucklander Bevan Holmes playing at No 8.

The All Black tour didn't get any better when it reached Wellington, to play a President's XV in what amounted to a farewell to Colin Meads, who captained the President's team. At halfback in

Peter Bush

Sid Going, backed up by Ian Kirkpatrick, tries to turn the tide against the '73 England team, but the All Blacks lost 16-10. It would be Wyllie's last test.

the Meads team was Sid Going, who had been unavailable for the All Blacks, but was apparently cajoled into turning out against them. The President's XV, an odd mixture of former All Blacks, provincial players and some overseas stars, beat the All Blacks, 35-28. Wyllie recalls that Sid Going was almost embarrassed at having to play against his All Black teammates.

By the time the All Blacks got to Rotorua to play the New Zealand Maori team, coach Stewart was getting desperate. He provided one of the great quotes of coaching history. "If the All

Blacks don't beat the Maori team," Stewart told journalists, "I'll bare my backside on the steps of the Auckland Post Office."

That embarrassment was spared Stewart when the All Blacks won 18-8, after the Maoris drew level, 8-all, early in the second half, and the last match of the scruffy little tour was won, 22-10, against an Invitation XV (the President's XV under another name), in Auckland.

Luckily for the people of Auckland, Stewart made no promises of public exposure, at the Post Office or anywhere else, before the All Blacks played England in a one-off test at Eden Park. The visit by England was a substitute for a substitute.

Scotland were to make an eight match, two test tour, subbing for the Springboks. The tour by the Scots fell through, and then, when a tour to Argentina by England was called off, after kidnap threats, the English, captained by hooker John Pullin, were jetted in for three provincial matches, and one test, at Eden Park.

The tourists lost to Taranaki, Wellington and Canterbury, captained by Wyllie, before they arrived in Auckland. At the end of 80 minutes the All Blacks had suffered an embarrassing 10-16 loss. It would be the last game Wyllie would play for the All Blacks.

In 1974 the All Black selectors, Stewart, Jack Gleeson and Eric Watson, deposed Ian Kirkpatrick as captain, replacing him with Andy Leslie, and dropped Wyllie, Hamish Macdonald, Mike Parkinson and Kent Lambert, from the tourists of '72-73 to Britain.

Macdonald and Lambert would be reinstated for the tour to Ireland at the end of the year. Wyllie was not.

Several years later Wyllie and Stewart were guest speakers at Macdonald's club in Kaitaia. At question time Stewart was asked why Wyllie had not gone to Ireland in '74, or South Africa in '76. Wyllie said he wouldn't mind knowing either. Stewart told the original questioner: "Grizz didn't go for the same reason you didn't go. He wasn't selected."

Today, with his tongue out of his cheek, Stewart says Wyllie's powerful personality was never a factor in him being dropped. "I'd had Alex with me on that stupid internal tour in '73, and I found him good company. I like him. Selection for a rugby team is very subjective. It isn't like the system the Americans use for the Olympic athletic trials, where the first three athletes past the post are in the team, and that's it.

"As a coach, I was looking for a more expansive game, and, at the time, Alex was playing off the end of the lineout, or one in. At the time he was being challenged in that position by people like Kenny Stewart who, quite frankly, could run considerably faster than him.

"It's always hard when a good player is dropped, but I think it's a fact of life in rugby, the young bulls are after the old bulls, and eventually the young ones take over."

Legend

THE LEGEND: *Alex Wyllie was such a brutal boxer, that after he fought in the heavyweight championship at St Andrew's College, the school banned the sport.*

WHAT REALLY HAPPENED: *As a 14-year-old, 13st 5lb fourth former, Wyllie did fight in the 1960 heavyweight final. He fought a sixth former, JAR Reid, who was a stone lighter. The school magazine said: "Wyllie had a hard punch, and the torrid first round was in his favour. But Reid, able to absorb punishment in the first round, then boxed his way into a winning position." Wyllie lost on points. The next year boxing was discontinued.*

VERSIONS: *Reid was going to return the following year, and a 15-year-old Wyllie, disgruntled at his loss, would certainly have been ready to make all three rounds "torrid." Old classmates favour the legend. Former teachers say the movement against boxing had been building up for some years, with the staff finally deciding that boys who might want to use their brains to make their way in the world shouldn't run the risk of having them scrambled at school. But the Wyllie style alone didn't close the sport down.*

SOURCES: *School magazine and former teachers Ian Clark and Frank Finnegan.*

CREDIBILITY RATING (OUT OF 10): *3. Boxing was certainly on the way out, but all accounts of the Reid-Wyllie final suggest it would have been a handy tool for the anti-boxing lobby.*

6

Murdoch and the mafia

A lex Wyllie isn't feeling too good. It's a Monday morning in Birmingham, in the Midlands of England, and he's nursing a torn rib cartilage, damaged in the test with Wales on the Saturday.

He's had a room to himself so he wouldn't be disturbed, but he's bemused when he hears on the bedside radio a story saying the All Blacks have had a quiet night, and held a team meeting. Jeez. What team meeting?

Wyllie hurries out of his room. At the lift he sees the Poverty Bay player, Mike Parkinson.

"What the hell's the story," asks Wyllie. "Was there a team meeting last night? Why didn't I get a call?"

"We checked your room out," says Parkinson, "but you were still asleep, and we knew you were crook with your ribs. We're on our way to training. You'd better let Ernie know what you're doing."

Going to see Ernie Todd, the manager of the 1972-73 All Blacks, isn't something that Wyllie relishes. To his mind, and to many others, the tour's just barely being kept together by coach Bob Duff.

There have been too many examples of disorganised management from Todd. Once the team sat on a bus getting ready to go to training. Todd arrived in collar and tie, and demanded to know why the players weren't dressed the same way. There was an official function to be attended after the training session. None of the players had been told, and they had to troop off the bus, get changed into formal clothes, and then leave for the training. It doesn't sound like much, but on a long tour, small irritations quickly become big ones.

When Todd opens his door to Wyllie he looks like a man in bad shape, and under pressure. Still in his dressing gown, it's obvious there's been late drinking in the room the previous night, and Todd hasn't had a good sleep

Wyllie asks: "What's going on?"

Christchurch Star

Bob Duff (left), with Ian Kirkpatrick and Keith Murdoch, was a man a heavy burden fell on in Great Britain.

"I've been up all night," says Todd, "talking to the English officials here, and to Jack Sullivan (the chairman of the New Zealand Rugby Union) on the phone. He's left the decision on Keith (Murdoch) to me. Keith's going home."

Wyllie is stunned. "Jeez, hang on. Don't do that."

"I've made up my mind. Keith's going home."

The last act of a tragic series of events starts to slip out of control. Wyllie goes downstairs, and finds Ian Kirkpatrick, the team captain. "What the hell's the story," Wyllie asks Kirkpatrick. "Ernie says Keith's going home." "He can't be," says Kirkpatrick. "We ended up with Ernie last night, Bob (Duff), Sid (Going), and myself, and it was agreed Keith would stay. We'd had a talk to him, told him if there was any more nonsense he'd go. But he wasn't being sent home."

But it is a fact. Kirkpatrick and Duff argue with Todd, but the manager is firm. Keith Murdoch will become the first, and thankfully, to date the only, All Black to be sent home from a tour for misbehaviour.

Murdoch himself has never spoken out fully on the affair. When he was found in Queensland last year by Margot McRae, an Auckland television journalist for the "Mud and Glory" programme, he talked with her in some detail about what had happened, but declined to be interviewed on camera.

Exactly what Murdoch did in the early hours of the morning at the Angel Hotel in Cardiff will never be really known. Several hours, and many beers, after an historic win over Wales at Cardiff Arms Park, many of the players who might have been around him, and seen what went on, cannot be the most reliable witnesses. Wyllie, full of painkillers for his damaged ribs, was early to bed.

It certainly hadn't, in some ways, been a pleasant night. Tane Norton recalls that at the cabaret in the Angel after the test there had been free drinks down one end of the room for the Welsh team. Down the other the All Blacks had been expected to pay. So most of the players took off to their rooms for a series of private celebrations. Murdoch went to find drinks, and possibly food, to fuel the occasion.

Who knows, or can remember clearly, what happened next? But it is a fact that a Welsh security guard, Peter Grant, was soon nursing a black eye, which came from a blow delivered by Murdoch in the kitchen of the Angel Hotel.

It took some time after that, but Murdoch was eventually persuaded by Duff to return to his room he was sharing with an old Otago friend, Lin Colling.

Murdoch, it would be fair to say, was not the first international rugby player to be involved in a scrap while on tour. But, while many felt the security guards at the Angel that night were behaving like thugs, thumping one inevitably led to serious consequences.

Duff tried to find Todd on the night of the incident, without success, and, when he went to Todd's room the next morning, found a couple of Home Union officials already there.

The Murdoch incident was being discussed. The Home Union officials were angry, and Duff says there was an immediate investigation. Murdoch was brought in. "He wasn't particularly communicative, but he didn't try to justify his behaviour. We got an undertaking from him that there wouldn't be any repetition, and we decided that the discipline would be decided in the bus on the way to Birmingham. At that stage we knew that Keith wasn't going to be charged by the Police. If there had been charges pending that might have put a different complexion on it, but that wasn't happening."

With the bus due to leave at 1 o'clock the tour leaders, Todd, Duff, Kirkpatrick, and vice-captain Sid Going, go and pack. On the bus Duff and the two players decide that the team for the next game, against West Midlands, will include Murdoch. "We had a tough game coming up," says Duff, "and Keith's form was on a high. After a bit of a slow start he was really playing well."

Todd hadn't finally decided on what would happen, but sending Murdoch home, in the memories of Duff and Kirkpatrick, was never an option being considered.

Duff went out for dinner with Tane Norton and a representative from Adidas. On his return to the hotel Duff was called to take a phone call from Jack Sullivan, in New Zealand. They talked for a while, and Sullivan told Duff he was trying to get hold of Todd. Sullivan said he would try for Todd later.

Next morning, at about 9 o'clock, Duff was called to Todd's room. "Ernie said, 'I've been thinking about this, and Keith is going home.' It knocked me over. I objected to it, and said it wasn't right, and argued the toss with him. I asked him why, and I got the impression, I should say it was just the impression, that he had been under pressure to do it."

Duff returned with Kirkpatrick, who was just as determined that Murdoch should be allowed to stay, on the promise of good behaviour. Duff says: "We made a last effort to get him to change his mind. I said, 'Ernie, this can't happen. Would you please change your mind? It isn't good for the team.'"

But Todd would not be persuaded.

Why did he, in effect, change his mind from one day to the next? Did new evidence emerge overnight? If it did, nobody has ever uncovered it since.

Wyllie and Grant Batty bailed up Todd on the night after the game with West Midlands, when the All Blacks lost, 8-16, and demanded to know why Todd had sent Murdoch home. Says Wyllie: "He told me that the England officials had pressured him into it. They'd insisted that Keith be sent home." Duff, the man in the touring party closest to Todd, was never told that, but is sure the English pressure was the key issue.

On the other side was the New Zealand Rugby Union. Todd told Wyllie that Jack Sullivan had left the decision to Todd. Did Todd get backing from the New Zealand union to resist the British pressure?

Duff thinks not. "They more or less left it to Ernie. He was in it alone. They hadn't given him any strong opinions, they didn't advise him on what they thought he should do. He was under a lot of strain on the Sunday morning, and under even more on the Monday morning."

The picture that emerges is of a manger being pushed very hard from one side, with no weight coming in from the other to help him push back.

There are many theories as to what could have prevented the Murdoch affair. One is that Murdoch should never have been sent on tour. Another that Todd should never have been the manager. Another that the team should have, in effect, gone on strike to demand that Murdoch stay. Yet another that one more very senior player, like the great Colin Meads, then in the twilight of his career, could have kept Murdoch on a shorter rein.

Of Murdoch himself, Wyllie says that his attitude had changed since the South African tour of 1970. Then Murdoch had been a

Peter Bush

Keith Murdoch on the way home in 1972. His departure was, Wyllie was told by manager Ernie Todd, demanded by English officials.

disappointing trainer. But in Britain he was training as hard as anybody in the team. "He'd be first out on the ground, and the last to leave. He was scrummaging very well. Had he got through the tour, how long he could have played for New Zealand would really have just been a question of how long he wanted to. He had the skills, the speed, and the strength, he was proving it game by game."

Duff says that all the players respected Murdoch. "I was happy to have Keith on tour. At times I could have kicked him in the backside for his behaviour, not things that were too far out of line, but I had to say 'Come on', and he'd react well, and do the right thing."

Wyllie says that Murdoch was not the most rowdy player at parties. "He was quite happy to sit in a corner. A lot of people might have got the impression that he wasn't the brightest, but he was far from dumb. At times he'd just play along with people who thought he wasn't too clever. Basically, he was happy to keep to himself, or just be with a couple of mates he got on well with."

Looking back now, it sticks in Wyllie's craw that the New Zealand Rugby Union selected Todd as manager.

Todd would die of cancer in November, 1974, and Wyllie is one who believes he was sick before the tour to Britain began. "I don't think it was Ernie's fault, so much as people on the council who knew he wasn't well and still sent him away to manage the team."

A team manager in Great Britain has a tough, tiring job. "It's damned hard work," says Wyllie, "and you've got to be on your mettle to keep up with everything that's demanded of you. There's a very heavy social schedule that a manager really has to do. Over there they make a very big thing of the official functions, and as well as that a manager has to be able to keep the team moving along as well."

Captain Kirkpatrick firmly believes the New Zealand union knew Todd was ill before the tour began. "It became more and more difficult, and Ernie became more and more divorced from us. I think the union had a lot to answer for. They must have known Ernie wasn't well."

Duff, however, is not sure that Todd was aware of his illness before the tour started. "There were occasions when Ernie had to go to bed for a day or two, but we had players with the 'flu, and there could have been times after a win, and a celebration, that some of us didn't look or feel very well either."

Duff does know that Todd "wasn't really the same guy" after Murdoch had been sent home. Todd was in a difficult position with the team after Murdoch had gone, with many, possibly all of them, blaming him for what they saw as the wrong decision.

In fact Duff had to tread a narrow line between Todd and the team. "I couldn't say to him, 'Ernie you were right,' because I didn't believe that what had happened was right. But if I'd sided with the team against Ernie that would have split the whole tour, so we had to work through the situation to keep the tour going. I think it's fair to say we got on okay after Keith had gone, and at times I suppose I virtually played the peacemaker."

Wyllie recalls that two Wellington players, Mark Sayers and Ian

Peter Bush

Ernie Todd...the New Zealand Rugby Union shouldn't have selected him for the '72-73 tour says Wyllie.

Stevens, would later say they believed that Duff was the man who held the tour together.

From the morning Murdoch appeared on the team bus, in an open necked shirt, and a plain blazer and said "Hooray, boys, I'm off," there was certainly a feeling in the team that they should have threatened to go with Murdoch unless he was reinstated.

Tane Norton says, "The doors should have been shut on the bus, and a meeting held. Then, if we accepted the decision, and believed Keith should be sent home, we carried on. Or, if we didn't, we should have gone home en masse. But whatever happened we should have had a meeting. You felt it had been done slyly, so Keith was gone before we could do a thing."

What about the suggestion that the team lacked senior players of the Meads stripe? Or that the senior players they did have were undisciplined, mavericks, who formed a black hat gang that threatened the stability of the whole team?

Wyllie, Norton, Alan Sutherland and Going were all under fire, from the British media, and from the senior New Zealand journalist on the tour, Terry McLean, for wearing the hats, or, in Going's case, a beret, instead of proper uniform.

The hats, says Wyllie, began as a joke in Vancouver, where they were bought from a shop in the foyer of the team's hotel. Certainly they were worn at team court sessions, and the men who wore them sat in the back seat on the bus. "But there's a back seat on every bus, on every tour. There's nothing unusual about that. The whole black hat stuff was blown out of all proportion."

Duff says he thought the hats were funny from the time they had been purchased. "When they did wear them for a photograph, with Alex's face underneath it, well, they did look a bit like the Mafia I suppose. Within ourselves it was always a joke. The young players tried to flog the hats, and the older ones fought like hell to keep them. But it was never anything sinister."

In fact, says Duff, the '72-73 team was never rent by divisions among the players. "They were all good friends. We constantly alternated roommates, and not once did anyone ask if he could have a rooming arrangement changed."

Duff, and captain Ian Kirkpatrick, both say they couldn't have faulted Wyllie's commitment to the team and the tour. In Kirkpatrick's opinion, Wyllie "was a help to me out on the paddock, or at training. Grizz was like he always was, in top gear all the time. There was no low gear, it was one hundred per cent whether it was a club game, a charity game, or a test match."

In Wyllie's view, the fact that the 1972-73 tour was the first time the test matches were shown live on New Zealand television led to a big change in the way print journalists approached the tour. There were a lot more than usual, and many, Wyllie was told, were under great pressure from their newspapers to provide sensational copy, to counter the fact that straight match reports, on the tests anyway, did not have the same currency they had in the days of radio reports only.

The idea of some sort of threat to Kirkpatrick's captaincy was nonsense, according to Kirkpatrick. "That was the British media looking in from the outside. There were no problems at all."

In a different environment the black hat gang would have been seen as the joke it was intended to be, says Kirkpatrick. "To paint those guys as the Mafia was just ridiculous. You wouldn't meet an easier going guy than Tane (Norton) for one. But if anything went wrong, those four, or Keith (Murdoch) seemed to be the ones who copped it. The British press niggled at Keith from the time we arrived in Great Britain."

What seems remarkable now is that the team peformed as well as they did. They were young, with an average age of 24, with only six players who had ever been on a major tour before. It was the first major tour of the captain, coach, and manager. Yet they beat Wales, 19-16, beat Scotland, 14-9, beat England, 9-0, and were leading Ireland until the last few minutes, when Ireland snatched a 10-all draw.

So the much maligned team was just a heartbeat away from becoming the first ever All Black side to beat all four Home Unions.

Two of the Black Hat boys, Wyllie and Alan Sutherland.

(The famous 1924-25 team did not play Scotland, apparently because the Scottish Rugby Union was still smarting from a poor financial deal set up for the test with New Zealand in 1905-06). The Irish test was the only occasion when Duff was angry and disappointed with the team. "We had the legs on them in the backline, but for some reason we tried to keep it in the forwards. The plan had been to move the ball." Only France, right at the end of the tour, would beat them in a test, 13-6.

Wyllie, with the hindsight of a man who has returned to Britain as an All Black coach, is very clear that the '72-73 team have carried an unjust reputation.

"We had big problems after Keith went, and Bob Duff was vital to us. He got on well with all the players, and he was well respected. He had such a young team, probably one of the most inexperienced the All Blacks have ever had on tour. For example, if you look at a player like Kent Lambert having to come on (against Scotland) to replace Jeff Matheson, Kent was just twenty-one, which is very young for a test prop. But Bob worked on getting the basics right, and that carried us through."

Duff may have been a powerful lock in his playing days, good enough to captain the All Blacks to the historic test series victory over the '56 Springboks, but he doesn't carry any abrasiveness off the paddock. Sitting in his Lyttelton office, there's a lot more of the reflective accountant than the rugged rugby player.

During the 1973 New Zealand season there was only one test match, against England, at Eden Park, lost 16-10 by the All Blacks. JJ Stewart was the All Black coach. It would be Wyllie's last game for New Zealand.

Duff was dropped from the panel at the end of the '73 season. "I'd thought it would have been a natural progression, having had me coach the team on a long tour in '72-73, to possibly have me continue as coach," says Duff. Was he disgruntled when he lost his place on the panel altogether? Duff smiles. "I'd be less than honest if I didn't say I was a little bit disappointed I didn't get the opportunity to continue."

In 1974 Kirkpatrick would be gone as captain, although still in the All Blacks. Wellington's Andy Leslie was the No 8 and captain. The All Blacks returned to Wales and Ireland, winning both tests, and drawing one match on an unbeaten eight game tour.

To some it was seen as a bold new All Black era, and the team did play well. But consider this: The side that beat Wales 12-3 in '74 contained 11 of the test players from the much-maligned team of 1972-73. At the core of the '74 team against Wales were Duff's men: Karam, Batty, Williams, Robertson, Hurst, Going, Kirkpatrick, Macdonald, Whiting, Lambert and Norton. The new look was very much like the old look.

THE LEGEND: *Alex Wyllie once punched the Wellington loose forward Mark Stevens during a game with Canterbury. As Stevens was being attended to, the outraged Wellington halfback, Dave Henderson, shouts: "Who was the dirty bastard who did this?" Wyllie pops his head up. "It was me." Henderson gulps, and says: "Nice punch Grizz."*

THE REAL STORY: *The same as the legend according to Henderson, now an advertising agency executive in Auckland.*

THE WYLLIE VERSION: *"It was sort of along those lines. It happened at a lineout where I'd thought that if all hell was going to break loose it might as well be there."*

CREDIBILITY RATING (OUT OF 10): 10.

Legend

7

Taking a chance with kids' games

Jim Blair, a physical education lecturer at Auckland's North Shore teachers' training college, was fumbling his way to the urinal at Lincoln College.

His hesitancy had nothing to do with the beers he'd been drinking. It was just that the light was so bad he didn't like the idea of bumping into a concrete wall, or stepping where he'd regret it.

He had found his way safely to his destination, when the light streaming through the door was cut off by the frame of a large man.

Blair recognised the voice from the opening words. "I want to talk to you, Jim."

Oh God, thought Blair, Alex Wyllie.

"I don't mind admitting it gave me a fright," says Blair. "Certainly not from any fear of being sexually molested, but I'd heard about Alex Wyllie, this hard man, and there was this big figure towering over me."

Blair had been in Christchurch for that Easter weekend in 1983 to speak at a promising players' school.

Wyllie was there by chance, asked to help with some coaching tips. "We were sitting round having a few drinks the night before the players assembled. I'd never met Jim Blair before, and I heard him talking. He was saying how players should prepare themselves not to just go out and run and run. You can keep going at that pace for a long time, but it's not what's needed on a rugby field.

"I thought I should have a yarn with him, but I left it for a while, because there were a lot of coaches there, and I didn't want them all on to it at once. So I waited until we could have a word in the toilet, then went to the Canterbury union and said, 'I want to get this joker down and do a few tests.' That's how it started."

Well, not quite. To be in a position to invite Blair to help with Canterbury, Wyllie had first to be elected Canterbury coach.

It wasn't a position that Wyllie had seriously thought about when he stopped playing for the province at the end of 1979.

He was still playing for Glenmark, and wasn't highly impressed when he wasn't selected for the Canterbury Country team, which lost to the Town side.

In the careers of successful people there is often a turning point, which doesn't seem extremely important at the time, but, in hindsight can be considered vital. Wyllie believes his non-selection for a Country team that would lose to Town was a vital moment in his career.

The non-selection, says the Country coach of 1980, Tom McLay, was probably a mistake. "I was under the impression that Alex had retired from all representative play."

Wyllie, who regarded Country losing to Town as the next worst thing to rugby being declared an illegal activity, decided to stand for the Country coaching job himself. A lot of ifs followed that decision, but, if Wyllie had not stood for Country coach in '81, he would hardly have been a candidate for Canterbury coach the next year. And if he hadn't coached Canterbury in '82 he might not have had a chance for two or three years, and he would certainly then not have been the All Black coach at this year's World Cup.

McLay, who had successfully coached the Marlborough team in the mid-60s, says he was "quite hurt about it" when Wyllie took McLay's position as Country coach in '81. "Alex and I have sorted it out since. He really had to be the Country coach to be able to take over the Canterbury team. I think a lot of other people were working towards that, even then."

That's overstating the case, but it is true, that, although McLay losing his job wasn't the result of a backroom plot, a group of Canterbury officials were growing increasingly concerned about what was happening to their representative team in the '81 season.

It was the man from the Apple and Pear Marketing Board (sponsors by then of Canterbury rugby), Mike Weir, who Wyllie recalls as being the one who actually suggested Wyllie should stand for the Canterbury job. Wyllie had grave doubts about it.

"I'd only had one year with the Country team, and although we'd played pretty well in the forwards, and cleaned Town out, I didn't really expect to have much of a chance. I knew Mike (Weir) from when he used to play with Amberley, and he was saying to give it a go.

"I was thinking that if I stood, and lost, then the next year there could be a feeling that I'd already been there, and missed out, so why bother with me any more? In the end I was late putting my name in. You had to have the form agreeing to stand at the union's office by 5 o'clock, and I was half an hour late. I was still wondering about it."

But not wondering were men like Weir, Murray Inglis and Les

McFadden, who all agreed that Wyllie was the man needed to restore Canterbury to the frontline of New Zealand rugby.

They lobbied for support for Wyllie, but not one of them could be sure that Wyllie would get the job when the Canterbury union voted for the position. It was touch and go. As captain of Canterbury, Wyllie would never have been confused with Henry Kissinger. As the future chairman of the New Zealand Rugby Union, Christchurch's Russ Thomas would note Wyllie never spared officials if he thought the team wasn't being treated fairly. Thomas was the manager of Canterbury when Wyllie, the captain, wanted a strapper to go to Dunedin to plaster some of the veterans together for the match with Otago. Thomas refused the request. For the whole trip Thomas and Wyllie had to converse through Fergie McCormick, Wyllie refusing to speak to his manager. "As it turned out, Alex was right, and I was wrong," says Thomas. "Physiotherapists are an important part of a team now. Alex got a lot of things for players, by taking an aggressive approach towards administrators."

So rather than sitting by the telephone, Wyllie was at a Lions club meeting in the Gretta Valley tavern when the call came from Canterbury president, Benj Drake, saying Wyllie had the job. To the media Wyllie said that he thought a bit of discipline wouldn't hurt the Canterbury team. He didn't volunteer the information that he was slightly shocked at the appointment. "I didn't think everyone on the union would have agreed with my ideas."

It took three ballots before Wyllie won the coaching job. On the first ballot John Creighton, Fergie McCormick and Laurie O'Reilly were eliminated. On the second, Andy Holland went. In the last round of voting Neil Cornelius and Ceddie Smith were unsuccessful.

Back to the soccer player from Auckland. Jim Blair travelled to Christchurch, in his own time (all his work for Canterbury was unpaid), and set up fitness tests for the Canterbury squad at the Albion club's gymnasium.

"I remember we had to do the aerobic tests outside, because someone had forgotten to unlock the gym. I was doing a step test with John Ashworth, and eventually I had to wipe it. He just could not keep in time, which you need to do as you step up and down in the same order, over and over. Well, John was as coordinated as an alligator with haemorrhoids. For a guy that was so well coordinated on the football field, he was a disaster. I'd just have to say he must be a terrible dancer."

Next day Blair worked the whole squad, showing them the grid games, in which players flick back and forth while running towards each other, and possible points of collision.

Wyllie was convinced. "What Jim was saying was exactly what I'd thought in the past. He was saying that just going out and running wasn't the answer. I'd known a couple of Canterbury players who did that, but I was able to beat them to the ball because they lacked pace. And that's the vital part of the game, being first man to the ball.

"Jim tested them, said what was right and wrong, and gave them all a training programme. The grid work was something totally different. I guess at school we'd played some games that were a bit like it, bullrush and so on. I think some people, even today, see the grids and say that it's kids' stuff. They don't realise how competitive it can be amongst the team, and how you improve the skills of handling and passing the ball.

"When I was playing we'd have one or two footballs at a training run. We'd warm up by running round and round the damn paddock, then a few sprints, a few sit-ups, some running as a team, no skill work at all."

Blair, who notes that he wasn't on hand for most of the Canterbury training runs conducted by Wyllie, says he was as surprised as anyone that Wyllie would embrace his ideas.

"Alex seemed to epitomise everything that was traditional and uncompromising and hard about New Zealand rugby. If you think about it, for someone like that to pick up what is supposed to be a radical approach, from a guy who had never played a game of rugby in his life, worse still, a soccer player, from the poof's game, is quite remarkable.

"He was taking a hell of a chance really. He accepted my ideas on one meeting, and at the time I had no experience with top rugby.

"I think he saw something, and grabbed it, and I'm eternally grateful to him for that. He set me on my way in rugby."

Blair today is on the staff of the New Zealand Rugby Foundation, spreading his fitness doctrine throughout the country, and he is an official member of the All Black World Cup squad.

But in 1982 such lofty heights were miles away, and playing "kids' games" didn't seem like the sort of thing an Alex Wyllie would go for.

Blair himself says there was "a fair bit of fencing" in the first couple of years of the relationship between himself and Wyllie. "We didn't know each other very well, and didn't have much of a chance to, because I was going down on a Friday night, and home on Sunday. During that time I was flat out with the players, and we didn't have a great deal of time to talk about concepts.

"I know now, as we've had the chance to talk over the years, that even as a young man Alex was intuitively doing the training that was right for him. I think what always stuck in his mind was that rugby training runs are for everyone, and some of the training wasn't suited to him. He knew, and his body knew, what was right for him. He picked that up by trial and error.

Rugby Press

For Jim Blair, meeting Alex Wyllie for the first time was a frightening experience.

Christchurch Star

Skills and "kids' games" were part of the Canterbury scheme. Don Hayes starts this "game".

"Once you get to know him you realise that Alex's a much maligned man as far as his intelligence goes. Basically I've always felt he was quite shy, and when he was thrust into a high profile public role he used gruffness to cover it.

"He has a very conceptual approach to rugby, and you can't have that unless you're a deep thinker, and have feelings."

It wasn't until Canterbury had whipped Auckland 31-9 at Lancaster Park in 1983 that Auckland coach John Hart decided to use his hometown man, Blair, with the Auckland team.

The grid training, the "kids' stuff," illustrated a difference in approach between the two.

Says Blair: "It's like looking at the same tree, and describing it in two different ways. I believe that what excited Alex was that the grids can be very aggressive. They encourage very aggressive running with the ball in hand, as well as the skill element. I think Alex, perhaps more than John, saw them relating to the aggressive running that he wanted for his Canterbury team. As a player Alex had been a very aggressive runner, and he enjoyed that sort of thing. He saw how the grids melded with what he wanted from the Canterbury team. His side was very similar to the Auckland side now. The only real speedster Auckland have is Terry Wright, and Canterbury didn't have any. So with Canterbury we had to develop acceleration, and be very quick over twenty metres, and then get the support play up to them. If you look at a lot of the tries Canterbury scored, not many were from guys running forty or fifty metres. They scored tries by jumps up the field, with the back row getting there in support."

Part of the Blair dictum is that team training doesn't go on for long spells. How does that square with stories of players staggering in legless after Wyllie training runs in the first couple of years with Canterbury?

"Intellectually Alex came round to my methods very quickly, but emotionally, I'm not so sure.

"There are a number of sides to that. Training for a country player is a bit different to training for a city player. Alex loves to be in that rugby atmosphere, and it doesn't matter to him how long he is there. My theory is that if you're in an area where you travel fifty or sixty miles to training, it must seem a hell of a waste of time to only do sixty minutes of training. A city guy, who drives twenty minutes to training, wants the training to be over so he can get on and do something else. All the country guy might have to look forward to is another sixty miles' drive home. So I think long training sessions were almost a social function.

"I'm very much against players training on the day before a game. I believe it can take the edge off a team. When Canterbury came to Auckland in 1984 Alex rang me and said they were going to have a training run on the Friday. I said, 'Alex, you know how I feel about that.' He said, 'It'll only be light, come and see for yourself.'

"Well, he really redefined the word 'light.' They'd trained on a fairly heavy ground, and I believe the match with Auckland was lost on the Friday. On the Saturday I felt they lacked in sharpness, they appeared dead in the legs, and the game was lost.

"I feel that training the day before a game is the result of Alex getting so worked up before a game, the session is for him to relax, more than for the players. He'll deny that, and he's being honest when he says that. Having the training run comes from an honest desire to do the best by the team, but what's really needed is for Alex to go and do something vigorous, like a game of squash, to relieve his own tension."

The biggest build-up of tension in New Zealand provincial rugby history must have been before Auckland's 1985 challenge for the Ranfurly Shield at Lancaster Park.

Blair was in a unique position. By then he had both teams on his programmes. He knew the differences. "Alex had a highly disciplined team. There was nobody who would think of questioning anything Alex or myself said. Auckland was quite different. A player like Tim Burcher (now part of the group that has set up and runs All Blacks Ltd, the commercial company that oversees money earned by the All Blacks from advertising and promotional work) told me he was a lazy trainer because he hated running. It hurt his legs. I looked at him, and he was right, he had leg splints. So I gave him a special programme, with exercises he could do at home in front of his TV. He trained hard after that.

"It would never have occurred to a Canterbury player to tell me that he hated running. It was just unthinkable for the Canterbury players to question what was happening.

"I realised before the game in '85 that it was going to be a Titanic struggle. I should mention the ethics of both Alex and John during that period. At no stage did either man ask me for any information about the other side, trying to check out fitness levels, or any injuries. They should be proud of the fact they were never tempted to even ask."

In Blair's opinion the sides were physically evenly matched for the '85 game. The superb start Auckland had could, he thinks, have been traced to the abuse heaped on the players by a crowd of Canterbury fans as the Aucklanders left their hotel to take a bus to the ground. "You could see their backs stiffen."

It was a high level of fitness that allowed Canterbury to dominate the last stages of the game. It was a high level of fitness that allowed Auckland to just hold them out.

As Wyllie's coaching career has progressed he has never lost faith in Blair's methods, evidenced by Blair's work with World Cup candidates. and the final squad.

Before the Christmas of 1990, 60 letters went out to the top players in New Zealand, advising them of what programmes Blair wanted them working on through the summer

For some it meant a big change in what they had been doing. North Auckland lock Ian Jones, for example, was firmly instructed to leave his road running shoes in the cupboard, and to get on to the track. Nine years earlier Blair and Wyllie had gone through the same process with Canterbury captain Don Hayes. Says Wyllie: "As captain, Don was working hard to set an example. But I had to

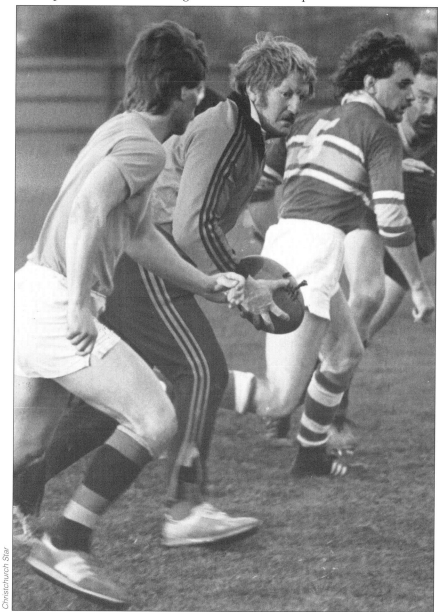

In 1983 Wyllie shows the way at a training school.

Christchurch Star

tell him to cut it out. We didn't want bloody marathon runners."

The grids still have their doubters, says Wyllie. "I remember once in Dunedin with the All Blacks we were running the grids, and I heard someone say on the sideline, 'Gee, they really do use those things.' It was almost like they were a bit of a joke. Some people still don't realise how competitive they can be."

And there's a bit more to it than competitiveness.

For all his reputation as a tough coach, Wyllie says training must be of a type that players can enjoy.

His views on training were formed when he was, at some stages in his career, training with Glenmark, North Canterbury, Country sub-unions, and Canterbury. "Sometimes you'd be training four nights a week, with four different teams. Today you wouldn't do it, but you tried to then, and it was really just about impossible. In the end it became a routine, put the boots on and go out and do the same old thing. You became sick of it. You've got to learn to adjust to methods that keep players interested."

Oddly, one aspect of modern rugby, fully used by the All Blacks, that Wyllie gives no great personal backing to, is stretching.

First universally used in rugby by the Counties teams of the early 1970s, the man who directed Counties, Malcolm Hood, would introduce his stretching methods to the All Blacks later in the decade, as a physiotherapist with the team.

Wyllie, coming from the old run up and down on the spot school of changing shed warm-ups, wonders whether there's such a huge decrease in hamstring and muscular injuries since stretching has become so widespread. "I still wonder how vital stretching is. You still see jokers pulling muscles after ten or twenty minutes of training, so how much stretching do you have to do to get things right? On the other hand, if a player feels that he's stretched, and that's conditioned him, he's right in his mind. So that's good."

But he's no conservative about getting new ideas to all coaches in the country.

"For a number of years, I've felt the idea of getting all the provincial coaches in the country together in Wellington isn't such a great thing. I know from experience that for the provincial coach to go back to his area and to try to tell the other coaches what should be happening just doesn't work. For a start there'll be three or four coaches who stood against the provincial coach, so they rate themselves as being as good as he is, and they're sitting there thinking, 'Who does this jumped-up bugger think he is?'

"I've also been at national coaching schools and looked around, and there are guys there who aren't the slightest bit interested. So I don't think the New Zealand union have always got value for money from having people in Wellington.

"I think it'd be a better idea to have some of the best players and

Peter Bush

"We should be giving coaches a real foundation for all their work."

coaches at national level going out to the unions, and getting all the local coaches together, and showing them what to do. It's the smaller unions that will benefit the most, and those are the ones we have to look to anyway. The game's falling away badly in some of those unions, and if we have to look after them. If they start to fall apart the game could be lost.

"It's amazed me, since I got to Canterbury and then New Zealand level as a coach, that some good players come through who have never really been shown the basics of the game. I think there are a lot of coaches at lower grade level who may not have played much themselves, and they're not getting the help, the advice, from experienced players and coaches.

"You can understand why a lot of the top players these days don't want to be involved in a hurry with coaching. They play so much rugby during their career that when they get free time they don't want to be automatically involved with it again. They want a break, which is fair enough, and then they say the game's changed too much for them to be back coaching again.

"I'm not knocking the people coaching rugby who didn't play it much. You have to admire them for their enthusiasm. But I think we let them down sometimes by not giving them a real foundation for all their coaching.

"If you look at the problems we have with collapsed scrums, and the injuries that can come from that, it all goes back to coaches who have never been taught the correct way to scrum, so they can't teach their players the correct way themselves."

For Jim Blair, the partnership with Wyllie and the Canterbury side proved to the rest of New Zealand that Blair's way was the correct way, and, while Blair did not prepare the fitness programme for Canterbury after 1985, he would continue in Auckland, to the present day, and be the fitness expert with the New Zealand America's Cup challenges in Fremantle and San Diego.

He was not officially involved with the All Blacks until the World Cup campaign, but was preparing programmes for all the Aucklanders in the team, and some individual players as well.

And while even Blair says the association with Wyllie looks unlikely to an outsider, they are both very basic, straight talking men.

As All Black doctor John Mayhew says: "Jim's personality is important. There may be fitness experts in the country with as good, or even better, academic qualifications, but Jim's been able to win the confidence of the players. They respond well to him as a person, and that gives them more faith in his methods."

The last sentence of Mayhew's words could, if you substitute Wyllie for the All Black players, sum up the reason a man who's never played the game is now at the heart of New Zealand rugby.

Alex Wyllie (at left) ready to snap up the ball that's eluded Brian Lochore, Ian Kirkpatrick and Sam Strahan (hand highest) during the 1970 All Black tour of South Africa.

Africamera

South Africa, 1970, as Alex Wyllie meets the local fans.

Ross Wiggins

Rugby Press

Wyllie (at left) during the test with England at Twickenham on the 1972-73 tour. The team came within a minute of a Grand Slam.

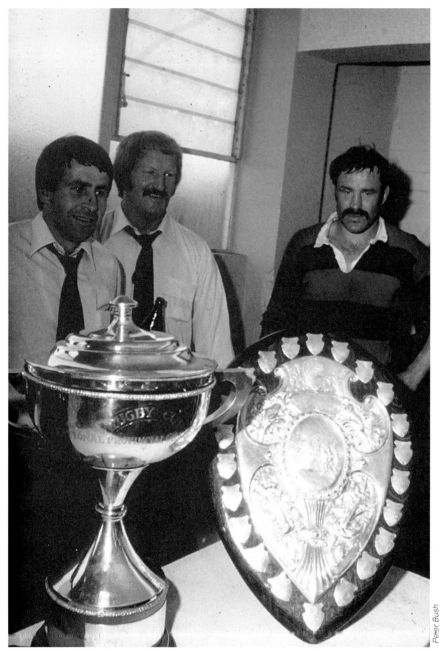

What made the hard work sweet. Doug Bruce, Alex Wyllie and Don Hayes with the spoils from the 1983 Canterbury season.

Peter Bush

Peter Bush

Bruce Deans gets plenty of altitude into a clearing kick against
Wairarapa-Bush in 1984.

Tips for Ron Goodwin are given by guest conductor Wyllie, about to lead the New Zealand Symphony Orchestra through "Give It A Boot Robbie."

Peter Bush

Not exactly Lord's, but Wyllie (with Bruce Deans keeping wicket) is prepared to deal with a damp pitch at Townsville in 1988.

Peter Bush

Being an All Black can mean you're on display when Expo '88 is being held in Brisbane.

"Over here should be the place to watch." Wyllie leads selectors Lane Penn and John Hart at a zonal game in Wanganui in 1989.

Peter Bush

8

Something
special beginning

Victor Simpson had a sneaky feeling he wasn't going to enjoy
playing for Canterbury with Alex Wyllie as coach.

He met Wyllie for the first time in 1981, under the stand at
Lancaster Park. Alistair Hopkinson introduced them. For Simpson
it was awesome. Grizz Wyllie, one of the original tough, hard
Canterbury forwards. A legend to a player of Simpson's generation.
And unlike most legends, Wyllie wasn't smaller in real life. Bigger,
if anything. This huge hand came out and enveloped Simpson's.
The voice was right too. Gruff.

Nothing went wrong that afternoon, but Simpson's University
clubmates got in his ear straight away when Wyllie was appointed
Canterbury coach in '82.

"No fun for you, Victor," they told him. "Wyllie hates Varsity
players. Hammered them on the paddock, ripped into them on the
team bus. He'll give you heaps, mate."

Then trial teams are named. Wyllie has decided he wants to
examine the best Canterbury has to offer, up against each other.
Four teams play at Kaiapoi and then Simpson is named on the wing
for the final trial under lights at Denton Park.

Simpson pulls a sicky. Leaves it until the afternoon of the trial,
rings after Wyllie's gone to the ground, and tells Keryn, "Could you
tell Alex I couldn't play because my ankle's not right." Then he slips
off to watch the trials, just to check out how the candidates are
shaping up. Out of the reserves comes a Canterbury B player, Gary
Hooper, who has problems getting sprigs screwed into a new pair
of boots and actually gets on the field a couple of minutes later. He
still manages to score three tries, and will go on to score 20 tries for
Canterbury, and play for the South Island in 1982.

Wyllie still finds a place for Simpson in the Canterbury squad,
so the Varsity man who doesn't want to play on the wing is one of
the players shivering in a circle at Amberley as Wyllie lays down the

rules at the first training run. Simpson is really not sure whether he should even be there.

Wyllie had heard how the season before some players turned up late for training, how others sometimes didn't turn up at all. That sort of thing eats him up. "Even when I played, it always seemed to be the ones who had to travel the most who turned up on time. And nine times out of ten, the one you want to see before you start training is the one that hasn't turned up on time. So the whole team has to wait. When I started coaching Canterbury, I was still living out in the country, so I couldn't see any reason why, if the rest of us could get there on time, everyone shouldn't be able to get there."

The players at Amberley get the famous edict on missing training. There are just two excuses: Death or docking. To be absolutely honest he might have said death and crutching. The players were too shell-shocked at the time to remember clearly now, and Wyllie says the important point was that "there were no bloody excuses at all really."

The ground rules for training laid down, Wyllie starts looking for Simpson, to establish early that from here on in there's just one man deciding what position players will have on the field, and it's not some clever dick back.

Wyllie fires a shot at John Ashworth. He'd heard how Ashworth, an All Black prop, had taken, the previous season, to missing a few training runs. "Ash, no more turning up just when you feel like it. Every run from now on. Every run."

Ashworth cops it easily. "I was pretty excited about Alex coming in to coach. I think the whole of Canterbury was. The season before it was easy to get a bit downhearted, you were battling, but no score was coming in. Yeah, I had missed a few runs. With Alex he'd been around so long, he'd heard every excuse, nothing was new to him. So he had the whip hand right from the start really."

While he's speaking Wyllie's looking for Simpson. Simpson is breathing a little easier. He's not going to have a go at me, he thinks. But Wyllie hasn't forgotten. "I just couldn't find the prick." Suddenly he spies Simpson, who has been easing in behind bulkier players while the verbal bullets are being fired. Wyllie swings round and snarls: "As for YOU Simpson, you'll play where I put you, or you can piss off right now." Other players look away, embarrassed, as the two glare at each other.

"He caught me flat-footed," says Simpson. "I didn't say anything. We just carried on with our training. I figured that if it came to a real clash of wills, it'd come later anyhow."

That real clash was avoided for a couple of months. Simpson sat on the bench, then was involved with Maori rugby at the end of June and into early July. "I just didn't want to play on the wing. I like centre because there always seems to be more action there."

Christchurch Star

When Victor Simpson and Alex Wyllie first clashed, the other players turned away.

Wyllie wasn't being bloody minded for the sake of it. For a start there just weren't that many wingers available in Canterbury, but players as good as Simpson, Craig Green, Warwick Taylor and Andrew McMaster all deserved to be fitted in somewhere.

There was also the question of players doing the best by the team. "One of the things I felt," says Wyllie, "is that if you're going to have players dictate to you where, and how, and when they're going to play for you, you're better off without them. If they've got away with it once off the field, they'll start doing it on the field. When you haven't got fifteen men out there all pulling their weight, you're wasting your time. I think most people would say that if you're going to put the provincial jersey on, you should be prepared to play wherever the coach wants you to."

Finally, in September, the Canterbury side lands in Whangarei, where Simpson plays on the wing. That night Wyllie suggests that's where Simpson will play for the rest of the season. Simpson bridles at the idea. He gets touchier and touchier about it. John Ashworth suggests he should cool off, and upends an ice bucket on to Simpson's head. That's it, says Simpson, get me a ticket, I'm going back to Christchurch, and you can stick this team. Later a Canterbury backline move will be named Qantas in honour of Simpson's desire to board a jet plane.

At Auckland airport the next day Simpson reconsiders. He tells Wyllie he will play on the wing, if that's what Wyllie really wants. "Too late," Wyllie replies. "And I'll tell you this. The player (Craig Green) who's going on the wing is going to go further in the game than you." Sure enough, Green will beat Simpson to the All Blacks by two years. Simpson gets the centre spot in the Canterbury team, but it will be in 1985 before he wears the All Black jersey.

Despite the initial battles, a mutual respect will grow into friendship over the years. And there was no real reason why the two shouldn't become mates. Wyllie's attitudes towards positions and training had never been anything personal.

His approach was always to start from basics, and build. With Canterbury he soon realised he had to. "When I took over (as coach) I found I was fitter myself than half the players. So we had some long and hard training runs at times to try to improve the fitness. We didn't do any moves for a start, because we couldn't pass the ball to the wings without dropping it anyway. So I said: 'Forget the moves until we can pass it out without dropping it.' Then we gradually brought in some simple moves, like bringing the fullback and

Wayne Smith (with Jock Hobbs in support) always remembers his first trip with the Canterbury team.

Christchurch Star

missing him with the pass. By the time we'd finished we had some moves you knew could only be used in a game you were completely on top in. We did a triple scissors, which we used once, against Otago in 1985."

A key man in the backline approach was Wayne Smith, who, after moving south from his home in the Waikato, had actually played with Wyllie for Canterbury in 1979. "I was nervous about playing with Alex, because a mate of mine, Gary Barkle, had played as a real youngster with Alex, and they say he called him 'Sir' or 'Mr Wyllie' for the whole season."

The first trip with the Canterbury team in '79 didn't help Smith's nerves. "I went to Ashburton as a reserve to Robbie Deans, who was playing at first-five. I didn't know a soul. I'd only been in Christchurch a few months. I sat on the reserve bench with John Ashworth, and wasn't sure who he was.

"We had a few beers after the game, and then got on the bus to go home. John Collinson came along and gave me a bottle of beer. He was handing them down the aisle. Then Alex got on and went to the back of the bus and yelled: 'Who's taken my beer?' Apparently he had this dozen of beer that was his. All of us who had a beer quickly stuffed the bottle under the seat, and hoped it'd roll down the aisle, because Alex and Bill Bush came down the aisle, looking under seats to see who'd taken the beer. All these bottles were rolling around under the seats. I was terrified."

Smith's first game for Canterbury provided a less blood chilling encounter.

"We played South Canterbury in my first game, and at one stage I cleared with a pretty good left foot kick. Alex gave me a quick pat on the back. It was a really big moment in my career at that stage."

What also stuck in Smith's mind from that winter of '79 was how Wyllie controlled the game, and how skilled the big No 8 was.

"I was actually surprised at how skilled Alex was, because I'd always thought of him as a crash and bash man, but he had a lot of fine touches. When we did a scissors move his timing and passing was excellent.

"When he got the job as coach in '82 I was pleased, because he'd virtually coached the team when he was captain, and he was thorough about defensive patterns, and our moves. So we knew, even though the training would be long, we'd cover everything, and that's what I wanted."

Smith found immediately that the sessions were tough, and that mistakes made them tougher.

"Alex didn't have to do a lot of shouting at training. He'd just make you do ten shuttle runs. After those you knew you'd done something wrong, and the threat was always there.

"He was short tempered with people who didn't pick things up quickly. People who were like that didn't stay in the team very long. So we ended up with a team of people who picked things up quickly, and worked hard."

Captain Don Hayes was another in the Canterbury team who had played with Wyllie. "It was so easy (as a flanker), all I had to do was pick the ball up, and he would run off it. He knew exactly how to control the game, how to spot the weaknesses. He didn't do a lot of running in '79, but when he did it was all on. He made tries on the short side look so easy."

Hayes was another pleased when he heard that Wyllie had won the Canterbury coaching job. "In '81, when he took Canterbury Country, I was really impressed with the way he ran things. He showed me how to stand in the lineout, and jump, how to do moves off the back of the scrum, and why. He was able to get technical, and to pass it on. I'd never had anything like that before. It all seemed to work, and everything finally made sense."

Victor Simpson says that, having seen how physical Wyllie the player was, he took some time to see past that. "We didn't really get into using skills until halfway through the season. And that's the way a team should be run. Get your basics right, and worry about all the fancy stuff at the end."

Robbie Deans had been through the two worst provincial seasons in living memory in Canterbury when Wyllie took charge. "We were a very young team, and there weren't very many new players. Alex ingrained the discipline and gave us the structure to succeed. It's easy to say the players were there, but he provided the format for us."

Smith says Wyllie was the first coaching "all-rounder" he'd ever struck. "He really was the complete rugby thinker. He could tell the backs what to do. He could tell the forwards what to do. He was very intelligent.

"He has a great knowledge of the game, and a simple philosophy, which has developed from when he was a player. He knows what he wants. The things he says are to the point and correct. There are not many times when I played under his direction when he was wrong," Smith smiles. "Of course, if he was wrong, he wouldn't admit it."

Into the mix of the Canterbury team Wyllie introduced Doug Bruce. Bruce is a man for whom they could have invented the word laconic. He never uses two words when one will do, and on a football field never ran two metres if one got him to where he needed to be.

Three years younger than Wyllie, Bruce had first encountered him when Bruce was a 19 year-old first-five for Mid-Canterbury, fresh out of Ashburton High School. Not that Wyllie got his hand on him that day. The one Bruce had to look out for was a young Ian

Doug Bruce and Alex Wyllie. They never had to argue about rugby.

Kirkpatrick running off the end of the Canterbury lineout.

On a football field Bruce wasn't a man to make a foolish move. Tactically he was superb, cool and controlled, with an accurate kick, quick hands, and the happy knack of always taking the right option. Fellow players joked about his heavy smoking, but they never joked about his match winning abilities.

Playing with Wyllie, for nearly a decade, Bruce certainly knew what he thought about rugby. "We'd be continually calling for the ball in the backline, and Alex would say: 'If you're going to make bloody use of it, you'll get the ball. Make a mistake, and you won't get it again.' It became a joke in the end, we had to laugh, it was so dictatorial. We couldn't believe he was actually saying that, but he did mean it."

Was it frustrating to play under such circumstances? "Not really, he proved his point. He was good, tactically, as a captain. He could sense the weaknesses in the opposition, and after the game, we might have moaned about him, but the result would be up there on the board. And it might have been a good thing, because when we did get the ball we made sure we made good use of it. We were going to make sure bloody Alex didn't dominate the ball all day."

Christchurch Star

No pushover tries for Canterbury, but plenty for the brilliant Craig Green.

Bruce was a logical choice as Wyllie's assistant coach, having spent two years helping Wyllie with the Canterbury Country team. "Doug had a quiet manner, which we needed out in the country. He didn't put too much pressure on the players, didn't expect great things, just to do the basics."

From Bruce's side there was no real hesitation. "If I'd had any doubt about the success of it I probably wouldn't have taken it on. But I had a fair idea Alex would do well. He's pretty clear in his mind about what he wants, and his picture of the game is clear."

Not that Wyllie and Bruce had to spend a lot of time discussing their thoughts on rugby. Says Wyllie: "Looking back, we didn't talk a lot about what sort of game we wanted to play, or what sort of player we'd need for it." Says Bruce: "We never sat down and talked about rugby in general. Alex would have his fixed ideas I'm sure, and never waver from them. He was pretty good at picking out talent, for a big, grumpy forward."

Just how closely the two saw eye to eye on talent would be revealed after the first set of trials in 1982. The announcement of the team was going to be made that afternoon, but Wyllie decided to wait until the next morning. When he rang Bruce the following day he asked Bruce to name the players he would have selected. On Wyllie's list there was a matching column of 15 ticks. The partnership was ready to go.

Bruce, typically, plays down his role in the team. "What did I do? I think I protected the backs from Alex. Most of the time at training when the backs were working on their moves, their patterns of play, I was with them. If they'd stuffed up something during a game, Alex would come over and tell the backs about it. I could see that as well, but it was his team, so it suited me to have him give them the edge of his tongue."

How much did Wyllie understand about back play? It's a question that Bruce never seems to have considered before. "Well, he holds it (back play) pretty highly in the team plan." Yes, but how much does he understand it? "Well...he knows a good back when he sees one. He can recognise talent. He often talked to the backs about the defensive side of things. That was an area we did concentrate on. But we never really talked about back play as a set issue."

Wayne Smith remembers some worries amongst the Canterbury backs that Wyllie the coach would revolve the whole game around the forwards, but that proved unfounded. "He soon showed us that there was no way he was going to produce a certain style just because he'd been a forward. He was always going to let us use our strengths."

Victor Simpson, as you might expect, comes out swinging. "You have to be very bright to pull one over Alex. People who don't know him might think he's a big rough farmer, with not much between the ears, but he's very clued up. When it came to how we played the game, we had to move all the ball we got. Since '85, Auckland have had so much firepower up front, they can rely on the forwards to grind the opposition down, and then move it wide.

"We only closed the game down when the opposition team wouldn't play the attacking game. We were more mobile than our opponents, we were fitter, and we ran it wider. In 1983 Craig Green scored more tries than any other winger in New Zealand. There were no pushover tries for us!"

Up in the forwards, prop Ashworth says there were no arguments. "Alex wasn't that subtle in those days. The mould for the coach was pretty much set as a captain. He told you what he wanted, and if you didn't do it you were in trouble. I guess there was a bit of fear and intimidation in that. But that's what rugby is about a bit at times."

Wyllie was sticking to his basic idea, that rugby is a simple game. "If you've got the ball, your opponent hasn't, so the first thing is to win the ball. Then, after that, if you keep hold of it, you shouldn't lose. It's easier to say than to do, but that's the guts of it.

"When you're coaching at a provincial level, I say it's simple, because you get the set pieces right, and after that it's up to the players themselves to show their ability and skills, whether it's their speed, their kicking, or jumping or scrumming.

"I've seen jokers go out and try and say to their players, 'Now in this position on the twenty-two we're going to do exactly this.' All you're doing is making your players robots. You're not achieving a lot at all. You put ideas to them, you give them advice, but they have to be able to make the right decisions under pressure, to be able to think under pressure. By saying that in this position you do that move every time, they get to be robots, and the opposition get on to it, and it's easy to nullify it."

Wayne Smith says he played the first game under the Wyllie regime in '82 in a confused frame of mind. "Alex thought everyone in the team understood what he wanted, but we didn't. He'd said to me: 'Only run twice in the game.' After five minutes I'd had my two runs, and I was buggered for the rest of the game.

"We won (30-6), and we had a do at the Hornby Lodge, and he got me in a corner, and poked the finger at me, and told me he was relying on me as a decision maker. I grew up a bit that day I suppose. He put a lot of responsibility on me.

"The next game was against Queensland at Lancaster Park, and it was a great game, probably one of the best games of that era with Alex. They came here with all the guns, Roger Gould, Brendon Moon, Andrew Slack, and we just took them apart (23-4). That day the waiting list for the supporters' club went up to about 150 people. Suddenly, people realised there was something special going on."

THE LEGEND: Alex Wyllie was in a huge brawl with Fijian tussock grubbers outside a hotel, in which he was knocked out.

THE REAL STORY: It happened on October 31, 1970. Wyllie and fellow All Black to South Africa that winter, Jake Burns, had been to the Amberley A and P show, and had adjourned to the Waipara Hotel, where the publican was Wyllie's father-in-law, Bill Smart.

An argument, not involving Wyllie or Burns, broke out over the use of the pool table. A group of 27 Fijian tussock grubbers were drinking in the hotel, and some of them traded punches with a couple of locals. Bill Smart ordered the men fighting out of the hotel. Wyllie went out to see if his father-in-law was okay. "I knew one of the Fijians quite well, and Bill and I were talking with him, trying to sort it out, when someone hit me on the

Legend

head. I didn't see anything." Later, some Waipara patrons would see Fijians tying the end of their jersey sleeves and loading the sleeves with rocks, while others put rocks into their socks, and used them as coshes. It was almost certainly a rock that felled Wyllie, and gashed open his head.

The most maligned man over the years has probably been Burns. He recalls a local saying Wyllie needed help. Burns, not realising how serious things were getting outside the hotel, joked: "Alex can look after himself." Told Wyllie really was in trouble, Burns went out, and was greeted by the sight of an unconscious Wyllie being dragged down the road by two tussock grubbers, one on each leg. Burns grabbed a crankhandle from his car, and the sight of the large All Black lock was enough to persuade the Fijians to drop Wyllie. Burns dragged Wyllie into his car, and headed north to Wyllie's home. Says Wyllie: "The first thing I can really remember is cleaning up in the washhouse." Wyllie, Burns recalls, was covered in blood.

Back at the hotel what almost amounted to a siege began, which ran for the 45 minutes it took several carloads of police to arrive from Christchurch. With no sign of Burns, some thought he'd slipped out and headed for home. In the confusion only Wyllie really knew that Burns had been a single-handed rescue mission.

Two days later five of the Fijians would leave the country. One was charged with assaulting Wyllie and Bill Smart, but he wasn't sentenced, and, along with his fellow workers, instead lost his work permit, and was immediately flown back to Fiji.

CREDIBILITY RATING (OUT OF 10): 9. Docked one because to say Wyllie was in a brawl implies he was fighting. He was actually trying to negotiate when he was blindsided.

9

We're all still mates

I f they designed a place where rugby players were sent to be punished, it would be just like the changing rooms at Athletic Park.

Players walk down a dank, concrete corridor, then push open ancient bright green wooden doors, and pick their way down worn steps into shadowy, stark rooms.

On the morning of September 18, 1982, the corridors were being prowled by Alex Wyllie.

He was feeling as good about the Ranfurly Shield that afternoon with Wellington as any coach could.

In fact he was confident, to the point where the night before he'd harrassed Canterbury Rugby Union chairman Russ Thomas into buying extra rounds of drinks because "we're going to win the bloody Shield for you tomorrow."

So confident that he hadn't been that twitchy about a Fresh-Up television commercial being arranged for immediately after the game. "Usually you'd hate that sort of thing, but I just had a feeling it'd be okay."

He'd travelled to Wellington to see Hawkes Bay almost win the Shield the previous week. He knew then that if Canterbury played well, they could take the Shield.

He left little to chance.

For a start, Wyllie got other Canterbury stalwarts to join in the preparations.

Alistair Hopkinson and former coach Jim Stewart spoke to the team at a midweek meeting in Christchurch. Hopkinson warned them about how quickly time would pass in a Shield challenge. Any scoring opportunity had to be seized on the instant. Stewart turned to the emotion of the challenge. In sport there was often just one chance for greatness, he told the team. Miss the chance, and you might regret it for the rest of your life.

Christchurch Star

Don Hayes (second from right) is a sore captain, or perhaps he's juice-logged. The Canterbury changing room after winning the Ranfurly Shield from Wellington.

Then Wyllie changed the Canterbury team's hotel.

The team had been booked into a city hotel just a drunken lurch away from Wellington's red light area.

Out in chaste surroundings at a hotel near the airport was a supporters' group, organised by 3ZB.

Wyllie arranged a swap.

Barry Corbett, 3ZB's breakfast announcer, says that was certainly a wise move. "In town, we were awake all night, with Wellington supporters singing and chanting outside our hotel, thinking we were the Canterbury team."

Wyllie also jacked up a tape that would help tweak his players up an extra notch on the day of the challenge.

Wellington's All Black fullback, Allan Hewson, a man with a keen sense of humour, had been interviewed by a Christchurch radio man, Ken Anderson. Hewson said the best advice he could give to the challengers would be to get back on the boat and go home.

Recalls Victor Simpson: "Grizz said, 'If you need any psyching up, have a listen to this.' You should have seen it. The boys went from about 70 per cent to 110 per cent by the time they left that room. The timing was perfect."

With it all running the way it should, it was a big shock to Wyllie when he peered in the Canterbury changing room in the morning, and found it crowded out with television lights and reflectors, and

Christchurch Star

The joy of winning the Ranfurly Shield, on the faces of Wayne Smith and Jock Hobbs.

electric flex snaking across the floor.

Advertising man Daryl Hughes and his crew were setting up for the Fresh-Up commercial shoot.

Wyllie appears at the door. "What do you think you're doing?" Hughes gulps, and starts to explain, about lighting set-ups and how long they take. Wyllie's answer is brief, and final. "You can get that bloody stuff out of here for a start." They do.

With the changing room restored to its normal state of cheerless damp, the Canterbury players stripped and started to focus on the game.

Simpson was one who knew what the formula had to be. "In a Shield game, she's real quick. You get to halftime, and, if you don't watch yourself, you don't really know that you've played. In the first ten minutes you've got to fire, go out full bore, then sort of cruise, and in the last ten before halftime, put the screws in. We worked to that. In the first ten in the second half, fire again, then hopefully in the last fifteen we'd give it the big grunt."

Playing into the wind, Canterbury were down 9-4 at halftime, but that wasn't any disaster. The Wellington pack was big and strong, and with All Blacks props Scott Crichton and Brian McGrattan, was able to dominate the scrums, eventually winning six tightheads.

But the highly talented Wellington backline never had the chance to fire. Robbie Deans, watching the Wellington attacks develop, and then get snuffed out, believes that Warwick Taylor and Victor Simpson virtually won the game for Canterbury. "Wellington had a great backline, but Warwick and Victor covered them like a glove. They had such a good understanding, and they'd do the damage, knocking the guys down."

It was Wayne Smith who would turn the game in the last five minutes, with a superb individual run, slicing past Wellington tacklers for a try, converted by Robbie Deans, that gave Canterbury a 16-12 victory.

Captain Don Hayes got the news huddled in the Fresh-Up set under the stand, when masseur Pat Long rushed in to tell him the game was over, and Canterbury had won.

Hayes had wrenched his ribs, which is why, in many photographs of him accepting the Shield from Wellington captain Paul Quinn, Hayes, wrapped in a grey blanket, looks more like a refugee than a delighted victor.

In his first season as Canterbury coach Alex Wyllie's team had won the Ranfurly Shield. They almost lose it in the first defence.

At the last training run before playing Counties, a week after the victory over Wellington, the last word from Wyllie was to meet upstairs at Lancaster Park at 2 o'clock.

So Wayne Smith, like all the other players, found himself cruising the streets around the park at 1.45, nervous sweat starting to stick his white shirt to his back, and not a parking space in sight.

"We had no parking stickers or anything, so when I finally did get a park, I had to race down the street, with people slapping you on the back and wishing you well, and it getting later and later. This was the most important game of our lives, and almost all of us were running late for it."

Wyllie, and the team, and the Canterbury officials knew that a Ranfurly Shield defence would attract a decent sized crowd. None of them had anticipated that 37,000 people would turn up.

Says Wyllie: "We were just looking around goggle-eyed. Canterbury hadn't had the Shield for so long, we'd forgotten what it was like."

But if Wyllie had underestimated the popularity of his side, he didn't miss the chance to plant a thought in the mind of the referee, Kerry Henderson, from Southland.

Henderson and Canterbury's top referee, Tom Doocey, bumped into Wyllie and a group of his friends on the night before the game. Doocey introduced Wyllie and Henderson. Wyllie said: "Keep an eye on those bloody Counties backs tomorrow, they stand offside a lot." Henderson brushed off the comment, and Doocey, who had known Wyllie for many years, told him he didn't need to talk to the referee, Henderson knew what he was doing.

Two minutes from the end of the game, with his team leading 15-

Robbie Deans has John Mills, Murray Davie, Bruce Deans, Wayne Smith, Warwick Taylor and John Ashworth hoping he'll land this last minute penalty against Counties. He did, and the shield stayed.

12, Counties winger Robert Kururangi grabbed an intercept, and sprinted off for what looked a certain try.

But back in the Counties half stood referee Henderson, whistling Kururangi back. The offence? Counties backs standing offside.

Robbie Deans placed one of the great pressure kicks of his career, and the draw kept the Shield in Christchurch.

After the whole nerve-racking day, there would never be disorganisation like it again.

Wyllie went to Canterbury president, Benj Drake. "This is hopeless," Wyllie told him. "From now on we're going to have to stay in a hotel." With tills jammed up with unaccustomed cash, Drake was more than happy to agree.

A pattern was then established that would be repeated over and over, through 25 successful defences.

The team would always be booked into a hotel on the Friday night. At first it was the Shirley Lodge, then the New Caledonian.

Six years after the last occasion, Wayne Smith can still remember the build-up clearly.

On a Friday there would be a very light run. Come Saturday the backs would get together and go through a few moves at the hotel, then the cars would be driven to the ground, and parked. Robbie Deans would go and have a few kicks, and most of the other backs would go on to the ground for a kick around too.

"Bruce (Deans) and I would go up into the stand, and visualise situations on the field. We'd talk about what the options were from a scrum on the ten metre line, a ruck near our line, a lineout near the line. We'd work our way through the whole field, so we were mentally prepared."

Back at the hotel the forwards would have worked through a few lineout drills, and there would be a team meeting around noon. Before the meeting players were able to prepare in their own time and way.

Simpson was a late riser, while Jock Hobbs and Don Hayes liked to have a cup of coffee together at the same time. Smith would be out the back of the pub, kicking punts against the netting fence on a tennis court.

At the meeting Wyllie would run through the game ahead, and sift through the team, man by man.

Like all good coaches, he treated each player differently. Captain Hayes often copped a rocket. That actually suited him. "If I'm complimented I tend to sit back and relax, and go to sleep. For some reason I react better if I'm being told off than praised." Warwick Taylor, who says he was usually "hiding in the background" was one who rarely suffered a verbal blitzing.

Taylor says: "That was the thing about Alex, he knew which guys he could rev shit out of, and which ones to leave alone. He never put down the guys who would have frozen. In the backs we found out very quickly that if you were trying you didn't get blasted. I remember after only three or four games, he blew us up because we hadn't attacked enough. He really got into us, saying 'It's all yours, I want you to attack, and you have an open hand to do it.' We all sat back and thought, 'Hell, if we get things wrong he won't come down on us, just as long as we're trying.'"

Prop John Ashworth actually advised Wyllic to "point the stick" at him. "It didn't really concern me. I knew Alex and I knew that I could wear it. Grizz needed to release some tension, and it was better on me than on a younger guy who might be threatened or intimidated by it."

Robbie Deans, who says that he was generally left alone in team talks, recalls how Wyllie, knowing Robbie and brother Bruce so well from Glenmark, could fire barbs at them if he wanted to, because "he knew we'd suffer it without any problem."

On the bus to Lancaster Park, the same route would be travelled every time. Says Wayne Smith: "It was comfortable, like going to the office every day. We knew it had been a successful time, and we got good memories every time we passed through. The same stop signs. The same little old lady working in the garden, sometimes wishing I was out there in the garden instead of on the bus."

There was one unfortunate bus driver who took a different route to the ground. "Alex would be ready to play the game by the time we got on the bus," says Smith. "When we were taken a different way, Alex almost floored the guy."

Usually it went like clockwork. "We'd get to the ground, drop our gear off, maybe look at the curtainraiser without really seeing it. Then, at two o'clock, we'd meet up above the stand, and Alex and Doug would have their say. The Shield would always be sitting there, and the seats were all numbered from one to fifteen, and the reserves.

"At about ten past two we'd go and get changed, and there would be another set of rituals. Victor would storm around the room with just his shorts on, and at a certain stage he'd pick up one of our management group, Les McFadden, on his shoulders, and he'd do ten squats with him.

"Alex would come through the room, and he'd have a word with each player. At times he could be inspirational.

"I especially remember when we played Auckland in 1983. We were in the tunnel, ready to run on to the field, and he suddenly grabbed my jersey and said, 'Run it from everywhere.' You know, he just had a feeling, maybe he'd seen something in the Aucklanders' eyes, maybe he knew we were at our peak, and we could tear them apart. We were just going to stick with our normal plan, but he'd suddenly decided it was on to just run all day."

Christchurch Star

Dale Atkins, a man Wyllie considers unlucky to have missed a shot at the All Blacks.

That 31-9 victory over Auckland would be rated by many as possibly the best victory of the Shield era, and it certainly reflected the fact that Canterbury didn't play stereotyped 10-man rugby.

Wyllie says that right from the start he had been determined not to have the team play negative football.

"I knew that outside Canterbury there were comments when I got the coaching job that Canterbury would go back to playing it tight. That was never the case with us."

His players soon found out that Wyllie's plans to use the backline weren't cheap talk.

Simpson gets almost as revved up as he used to on the field when talking about the Canterbury Shield style, and the way mobility would overcome sheer strength.

"I used to admire our forwards. They'd take a pounding for sixty minutes of a game, then get up and bend the other side. In '83 when we played Wellington they had us down and out, they'd shunted us all over the paddock. Most teams would have stayed out.

"But we had the mental attitude to take it back to them. In the last ten minutes Wellington didn't know what happened. They'd had the champagne organised, they'd come down to take the Ranfurly Shield back."

Wellington led 12-9 at halftime, and 16-13 going into the final quarter.

A huge crowd of 45,000 was almost silent for much of the game, but Simpson recalls how one man in that crowd wasn't down-hearted.

"I was just getting my sprigs tightened. As Alex was going off at halftime he said, 'We've got these pricks. Get into them.' I thought to myself, 'You've got me.' We finally nailed them, you could feel it."

Smith says the Canterbury pattern at first was heavily based on support play. "By '84 we'd reached a stage where we wanted to play Alex's tactics, to try to play the perfect game, with as little kicking as possible. Really only one major union didn't stand up flat in the backs against us, but tried to take us on through the backs, and that was Otago. We had a great game against them (won 44-3) in '84, but it was obvious that most teams came down and stood up on us, so we had to develop a kicking game.

"We hadn't been a kicking team at all, but Alex developed the high kick, and we worked and worked on it. Eventually we reached a stage where you could nominate which post you were going to hit.

"He'd read it right again. When we played Taranaki (in 1985) they stood right up on us, and we won that game through kicks."

Robbie Deans says that Wyllie's coaching during the Canterbury Ranfurly Shield era was never fully appreciated outside the province. "If you believed the media you would think he was just a rough oaf. His tactical appreciation is often underestimated. He's forever thinking about the game, and areas that can be exploited. With Canterbury he looked at what he had, and where he wanted to go. He wanted to play fifteen man rugby, and he slotted those players in to fit.

"In his last days as a player that wasn't how the game was played. It was possibly a reflection of the state of his own body, that he didn't look for a lot of running. Anyway, Canterbury had a giant pack, and they'd take the ball as far as they could, then come to a standstill, and give it to the backs. It was like, 'Okay, see what you can do.' And if the backs didn't make the advantage line, it was the last time they saw the ball."

Wyllie the Canterbury coach made extensive use of the blindside. Robbie Deans says "he's a master of the blindside, and that was where Canterbury did most of the damage. He used the blindside like it hadn't been used for ten years in New Zealand rugby."

Warwick Taylor, a schoolteacher who had moved to Christchurch from the physical education school in Dunedin, says all the basic patterns for the Canterbury team, including the backs, were set by Wyllie. "He knew what he wanted, and knew how it should be achieved. Then he left it to others to fill in the fine points. As a player to a high level, he knew what other people should be doing, and with himself, Doug Bruce and Wayne Smith, there was a great wealth of knowledge being applied."

Taylor remembers how Wyllie insisted that nothing in a training run be left half-done. "He was a hard bugger with training. He drummed into us that if we cut a corner in training, we'd cut corners in a game. He drummed that into us."

There was usually no need for Wyllie to shout at his players. He had a quieter, but tougher way of making a point. Recalls Wayne Smith: "If you did something wrong there'd be ten shuttle runs. The threat was always there. Sometimes I used to think that if it hadn't been for Albert Anderson and Kerry Mitchell we'd have all been dead. They were the biggest, and they were often last in the sprints, so Alex would say, 'Anderson, I told you not to be last, and here you are at the back. Do it again.' We'd have a bit of a break. Time and time again I'd look at Victor (Simpson) and say, 'Thank goodness for Bert and Mitch.'"

Simpson was one who virtually challenged Wyllie to make the training extra hard. Says Smith: "Victor used to call himself the Man of Steel, and he called Grizz 'Dad.' One Sunday training we had at Glenmark was just terrible. I heard one cocky, who was standing there in his hat and swandri, just looking, say, 'Bugger that' after he'd seen what we went through.

"That day we did more than an hour-and-a-half, it was shocking. All our legs were buckling, getting wider and wider apart, and

Alex came past Victor and said, fairly quietly, 'How are you going...tinfoil'."

Oddly enough, most players from the Canterbury team say that winning wasn't the start and finish of Wyllie's approach to rugby. "Losing is worse than death," an American football coach is claimed to have said. "You don't have to live with death."

It isn't a phrase that would automatically spring to mind when talking about Wyllie, but in many ways he's a rugby purist. He intensely dislikes boring football, and has little time for matches dominated by penalty goals.

Captain Hayes soon found out how serious Wyllie was about quality of performance. "We'd played Fiji in the last game of the first South Pacific tournament (in 1983) and we won it, and won the championship. Alex was really shitty. You'd have thought we'd lost the Ranfurly Shield. It took half the night to talk him around a bit, but he wouldn't concede that we deserved the title, because we'd played it wrong."

Captaining Canterbury was, to Hayes' mind, basically an easy job.

"I always had doubts about my own abilities as a captain, and if it had been any other team, or a coach other than Alex, I don't think I'd have been able to play as well as I did. But every time we had a problem Alex had the answer. It was a real breeze as captain. All I had to do was keep it organised on the field, and I knew how we wanted to play the game.

"It was an easy team to captain. There was no bitching. No one thought they were better than anybody else. If they did, they certainly got brought down quickly."

You could argue forever about whether team spirit develops because a team has success, or if developing team spirit is the reason for success.

Hayes believes the Canterbury team had more than victories on the field holding them together. "Success certainly helps, but we had a feeling in the side like a good club team. The way I saw it, everyone had an enormous amount of respect for each other. In the end, I'd say he picked the guys on character, and that came out when we were under pressure. The guys would dig deep. Not just two or three, but everyone.

"How did he judge the character of a player? Perhaps it was his training, sorting out the ones who couldn't, or didn't want to, keep up." Hayes smiles. "Or maybe it was a test of their drinking abilities."

Through the four years the Shield was in Christchurch, Wyllie worked to draw the team together in ways that people who had been around the Glenmark side over the years might have recognised.

Christchurch Star

Captain Don Hayes, who led a team where there was "no bitching, and nobody thinking he was better than anybody else."

The Sunday blowout became a pretty regular feature for the Canterbury squad. "That was our safety valve," says Warwick Taylor. "After having had rugby all the week, we'd let go after Sunday training."

Wyllie was always in the middle of the action, although Wayne Smith remembers that there was usually a certain amount of respect shown by the team. "There was that aura about him. A lot of coaches aren't respected the way he was. It was a mixture of what he'd done as a player for Canterbury, what he'd done in the All Blacks, how the media built him into a god, it all added to the respect. He was a sort of legend, even to us."

There were exceptions to that rule. After the thrashing of the Auckland side in 1983, the team gathered upstairs at Lancaster Park for a big Sunday party. Smith and wing Gary Hooper performed a skit as Keryn and Alex. Wyllie laughed as loud as anyone when Hooper mocked the Wyllie habit of saying "yes" and "no" in the same sentence, meaning the same thing...something virtually repeated by All Black Graham Purvis in the "Blood, Sweat and Touring" video.

Later in the day the big boys in the team were drawn into their version of big time wrestling. Hooper nudged Smith. "Watch this." The winger moved up to the group, in which Wyllie was buried under five or six large forwards, and gave Wyllie a gentle kick in the rump. No reaction. Hooper nudged Smith again. A bigger kick. No reaction. Disappointed with what had happened so far, Hooper took a pace back, aimed carefully, and sunk a kick with all his might into Wyllie's backside.

Players there still look bemused at what happened next. "It was like an explosion," says Smith. "All the guys on Alex, and some of them were big, just flew in the air," says Taylor. "It was like a cartoon," says Simpson. "We just scattered."

Hooper, a quick mover, was running by the time Wyllie's feet hit the floor. By the time they were outside, Wyllie, armed with a muddy football boot he'd grabbed by the door, was about 30 metres behind Hooper, who couldn't resist pointing a Wyllie-like crooked forefinger and chiding Wyllie for his lack of humour.

"If you can't take it, you shouldn't be here," cackled Hooper, as the boot whizzed past him, and crashed into Wyllie's own car. For the rest of the morning Hooper would duck in for a beer while Simpson sweet talked Wyllie at the bar.

There was a less dramatic reaction from Hayes when he and his wife found that the devilment abroad that afternoon had led to Hayes' car being filled with rubbish from a skip at the park. "To this day," says Smith, "Donny's never said anything to us about it. He just got in the car, pushed the rubbish aside, said to his wife, 'Gee Jenny, the car's untidy', and took off. You couldn't open the door without having rubbish fall out!"

Through it all, the victories kept stacking up, until, by late afternoon of September 7, 25 successful defences had been notched up, with a 29-3 victory over North Auckland.

All had been set for a new record of 26 defences, if the challenge the next Saturday from Auckland could be rolled back.

Wyllie remembers the week as offering pressure the team had never felt before. "I know I didn't get a minute to spare, and of course the players were the same. It was very obvious with the team, they'd make mistakes they never made before."

Auckland slipped quietly into Christchurch on the Friday. Their last, light, run under coach John Hart had been at Eden Park before they joined members of the Fred Allen era Shield team, whose record they were defending, for lunch.

In Canterbury, remembers Don Hayes, the week before the Auckland game didn't click the way things usually did before a Shield game. "It was just a lot of little things. Dale (Atkins) hurt his ankle at training, and I think we got carried away a bit with beating North Auckland. The days you play very well, everyone has thought about the game, and everything seems to go right, all down the line. It's an attitude thing."

Wyllie knew how much pressure his team was under, but there wasn't much he could do about it. "Our fellows were at home, we couldn't keep them out of things the way Auckland could."

The tension was so great that some in the Canterbury team can't really remember the way they ran to both sides of the ground to applaud their supporters.

The first half was a nightmare. "It could be that the opposition forced us into the errors, or it may have been the tension," says Wyllie. "But we didn't win any lineout ball, and we generally played like a team that was going out to challenge for the Shield. It often happens with a challenger, the first half is gone before they realise what they've got to do, and what it's about, and by then it's too late, there are too many points against them."

Wyllie wasn't angry about his team being down 24-0 at halftime, more sorry for them. They weren't losing with dignity. Simpson says at halftime there were no recriminations. "He came out, grabbed the ball, said, 'Look, they scored their points with this, so can you.' If he'd pounded us, that would have sent us straight down the tubes."

Canterbury would concede one more try, but score 23 points in the second half, in the greatest comeback in Ranfurly Shield history, finally losing 23-28, with ardent Canterbury supporters, and many of the players, believing there were two minutes still to play when referee Bob Francis blew for fulltime.

Warwick Taylor says Canterbury were lucky. Not in the way

Christchurch Star

Bruce Deans begins the amazing Canterbury comeback that almost won the day in 1985.

points were scored, but in the way the game was played. "Alex had always said he didn't mind if we lost it, just as long as we lost it playing well. And we did play well. The Shield had been a big part of your life, you'd lived it for three years, and then it was gone. If we'd lost it playing badly we would have all been bitter about it. But as it was, it hurt, but we didn't feel let down."

Simpson says: "The biggest thing was the friendship. We're all still mates. We've gone our ways, because some aren't playing, but when we get together, we're like a set of brothers. Alex had a big hand in that closeness."

Prop Ashworth goes even further. "A lot of things contributed to those times. I think it was something that came along when a lot of people, especially in the rural community, were hurting. When the Shield came along it was something that everybody could grasp a part of and share in the pleasure. People could take their minds off the daily struggle, and identify with a physical thing, where everyone could express themselves during that eighty minutes. So it was more than just rugby."

THE LEGEND: Alex Wyllie once straightened out the S-bends at Leithfield, driving straight through a couple of fences, and across a paddock before he woke up.

THE REAL STORY: Canterbury beat Auckland 42-3 at Lancaster Park in 1973, and the next day had to travel to the West Coast for the annual game. "It was a reflection of the attitude of the administration in those days. I think we left Christchurch for the Coast at about 6.30 in the morning. We travelled over there, and it's a long trip coming back from the Coast. At about 1 o'clock in the morning I dozed off driving home. I was heading for a bit of a pond on the side of the road at Leithfield. That looked a bit wet, so I swung it hard round the other way. It looked as if I was going to go through a gateway, which would have been okay, but I went a bit further and hit a pole. I had a run for a couple of miles to my cousin's place, and he took me home." Later Wyllie would find out that the local policeman, on hearing of the accident, was determined that Wyllie would face prosecution. The policeman went to the telephone exchange, to listen for a Wyllie call home (assuming that Wyllie would have gone to a friend's place, and would later call Keryn to come and collect him). It was quick thinking, but too clever. There was no phone call because Wyllie was already home. "He (the policeman) didn't think to look in the most obvious place."

CREDIBILITY RATING (OUT OF 10): 10 for Wyllie's version.

10

Feeding
the passion

'We were all excited when the Ranfurly Shield returned to Canterbury, but I was disappointed that you printed the picture of the well wishers holding the banner "Grizz is God." I trust Alex Wyllie will publicly refute that inscription. The Bible tells us: "You shall have no other gods before me." Exodus xx.3. A visiting English Bible teacher, David Pawson, pointed out that the popularity of the Beatles began to wane once they stated that they were as famous as Jesus Christ.
Mrs M.H. Sanson (Christchurch Press, September 21, 1982).'

The elevation of Alex Wyllie in Canterbury rugby might have disturbed the correspondents in the city's newspapers (Mrs Sanson was not the only one to complain about the Grizz is God notice), but it might have disturbed them even more if they had known that it was no accident, but, to a degree, the result of a determined campaign.

During Wyllie's time as Canterbury coach, the fortunes of the rugby team and the fortunes of Radio New Zealand's 3ZB were intertwined. Both had been through tough times. Going into the '80s, the station was losing money, the team was losing games. The low point for Canterbury rugby had been in 1981, with Christchurch a city divided over the Springbok tour. In Cathedral Square the sister of Canterbury's delegate to the New Zealand Rugby Union, Russ Thomas, would tell an anti-tour demonstration that she was ashamed of her brother. At Lancaster Park usually loyal fans were embarrassed by their team.

In the middle of it all were a couple of shrewd promotional people, a couple of talented radio performers, and some rugby administrators who were prepared to try something different.

Mike Weir, the Apple and Pear Board man who had just pushed the board's money away from John Walker, and into Canterbury rugby, had canvassed Radio Avon about placing $10,000 worth of advertising on their station in 1982, on the basis that the station would promote the Canterbury team as well.

With an arrogance that isn't uncommon among radio management, Weir was told that rugby wasn't Avon's market, but he was still welcome to spend some money in advertising. Well, said Weir, it looked as if Radio Avon wasn't the Apple and Pear Board's market either. He wouldn't spend a penny with them.

Waiting at 3ZB, with an on-air schedule full of spots for Fresh-Up rugby ads, was Bernie Brown, a Taranaki born rugby fan, who had been keen to see the station backing rugby when he had arrived in 1979 from 1ZH in Hamilton.

But '81 hadn't been the year for it. "It had been a really heavy time for rugby in Canterbury," says Brown, now heading a group due to run a music television channel in Auckland. "The grandstand at Rugby Park had been burned down, there were rumours of anti-tour protestors putting poison in the city's water supply. We did have signs up at the Park, but really we backed off a bit from our rugby campaigns."

The election of Wyllie as coach had changed all that. Brown wanted 3ZB in rugby up to their neck. He went to the union and promised that when there was a big game on the Saturday, breakfast announcer Barry Corbett's Friday show would be like the world's longest rugby commercial. The station also wanted cheerleaders, which started to lead to some muttering among the union conservatives. In stepped Russ Thomas's brother, Vic, who told the dissidents, look, these people are the experts in promotions and publicity, let's leave things to them. The union members agreed.

Enter Corbett, a slight, bearded radio veteran, whose breakfast show remains No 1 in Canterbury after a decade of intense competition from such heavily publicised rivals as James Daniels and Ken Ellis.

Nationally he's probably best known as the man who introduced American television star Leeza Gibbons to her future (now former) husband Chris Quinton when Gibbons and Quinton were in Christchurch for Telethon, but Corbett is a rugby fan too. When the Ranfurly Shield came back to Christchurch in 1982, he recalls that the rugby union threw the gates open for the station. "We started up Corbett's Corner in the stand, with seats for listeners to win, and we began to use Alex more and more on air."

Wyllie was the choice to be featured for several good reasons. One was that he had a higher profile, as a very recently retired Canterbury rugby hero, than most of the players in the '82 team. Another was that by concentrating on Alex the heat in the pre-game hype went right off the players. That especially suited a man like captain Don Hayes. "They wanted Alex more than me. He and Doug (Bruce) fronted everything. It kept the pressure off me. Also

Alex's memory is better than mine, and he can sum up a game better afterwards. When you're playing you don't see the whole picture."

At 3ZB Corbett could see, as time went by, that Wyllie was settling into the style of keeping things rolling on air. One moment sticks in Corbett's mind. Canterbury were playing in Blenheim, and Corbett called Wyllie at the team's hotel. The opening dialogue went like this.

Corbett: "Pretty flash hotel you're staying at by the sound of it. It must be very classy."

Wyllie: (Long pause). "It's condemned."

"I knew then," says Corbett, "that Alex was going to be good for us."

To make sure things stayed good the station kept popping up with the gimmicks. There was a one-eyed Canterbury supporter's eyepatch, that went into a one-eyed Canterbury supporter's pack, which, naturally, included a can of Fresh-Up.

Then there was the cardboard Grizz mask, an idea that Brown says originated with Chris Muirhead, then the programme director of 3ZB, now managing a new FM station in Wellington.

Wyllie was quizzed, late at night, and in front of witnesses, as to how he'd feel about a promotion that potentially could put 20,000 Wyllie look-a-likes on the bank and in the stands at Lancaster Park. "Do what you like," he said, not taking much notice. He had a later chance, says Brown, to turn the idea down, which would have prevented Keryn Wyllie from asking one of the great questions of the Ranfurly Shield era in Canterbury: "Why are people wearing Alistair Hopkinson masks?"

There was also a 3ZB front row, in which a pencil sized cardboard Corbett swung on a rubber band between a Ranfurly Shield toting Wyllie, and a broad shouldered Ken Anderson, the commentator for all the Shield matches.

Corbett didn't mind the fact that there was a noticeable contrast between his physique and Wyllie's. "We had Alex on almost every Friday through the winter, and it'd usually end up in a session at a pub that night. When Alex started pushing that big finger into chests, he'd go, push, next man, push, next man, push, then me, and the finger would stop about an inch from the front of my chest. I guess he knew I was such a weak little bloke he might kill me!"

It certainly helped the publicity machine that the Canterbury Ranfurly Shield era had enough excitement and plot twists to rival the old Saturday morning movie serials. Even better, for Canterbury fans, the guys in the white hats always won. Says Bernie Brown: "It was nothing like the Ranfurly Shield matches are in Auckland now. There was real passion among the supporters, and many of the games were close enough to be a worry. Week after week these guys would get out and beat off another challenger. It was a wonderful

3ZB Christchurch

Barry Corbett, the ultimate one-eyed Cantabrian.

atmosphere to be involved in. Personally I was never crazy on the cheerleaders, but the crowd loved them."

Running a Saturday morning sports show on 3ZB, and then calling the matches in the afternoon, was Ken Anderson, a successful business man in his own right, who says he didn't know Wyllie especially well when the Shield era began.

"I'd been broadcasting for nearly 20 years, and we had just got through the barrier of radio being very proper, very bureaucratic. The image of Alex might have been that he couldn't string four words together, which of course wasn't the case at all.

"I think Alex did a tremendous amount for sport in the news media. The trick is to find people on radio who will interest people who aren't really fanatics about rugby. He proved to be enormously popular.

"Bernie Brown told me what 3ZB wanted to do with Alex, and Alex got better and better. Let me put it this way, if you have somebody who really is an expert in his or her field, if they're fascinated by it, they can make it interesting for anyone else. If you take Alex's case, he'd watched his father coach, played the game to the highest level, seen the administrators at close hand, he'd really been involved, or close to, every aspect of the game.

"And he had a view on everything. That was what I think made him unique. As a group, New Zealanders tend not to have a viewpoint. We agree with everyone else. Not Alex.

"He was also very good at knowing what to say without actually saying it. He wasn't backward about speaking his mind, but he knew how to phrase things.

"What he did demand from journalists was that we knew we carried a great responsibility for the game. If you were criticising from a point of weakness he'd expose you for what you were."

What effect did all the attention have on Wyllie?

Very little, says Corbett, possibly because Wyllie, in Corbett's view, never grew to love the limelight in the way that some sporting personalities can.

To Wyllie, says Corbett, working with the media was part of what he saw as his duty to rugby. In a separate conversation Wyllie acknowledges that "the media is part of the job of being coach. You have to have it, whether they're praising you, or being critical."

Final proof for Corbett that Wyllie saw his involvement with 3ZB as a partnership, rather than a big favour Wyllie was doing for the station, came when Joe and Jean Wyllie had their 50th anniversary.

Alex asked Corbett if he'd mind mentioning the anniversary on air. Corbett duly made the dedication. At the time Corbett was in an indoor cricket team that included Wyllie and Doug Bruce. That night Wyllie said, "I've got something for you in the car." When they were outside Wyllie handed Corbett a parcel. When Corbett went to open it, Wyllie muttered urgently, "Don't open it here in front of the guys." By now very intrigued, Corbett went to his own car, and privately opened the small package. Inside was a slice of the anniversary cake.

As well as the hype being manufactured by the radio station, there were plenty of extra promotions that kept Christchurch people constantly aware of the fact that the Ranfurly Shield was in the city.

But the most unusual attention to focus on Wyllie during the Shield days came from Jesse Irene Sparrow, a Christchurch spinster who died in 1976, at the age of 84.

Miss Sparrow, confined to a wheelchair in the last years of her life, became a great rugby watcher, and so, as well as her milkman, and her nephews, she left $300 to Brian Lochore, and what was left would be for Wyllie and Sid Going. When the estate was completed, it was discovered that Wyllie and Going could both get $16,000 each.

The Public Trustee contested the will, with their lawyer arguing that as Wyllie and Going were known to Miss Sparrow only by their images on TV, it was a bit strong to suggest they should get 16 times as much as her nephews whose $1000 each was specified in the will. (So was Lochore's figure, so $300 duly winged its way to his Wairarapa farm).

Wyllie told a *Christchurch Star* reporter he had "more or less given up" on the hope of getting the money, but it had come as a hell of a surprise when he had been told there might be a nest egg from an unknown person.

It was a very sensible attitude for Wyllie to take...the bequest would eventually be denied to himself and Going.

There was a mix-up of another kind that saw Wyllie, in full evening dress, conducting the New Zealand Symphony Orchestra at the Christchurch Town Hall on a February Friday night in 1984.

Toyota were launching a new Corolla, and the fifth-generation machine was to have its first unveiling in Wellington. The booking was supposed to be at the Michael Fowler Centre's reception area. To their surprise, Toyota New Zealand found they had booked the huge auditorium instead. Nothing daunted they lashed out and hired the orchestra.

It seemed such a good idea in those pre-stockmarket crash days, that the whole exercise was repeated in Christchurch. Wyllie was handed the baton by English conductor Ron Goodwin to lead the orchestra in an instrumental version of "Give It A Boot Robbie", the tribute to Robbie Deans, recorded, with perhaps the worst vocal ever heard on radio, by Corbett and his team at 3ZB.

A critique of Wyllie's conducting suggested that he appeared slightly unaccustomed to the baton, but that "his punches in the air were superb."

And, as what could probably be called the ultimate accolade, Lancaster Park was renamed the Alex Wyllie Stadium for the last challenge of the 1983 season, against Manawatu.

At that time the Member of Parliament for Manawatu, Mr ME Cox, had moved a notice of motion in Parliament that "after

The sign that stirred the Christian letter writers.

recently making the Waikato representative rugby team look like a fourth-grade outfit, and then severely embarrassing the pride of Counties, the green and whites from Manawatu, after thrashing the Cantabrians this Saturday, will be returning the Ranfurly Shield to its rightful home - the Manawatu."

Undeterred, the Mayor of Christchurch, Sir Hamish Hay, suggested the one day name change for the Park, and the chairman of the Victory Park Board, that controls Lancaster Park, Mr D.L. Gallop, said the board was happy with the temporary change. "After all," said Gallop, "the board has good reason to be grateful to Alex and the team for what they've done for the board's finances."

To make the day complete, Canterbury held off a strong challenge from Manawatu, 28-15.

The attention that the Ranfurly Shield era focused on the Canterbury team made some of the players uneasy. Craig Green was quoted in Lindsay Knight's "Shield Fever" as saying: "I got to the stage where I stopped listening to 3ZB. At times you used to get sick of it."

Corbett, at the centre of the hype, makes no apologies. "We told the players not to listen, that we were going to go right over the top with the whole thing. We were going to say the team walked on water. We were so one-eyed from the start, but that was always the plan. It wasn't just the players who got sick of it at times. We certainly lost some listeners with the way we carried on, but we also gained plenty. I certainly never tried to pretend that I was a journalist being unbiased about the whole thing. I was an entertainer, and that's what I was trying to do, the ra-ra thing, let's stick it to the opposition."

They did. Auckland, when they arrived for the challenge in '83, found a bag in their rooms with red and black plastic razors that it was hinted could be handy for their wrists after the match.

At the centre of the campaign, which Bernie Brown described as a "boomer" for advertising revenue, was Wyllie.

"We needed a cult figure," says Brown, "and Alex was the perfect man for the job. It was obvious when you sat down and talked with him that the popular image of him then, as a rough, punchy bastard, wasn't right. What he was was a real salt of the earth person, from the third generation of a North Canterbury family of good Scottish stock.

"He was straight up and down, said what he thought, and underneath it all was a really decent bloke."

A test of that decency came when Wyllie was told by Brown that the radioman was opposed to the '81 Springbok tour.

Says Brown: "He asked me what the matter with me was. I told him I just didn't think it was good for the game, that I saw the tour as being an election bribe for Muldoon, and that I didn't like to see New Zealanders beating each other to bits over a game.

"We argued politics over it for a while, but eventually we reached a stage where he thought I was wrong, and he was right, but it didn't matter. He was prepared to tolerate my opinions. It didn't affect our friendship. I had my reasons, he had his, so what?"

As well as the radio work, Wyllie has had a ghostwritten column in the *Christchurch Star* for many years.

Unlike the radio work, the column began by chance.

Wyllie was talking with a Star reporter at an aftermatch function, and said he saw no harm in people close to the game writing about it. "After all, the ones directly involved in rugby know what's going on, both on and off the field."

If that was Wyllie's view, said the journalist, how would he feel about doing a column in the *Star* himself. "It started there," says Wyllie. "I was the Canterbury selector, and I gave my views of what was happening in club rugby, and the game in general. It doesn't matter to me whether people who read the columns agree or disagree, just as long as things are done in the right way, and you're not letting your teammates down by attacking them. I can see no harm in having a column, you're putting the game in front of the public, and it's the old story, any publicity is good publicity."

Christchurch Star

The best fish and chips in New Zealand, they claim in Canterbury, come from Cheviot Takeaways. And this is the painting on the wall of Graham and Pat Powell's shop.

His columns, "The Wyllie Way", were, especially when they began, more revealing of the man than many of the celebrity columns that have sprung up in the last decade.

They weren't controversial, but they did provide more information than many similar columns.

After an All Black-Australia test match at Lancaster Park, Wyllie said: "The wind was a major element in the game, as it turned out, and when Graham Mourie won the toss he faced a hard decision. I'm not sure what I would have done in the same circumstances. Usually it's regarded as better to play into the wind first, as long as you are confident of winning enough ball to keep the opposition in their own half.

"But if Mourie had played against the wind in that first half, the Australians might have had 16 points or more on when the change-round came.

"Obviously the Australian inside backs didn't run or pass as well as hoped. They need somebody stronger in midfield with Michael Hawker. Bill Osborne made the difference to our line, on attack and defence. Once I saw one of the Ellas stop dead in his

Christchurch Star

Everyone came out to support Canterbury in the Shield era, even an Englishman called the Wizard.

tracks when he saw Osborne lining him up."

On the second test in the '83 series, at Athletic Park: "I'm a bit surprised the All Black selectors didn't look at changes in the loose forwards for the third test in Auckland. I notice that Graham Mourie said after the Wellington test that the Campese try, the one that wrapped up the game, came through the New Zealand backline's mistake when they lost the ball.

"If Mourie had looked harder he would have seen the real cause of that try was the winning of good ruck ball by the Wallabies."

On Frank Oliver's play for Manawatu against Canterbury: "Frank Oliver had a great game, taking a lot of lineout ball, much of it two-handed. Later I asked him who had been doing the lifting."

Rugby Press

Don Hayes, left, and Wyllie reflect on one of the great shield eras with author Kevin McMenamin upon publication of "Glory Days" – a celebratory volume, chronicling a great chapter in Canterbury rugby.

On the expiry of the Wellington Rugby Union's lease of Athletic Park: "The park is Maori land, I believe, and I would expect the lease to rise quite a bit. This being the case, with a bit of luck, someone might consider changing Wellington's rugby venue from Athletic Park to somewhere else. After all, apart from the Millard Stand, there isn't much of value there. The old stand has seen better days, the dressing rooms are among the worst in New Zealand, the after match function area is pretty pokey, and the wind problem there has got worse since the Millard Stand went up."

After almost losing the Ranfurly Shield to Counties: "We won enough ball to score more points, but we just didn't use it the way I would have liked. The moves we had practised weren't used, because I think the players were too scared to use them for fear of mistakes.

"To help overcome this, for tomorrow's game against Wairarapa-Bush we are meeting tonight, and will stay as a team in a hotel. It is worth the trouble and the cost, and I would ask people to respect what we are trying to do by not annoying the players."

On one of his players: "Robbie Deans has certainly matured over the last couple of years. Anyone who could take that deciding kick as coolly as he did, and could stand up to the pressure he was put under, has certainly come on well.

"I see that Allan Hewson has been named New Zealand Player of the Year, but I can say one thing for sure - I wouldn't be swapping fullbacks with Wellington at any price."

And even a word for a referee: "The old television shows up every mistake, but what it does not make clear is the immense pressure a referee is under. In games like Saturday's, with a patriotic crowd, and scores so close, the pressure must be tremendous for a ref.

"It's something like a rugby player in his first big game, except that a player has fourteen other guys to help him. A ref is there all by himself."

As an All Black coach Wyllie has dropped his *Star* columns, but his views in them, rather like his radio work, had a much more free and open air to them.

If Wyllie chooses to stonewall an interviewer he has developed a masterful use of silence. It's turning an old journalistic trick back on the journalist.

Watch most tough television interviews, with anyone, not just a famous sporting figure. A difficult question is asked. Was this election promise broken? No, replied the politician. The interviewer then sits, and looks the person being interviewed straight in the eye. To fill the silence, the politician keeps talking. It's how Ben Couch was led into saying he wasn't opposed to the idea of apartheid by Ian Fraser.

Wyllie can sit out such difficulties. I once asked him, on radio, why a certain All Black hadn't been included in a touring team. A day before I had written my theories on those reasons, basically that the man was regarded as a disruptive off-field influence by other players. His rugby was quite good enough to be there. Wyllie laughed at the question: "Well, you seemed to know the reasons in the paper the other day, why don't you tell me?"

The chance of an unguarded comment for the Auckland radio audience had slipped by.

On the other hand, if you're a visitor to Christchurch, especially in the summer, tune in to 3ZB at about 10 o'clock on a Saturday morning, and you'll hear Wyllie in a way you probably won't hear him anywhere else. He loves cricket, and will discuss the game, the matches, and the players, for hours. His knowledge of the game is considerable, his enthusiasm for it likewise. A fellow All Black remembers Wyllie staying awake all night in a hotel room, listening to a radio commentary on an Australia-England game. "It wasn't even a bloody New Zealand game," grumbles the former roommate.

The contract says that Wyllie is obliged to be available for 10 minutes on the telephone. The reality is that after 30 minutes he's often still there, putting forward very convincing sounding reasons for why the cricket selectors need to look at a certain batsman, or why a bowler should think about altering his run-up to the wicket. Wyllie, you see, doesn't enjoy being the centre of attention, but he does love to argue the toss over sport.

Alex Wyllie isn't as difficult with the media as some might say.

Bob Templeton, currently the Wallabies' assistant coach, and Wyllie share a warm friendship.

Autographs are constantly being sought from a man everyone in New Zealand recognises.

Peter Bush

It's tense before a test. Grant Fox, Gary Whetton and Wyllie before the first test in France in 1990.

But it's enjoyable when you've won. Wyllie, Whetton and manager John Sturgeon after the 6-3 victory over the Wallabies at Eden Park this year.

Kenji Ito

Peter Bush

Grizz the coach...cracking the whip.

The omission of Buck Shelford from the World Cup team had the media rushing to get his reaction at Athletic Park.

The team is named for the World Cup and Wyllie, NZRU chairman Eddie Tonks, John Hart and Lane Penn can consider the next stage - the Cup campaign itself.

Craig Innes veers past French halfback Aubin Hueber and on to the goalline for a sensational early try against the French at Nantes in 1989.

John Kirwan proving typically hard to hold - against the Pumas at Athletic Park in 1989.

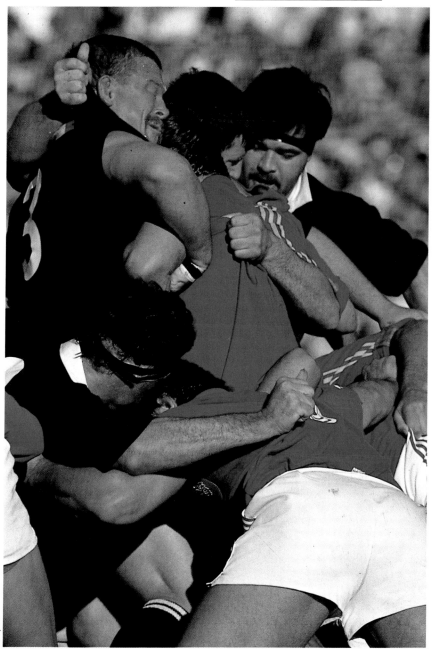

Kenji Ito

It's tough in them thar scrums. Richard Loe and Steve McDowell go upwards instead of forwards against the French at Eden Park in 1989.

Buck Shelford plays halfback during the 1989 Bledisloe Cup contest at Eden Park, a tough encounter the All Blacks won 24-12.

Watch out, here comes Stevie! McDowell prepares to take on a fair percentage of the Australian defenders during the 1989 Bledisloe Cup contest at Auckland.

11

The band of brothers

When Alex Wyllie took over the Canterbury team in 1982 the province had two test players, Graeme Higginson and John Ashworth.

In 1984 the All Blacks would play a test against Australia in which seven Canterbury players would be included. In all, nine of Wyllie's Canterbury players would play test matches during his five years as provincial coach.

There could have been even more wearing the silver fern, from a group of players who became not so much a provincial team, more a super club side.

Sifting through the names with Wyllie recalls the era when all of Canterbury turned to Lancaster Park Saturday after Saturday, with a fervour that was constantly rewarded.

Robbie Deans, the record breaking fullback, was a player whose selection, says Wyllie, was never in doubt. Like so many in the Canterbury backline Deans could have played in other positions. "That was the beauty of many of the players, Robbie, Craig Green, Andrew McMaster, Gary Hooper, Warwick Taylor, Vic Simpson, they could all adapt to other positions if we'd needed it."

The tragedy of Robbie Deans, says Wyllie, was that his knee was badly injured when he was at his very best. "Who knows how long Robbie could have gone on for? He was putting it all together, running into the backline well, playing with plenty of confidence. He had the guts to come back, but if he hadn't been injured there's no end to what he might have achieved."

Rod Latham, later to become a New Zealand cricketer, was the man who replaced Deans when Deans suffered his injury, at the end of the '84 season. "He was a player who could have gone further in rugby," says Wyllie. "He could goalkick, and had a really big punt."

Craig Green probably stands as the single most inspired selecting decision of Wyllie's Canterbury coaching career. "I'd never seen

Craig play on the wing when I put him there," says Wyllie. "But we had Warwick and Craig at second-five, and I wanted to give them both games. I was really waiting for Vic to say he wouldn't play on the wing, so I could play Craig at centre. When I asked Craig if he'd play wing he said 'yeah' straight away, so that was that. He was quite happy to play anywhere, just to put the jersey on."

Why did Wyllie believe Green would succeed on the wing? "He was a strong runner, and he had the ability to stand on his feet in a tackle. Those things are always going to help a winger."

Gary Hooper was 28 when he was first selected by Wyllie in '82. Old for a wing, but, in Wyllie's view, not a comment on Hooper's lack of form in past years, but of selectorial oversights. "He had great skills, and he put a lot of thinking into the winger's game, what should happen on attack, what patterns are needed on defence. There wouldn't be many wings around with a better knowledge of the game." Hooper played for the South Island in 1982, and retired from rugby at the end of the '83 season.

Hooper's place in the Canterbury lineup was basically taken by **Andrew McMaster**, a highly versatile player, who was actually playing at fullback in club football. At the end of the '84 season McMaster would move north, with the Royal New Zealand Air Force, and, after just two games for Manawatu, go to England to complete his training. Wyllie believes McMaster was a leading candidate for the proposed '85 All Black tour to South Africa before his move overseas. "He was probably one of our biggest losses. He had terrific skills, he could kick with both feet, he could cover fullback, wing and centre."

Adrian Boyd was a young winger from Nelson, a useful player, in Wyllie's mind, who never reached his full potential. Another winger was New Zealand track sprint champion, **Joe Leota**, who made the All Black reserves. Says Wyllie: "I don't think Joe ever really showed the qualities that I think he did have."

For **Victor Simpson** the path to the All Blacks would be rockier than Green's, but the fierce confidence that led him, in a move he would later admit wasn't smart, to turn down Wyllie's request to play on the wing was also a strength on the field.

"Put a challenge up to Victor, and it's all go. That's the way he is," says Wyllie. "He backs himself in confidence, and he's competitive with everything. That's a good quality to have in a player, because if you haven't got some confidence in your ability, you're wasting your time."

Warwick Taylor was one player who never quite got the attention others did, but in Wyllie's mind he helped others succeed. "I'm not saying others in the team weren't dedicated, but you wouldn't have found anyone more dedicated than Warwick. If he missed a tackle, missed a pass, missed a try, he really wanted to come to grips

Christchurch Star

Warwick Taylor, driving between John Kirwan and Sean Fitzpatrick, "put challenges on himself, and lifted his game that way."

with it, make sure it didn't happen again. To develop his kicking he used to work by himself with an old ball filled with wet hay. That's the sort of effort he made."

Wyllie says there was more to Taylor's game than reliability. "He had flair too. In fact, there wasn't much he couldn't do." But if there was one special skill that set Taylor apart it was chasing, and grabbing the ball, from up and unders. "I remember in 1983, in a Shield game against Hawkes Bay, Warwick came on as a replacement. He'd been on the field less than a minute when Wayne Smith kicked an up and under. Warwick followed it up, and scored near the sticks. He put challenges on himself, and lifted his game that way."

Taylor's partner in the five-eighths, **Wayne Smith**, is a player Wyllie would have liked to see stay in the game longer than he did. Smith retired after touring South Africa with the Cavaliers in 1986.

"As far as speed off the mark, seeing a gap, making a break at the right time goes," says Wyllie, "I don't think you could find many better. He'd moved to Canterbury from the Waikato because he couldn't make the team up there. He certainly proved his point with Canterbury."

Covering both second-five and first-five was **Wayne Burleigh**,

Christchurch Star

Bruce Deans had the variations in play that Canterbury needed.

who made a South Island team, but was unlucky enough to be playing in the shadows of Taylor and Smith. Smith had actually displaced an All Black, in Kieran Keane who would make five appearances in Shield defences.

Another All Black, **Steve Scott**, had to be dropped to make way for **Bruce Deans**. It was a selection that many in Canterbury were initially outraged by.

Wyllie had played for Glenmark when Deans was first in senior rugby. "I knew Bruce's game pretty well," says Wyllie. "He had the variations for what we wanted to do on the field. He was strong, he could run, he could kick over the top, and he had a pass that was a lot quicker than people initially gave him credit for. He wasn't just a halfback for the forwards. We were able to use the backs with him as well." Deans would become an All Black squad member in 1987, when Brian Lochore was All Black coach.

Canterbury's captain, **Don Hayes**, is a player Wyllie believes should have made the All Blacks. "Don played for the New Zealand Juniors in 1978, but, perhaps because the Canterbury team didn't perform in the next few years, he never went any further. I think he deserved to."

At the time Wyllie became Canterbury coach, it would be fair to say that Hayes wasn't fired with enthusiasm for provincial rugby. Wyllie heard stories of Hayes chatting outside the stand at Lancaster Park, telling retired Canterbury players he was at a stage where he wondered what it was all about, and was considering his own future in the sport.

Wyllie says that in '82 there was no other choice as Canterbury captain. Jock Hobbs, who would later captain New Zealand, was out of form at the start of the season, with the Marist flanker, Kevin Flood, playing against Queensland. So Hayes, not a man to rush to the front of a crowd, was captain whether he liked it or not.

"Don had the respect of the players. In fact you wouldn't ever get a more respected captain. He led by example. Don did the grafting stuff, not the sort of fancy stuff that shines for a lot of people. He was always right in the thick of it, setting up the ball for others to work with."

Tactically, Hayes worked to a Canterbury plan, and while he sometimes had critics who suggested the team was occasionally slow to adapt to changing circumstances on the field, in Wyllie's phrase, "it's damned easy to sit in the stand and ask questions about decisions that are made."

An unusual footnote to Hayes' time with Wyllie was Hayes' omission from the Canterbury team that challenged for the Shield in 1986 at Eden Park.

Even staunch Wyllie supporters question the decision, and some say it is one action as Canterbury coach that disappointed them. Loyalty is such a big part of the Wyllie code, they find it astonishing that Hayes should have lost his spot in his last season for Canterbury.

Wyllie says, and Hayes confirms it, that it was Hayes who suggested he be left out of the team, in favour of Grant Mickell, a much taller forward.

"We'd been thinking about what to do to combat a lack of height in the lineouts, and we decided to leave it until we got up to

Auckland. Up there Don came to me and said: 'You have to leave me out, because you need the height.' I would hope he was being honest in the way he was looking at it, and we were looking at it from a team point of view. It was one of those hard decisions you have to make at times.

"It's why you can't afford to get so close to your players that you might play them for sentimental reasons, rather than form. Your duty is to the team, not the individual. You have to play the team you think will do the best by each other on that day. So we didn't play Don."

Hayes says he hadn't been happy with his own form for much of the '86 season. "I told Alex I wasn't playing well. I'd probably annoyed him during the '86 season, because I just didn't have the interest, and on the field I just wasn't trying. In the end the decision (to drop Hayes for the challenge) had to be his. Alex is very loyal to players, but he's loyal to the team as well, and he picked the team he thought was best for the job.

"Looking back I suppose I wish I had played...but I suggested to Alex that I should be left out. I do know that I wish I hadn't gone up to Auckland as a reserve. It was bloody terrible, just watching it."

A lot of work went into turning **Dale Atkins** into one of the country's most dynamic back rows. "There were simple things for a No 8 that Dale was doing badly, and we spent a lot of time with him, until he could stay on his feet in a tackle and make the ball available. He developed into a very good No 8. In the end there was only one other around with the ability to drive like Dale did, and that was Buck Shelford. Why Dale never went closer to the All Blacks I'll never know."

The other man in the loose forward trio, **Jock Hobbs** complemented the other two, quick over the first 20 metres, a good tackler, able to set up play for others. "There are some players who have a bit of a burst, then stop, and have another burst later. Jock was never like that. He kept on going. He was very fit, and never hesitated to put his body on the line."

Albert Anderson was an important figure at lock, because Wyllie never had the luxury of two test sized locks. "Albert was on his way up, he was keen for work, and he got through a lot of it. We shifted him around a lot in the lineout, and he proved a few things in '83 against Auckland, when he did a great job. In some ways he may have been unlucky not to get more internationals."

An unlucky player was lock **Kerry Mitchell**, who played in the team that won the Shield, and then, says Wyllie "because of the very mobile way we wanted to play the game," didn't get many more chances to wear the red and black jersey. In fact, Mitchell would play in just six defences.

All Black prop **John Ashworth**, says Wyllie, was highly re-

Christchurch Star

Jock Hobbs (with the ball) was a player who didn't take any spells.

spected as a player throughout New Zealand. "Nobody ever beat him." The surprise in that was Ashworth's technique. "If you looked at him as a prop," says Wyllie, "he did so many things wrong. He didn't even pack with a straight back sometimes. So there must have been a lot of pressure there. But he must have had enormous strength, and he was hard. At the front of the lineout he was very good, and his handling and mobility were better than a lot of props."

Murray Davie, also an All Black, started as a loosehead, was switched to tighthead to accommodate Ashworth, then switched back to loosehead when Ashworth went to Hawkes Bay in 1985. "Murray did his job very well," says Wyllie, "and once again the mobility of players like Murray helped us get the ball back quickly."

When lock **Tony Thorpe** was selected many believed that, at 14 1/2 stone, he was too light for first class locking duties. "It is very light," says Wyllie, "but it's the old story, it's not so much a matter of how big you are, but how big your heart is. He had a big heart. You couldn't ask for a more honest forward." Wyllie thinks Thorpe was a little unlucky when, in 1984, he was selected for the New Zealand Juniors, and played five games in quick succession on a

Peter Bush

John Ashworth (grabbing Paul Quinn) was never beaten by a rival prop, even if, says Wyllie, he did so many things that were technically incorrect.

New Zealand tour in the middle of the season. "When he came back he was worn out."

Andy Earl was the man most often called on to fill in for Thorpe, or Dale Atkins, and Earl would eventually establish himself as Anderson's locking partner. "He always provided tough competition and we all know what he's gone on to do since," says Wyllie. "When you look back at it now, that Canterbury pack was very mobile. We had to be."

Hooker was never an easy position to fill. Wyllie worked with **John Mills, John Buchan, Gwyn Williams, Andrew McKellar** and **Brett Dixon**, but nobody ever guaranteed his position.

Over the Ranfurly Shield days, several good players would play in defences. The depth of reserves is often the measure of a good team, and Canterbury could look to people such as wing **Dennis Woods**, second-five **James Leggat**, first-five **Colin Williamson**, loose forwards **Barry White** and **Pat O'Gorman**, props **Phil Robson, Mike Taylor**, and **Chris Earl** to repel challengers.

THE LEGEND: *John Phillips, who would coach Canterbury in 1991, once booted Alex Wyllie in the face in a Town-Country game at Lancaster Park, slicing open Wyllie's cheek so badly it needed 15 stitches. But Wyllie never did anything about it, on that day, or in the future.*

ONE VERSION: *Phillips says Wyllie had thumped the Town prop, Alan McLennan, who had been unsettling the Country scrum. So Phillips stopped packing on the side of the Town scrum, stepped back, and booted Wyllie. "I expected him to stand up, but he just stayed down. They just about had to cut my boot out of his cheek. I didn't mean to kick him in the face. It was almost supposed to be a joke."*

THE WYLLIE VERSION: *"I'd reached out and given John a friendly sort of tap on the side of the face with my hand. Almost a 'G'day, how are you' sort of thing. I saw him stand up and pull his boot back. I didn't move because I never dreamed he'd do it. It took a few stitches to close it up. From then on, whenever we played against each other I'd say: 'It could be the day today, John. Could be the day.' Kept him on his toes, but I never did anything about it."*

CREDIBILITY RATING (OUT OF 10): *10. It certainly happened. The only dispute is over whether Phillips meant to kick Wyllie in the face, or in some other part of the body that would have been exposed when Wyllie stood up.*

12

Power games

A ll Black selection panels have sometimes been hotbeds of
argument, division, horse trading and deals.

Alex Wyllie can recall sitting in a hotel room in Hamilton, which
happened to be next to a room in which the All Blacks selectors of
the day were debating the naming of a touring team.

As angry words crashed back and forth next door, with Wyllie's
name popping up on occasions, the overall impression was certainly
not one of calm, logical discussion, making sure that the very best
players were being named in every position. It was more a case of
one selector being allowed his man, if in exchange another could
pick his favourite.

Such closed door bickering horrified the late Jack Gleeson when
he first joined the national panel in the 1970s. "I expected us to try
to work things through," said Gleeson, "but it felt as if we spent
more time negotiating over one or two fringe selections than over
the backbone of the team."

Wyllie joined the All Black panel in 1987, taking over from
Canterbury's Tiny Hill, who had stood down.

Wyllie had stood for convenor of the panel for the 1985 season,
in the expectation of the All Blacks touring South Africa that year.
He knew it was a million to one shot, but felt very strongly that for
the All Blacks to succeed, it was important that the tour was run by
as many men who had toured South Africa as possible. Two of the
New Zealand selection panel at that time, Bryce Rope and Hill, had
not played in South Africa.

Wyllie's hope, unfulfilled, was that he would be coach, with
Brian Lochore manager. As it was, the tour to South Africa, which
would have been coached by Lochore, managed by Dick Littlejohn,
was stopped by a court injunction.

There was no attempt by Wyllie to stand for the 1986 season, but,
with the Ranfurly Shield gone, and the World Cup coming up, he

was definitely a starter for the '87 panel. So too was Aucklander John Hart.

Hart's provincial coaching career with Auckland ran almost in tandem with Wyllie's in Canterbury.

It was 1982 when Hart won the Auckland job. He won it narrowly, which was no surprise to many who knew him. As a player-coach for the Waitemata side he was an excellent club player, but he also drove many of the people he played against crazy.

At halfback he was blessed with a very powerful voice, and a quick mind to drive it. He had a genius for niggling opposing players, and even his praise for good play by his own men could grate on rivals' ears. Such a voluble person couldn't help but pick up some enemies. On the night the Auckland Rugby Union was voting on the coach for 1982, I spoke with him at Alexandra Park, where a trotting meeting was being held. He asked: "How do you rate my chances?" I told him that in all honesty they were slim. I would probably have voted for him, but he'd rubbed a lot of rugby diehards the wrong way. He just nodded sombrely.

What I did not know at the time was that Hart's cause had been taken up by some powerful allies, most notably by Eric Boggs, considered by many one of the best talent spotters in New Zealand rugby. Boggs was the man who would suggest to Hart he take a close look at a Marist third-grader called John Kirwan. And Boggs was a man who, through a long, distinguished rugby career, from playing for Auckland and the All Blacks through writing about the game, to coaching Auckland to a Ranfurly Shield victory in 1974, had the contacts to give Hart just enough shove at the right time to clinch the Auckland coaching job.

When he was voted in, the result wasn't greeted with delight by Auckland's senior player, Andy Haden. Haden told Wellington journalist, Joseph Romanos: "I was a strict opponent of him (Hart) getting the job. I'd heard his team talks two or three dressing sheds away when he was ranting and raving as the Waitemata coach, and I'd seen his behaviour in club games."

Hart, who had been out of senior coaching for a year in '81, made his first move something that echoed what Wyllie was doing in Christchurch - he held trials.

The motives were slightly different. Wyllie just wanted to see the best players in Canterbury in direct opposition to each other. Hart wanted the same in Auckland, but it was also part of a move to ease the fierce internal politics that have often handicapped Auckland rugby. By calling in eight club coaches to help run the trials, and by gathering all the first division coaches in at the start of the year for a meeting to hammer out problems with training times, Hart mended fences. And it worked.

Alex Wyllie, Brian Lochore and John Hart, a combination that worked well at the 1987 World Cup.

In his five seasons with the Auckland team they would play 90 games, win 78, draw one, and lose 11. (While that was happening in the north, Wyllie was compiling an almost identical record, of 92 games, 76 victories, four draws, and 12 losses).

The Auckland-Canterbury games in their coaching careers were highlights of the New Zealand season. There were six games in those five years, and the teams emerged with three victories each.

They would even, after the first two seasons, share the same fitness expert in Jim Blair, first used by Wyllie, and snapped up by his hometown coach, Hart, the following year.

They had met in their playing days. Wyllie remembers Hart playing for an Invitation team against Canterbury at Denton Park in Christchurch. But they didn't really get to know each other until they were coaching their provinces.

It was 1986, with the Ranfurly Shield in Auckland, that they spent some time talking by phone. Both were disturbed by the Cavaliers tour, and, in the days before the tourists would slip out of the country, kept each other in touch with the latest on their vanishing players.

There were many who believed that the decision by Wyllie and Hart to both stand for the All Black selection panel for 1987 was by mutual decision. Both had been expressing privately during 1986 their reservations about some of the decisions made by Lochore, Hill and Colin Meads. Wyllie, for example, was surprised that 10 Baby Blacks were dumped when the Cavaliers became available for the second test in '86 against the Wallabies. Considering the All Blacks had lost the first test by only one point, he says he would have made no more than three or four changes for the second test.

Wyllie says that it would be "overstating it a bit" to suggest the move was a joint venture. "We both knew the other would be standing. I was a little surprised John was, because he had the Auckland team, and they had the Ranfurly Shield, and I thought they were improving. John stood in the north against Colin Meads, and I guess you could see that Colin wouldn't be in favour, after coaching the Cavaliers. John and I hadn't talked, either on the phone, or at coaching schools, over players, or what we'd thought was needed for the World Cup. We just let each other know we were going to have a go at the panel."

Once the new panel was together, there was plenty of work to do. The All Blacks had lost the test series with the Wallabies in New Zealand, and lost the last game of 1986, against France in Nantes.

The sessions the trio had together produced well-balanced trial teams. There was obvious common sense being applied to selections. Says Wyllie: "For the trials in '87, there was no doubt that we picked the players to play the type of game we wanted. Right down to the final trial we were looking at who would best fit the team's style. We were all very much going along the same lines. If there was a player who we didn't all agree on, it was down to BJ (Lochore) to make that choice. In the end it was going to be his team, so we'd discuss which player would do the best job for him and the team."

Mercifully free from the discussions was any hint of player trading. "Not once did we say 'I want him, so you can have someone else.' It's stayed like that ever since," says Wyllie.

Lochore, who'd made it clear 1987 would be his last year as All Black coach, involved Blair in the fitness training. The coaching of the New Zealand Colts team, and a New Zealand side to go to Japan at the end of the year, was going to be divided between Hart and Wyllie.

"At the time John wasn't going to be available for the tour the Colts made in New Zealand," says Wyllie, "so it was agreed that I'd take the Colts, and he'd come to help when he could, then he'd take the team to Japan, and I'd help."

Originally, says Wyllie, it was planned for the team to tour Japan to be very much a development team, with only half-a-dozen All Blacks involved. "John made it clear to the union that he wanted what would basically be a young All Black side, and eventually fifteen of the World Cup squad were included."

The chairman of the New Zealand union at the time, Russ Thomas, says there was also pressure from Japan to see more All Blacks included in the team. The New Zealanders were captained by Buck Shelford (who would say in his biography that he didn't consider he was captaining an All Black team) on their five match tour to Japan, in which the second game with Japan was won 106-4.

Hart was the coach, and Wyllie was designated assistant-coach. Wyllie's role would prove to be quite minor. That, says Wyllie, was almost inevitable with just 26 players in the squad.

"When you have two coaches in that situation, one is the head coach, and one does the bits and pieces, who takes the backs or the forwards away now and again. There weren't really the facilities to do that in Japan. When the head coach has the playing XV working with him, you only have nine or ten players left for the spare coach to do something with.

"With the opposition we had it was obvious we were going to do well, as long as we didn't loosen up and let ourselves down, but worked as a team.

"In some ways I think it was a waste of time taking another coach along. I don't know that at the top level you really need two coaches. The job there is to more or less mould the team together, not to coach them as such. Some players do come through that are lacking in skills, but mostly the players that get in the All Blacks are skilled, and coached in the basics."

One of the players on that Japanese trip was John Gallagher. Now in England playing league, he says in his book, *The Million Dollar Fullback*, that he had expected Hart and Wyllie to be equal partners in Japan. Equality would have been the best thing, says Gallagher. "Once the tour had been completed, Harty seemed to assume that he was going to stay the 'senior' coach/selector and he gave several press interviews pointing the way ahead for New Zealand rugby. I didn't know what was going on in Harty's mind, but I thought that he would have had more intelligence than to come out with those sort of comments. Perhaps the media were stitching him up, but it looked as if he was singing his own praises."

After the tour to Japan, Wyllie and Hart were both candidates for the All Black coaching job. Tipping who would win it depended on

Alex Wyllie (left) with Aucklanders Malcolm Dick, Gary Whetton (obscured) and Sean Fitzpatrick in Japan in '87. In some ways, says Wyllie now, it was a waste of time for him to be on the tour.

Peter Bush

Delighted to share in the 1987 World Cup victory. But at the end of the year Alex Wyllie and John Hart went head-to-head for the All Black coaching job.

where the person speculating lived. Aucklanders presumed that Hart, seen as the All Black coach after the trip to Japan, would get the job. In the South Island, people who worried about an Auckland takeover (Aucklander Malcolm Dick was Hart's manager in Japan) were backing Wyllie.

What nobody would know, until the New Zealand Rugby Union's council met to vote on the selection panel for 1988, was that Hart had his own plans.

Since Wyllie had challenged for the convenor's job in '85, the way the council decided the three man panel had changed. First, the convenor would be appointed, then the two who would join him.

In Wellington on Friday, December 4, 1987 Malcolm Dick may have been the only one of the 16 council members voting on who would be convenor who knew what would happen if Hart did not get the job.

Certainly chairman Russ Thomas says he was surprised when Dick said he had a statement to make, that Hart was no longer available to serve on the panel as a selector. "I asked Malcolm to write it down, to make sure the situation was quite clear. I felt it was sad, as John had capabilities."

The voting continued. Lane Penn, from Wairarapa-Bush, and Earle Kirton, from Wellington, joined Wyllie on the selection panel.

Hart was devastated by the news, although you had to hear the tenseness in his voice that afternoon to know what a blow it had been. The words themselves were considered, and, on paper, almost emotionless. Taking time out from a seminar in Queenstown with his firm, Fletchers, he spoke to me on Radio Hauraki in Auckland of how pressure of business had forced him to decide that he could not justify the time needed to help select, but not coach, the All Blacks.

Hart explained that he had taken the course he did, of councillors not knowing he wasn't available for anything except the top job, because if he had made that known he could have been accused of trying to blackmail them into voting for him.

He did not publicly condemn the decision, saying he was sure Wyllie would do a "fine job" as coach.

In Auckland, Hart supporters were not so discreet. Andy Haden called the decision "a terrible blow for New Zealand rugby. New Zealand rugby has a long history of choosing the wrong man. There is no doubt in my mind that Hart was the man for the job." And then, rubbishing Lochore, as well as Wyllie, Haden said that "the real force behind the All Blacks this year was John Hart."

The secretary of the Auckland supporters' club, Terry Dunleavy said: "The Kiwi clobbering machine is obviously still alive and well in the last bastion of backwoods conservatism, the New Zealand Rugby Union. This is not only anti-Auckland, but, more sadly, anti-excellence."

Chairman Thomas, on the other hand, said it was almost inevitable that such strong personalities as Wyllie and Hart, both highly successful as individuals, solo performers, would not easily mould into a coaching duo.

"It was like that on the tour to Japan. There wasn't any real need for the two men there, and when you have two aggressive people, very explosive characters, with different motivational skills, they won't work well together. I'd always said with Alex, that he's basically a loner, and he succeeds without a great deal of help from anyone else."

Wyllie, who points out that by not making conditions on his own nomination for convenor he'd implied he would be prepared to work with Hart as his boss, says he had no idea of the course of action Hart would follow. "I suppose you could say that, in the way he approached the thing in Wellington, that John didn't want to work with me."

It's not something Hart and Wyllie have ever discussed. At the time of Wyllie's appointment Hart left a message at Wyllie's home, but when Wyllie rang back he was unable to get hold of Hart.

Hart would not drop from sight, as he hinted he might at the time of his boardroom defeat. He spent a lot of time in 1988 working at coaching clinics, in several different unions. There was no doubt that in some quarters he'd lost a lot of ground over his approach to the convenor's job. Rugby here has never worked on the basis of picking up your ball and going home if things didn't work out. It was something Hart had 12 months to consider. He was hired as a comments' man by Television New Zealand, and did not use the position to carve up Wyllie in any way during the All Black tour of Australia.

At the end of '88, Hart displaced Kirton on the All Black panel.

Stories of divisions between them have never quite stopped since. One thing that Wyllie is emphatic about is that there have never been ugly scenes behind doors when the panel has been selecting the All Blacks.

"There's never been any of that, 'you can have that joker, I'll have this one,' going on," says Wyllie. "All of us (Wyllie, Hart and Penn) have worked easily together. There's never been a player in a side that's led to any personal arguments. It's been good."

At the time one Aucklander, involved with Hart from Hart's playing days, said to Wyllie: "I've got just one thing to say about what it'll be like with Harty: Always remember, rust never sleeps."

What has continued are constant media questions, almost all of them posed in Auckland, over whether Wyllie should be the All Black coach.

Often leading the charge is Haden, who works on radio for 1ZB. Little was heard of him in other media on the topic of Wyllie's coaching in 1988-89, but when the All Blacks started to stumble in France at the end of 1990 he was frequently quoted in print on the shortcomings of the tactical approach of the team.

The rest of the world, Haden suggested, had caught up with the All Blacks, and we hadn't advanced our thinking to keep ahead. When the All Blacks won the two tests in France, 24-3 and 30-12, there were no publicised statements from Haden.

What did happen after the tour was a strange batch of rumours about Wyllie's behaviour on the tour to France. If the more lurid were to be believed Wyllie had hit people, drunk too much, and even, in the most potentially damaging of all, been in a car accident and fled from the scene. All were untrue, but they were freely discussed in many rugby circles until manager John Sturgeon demanded they be cleared up before voting began on the All Black selection panel for 1991.

Once reporter Wynne Gray (see Legends) had told his story, and All Black doctor John Mayhew had explained in a conference call that a hangover had never stopped Wyllie from running a training run, the ballot for the panel was apparently over very quickly.

Peter Bush

The 1988 All Black selection panel, with former All Black coach JJ Stewart (on right in dark glasses). Wyllie, Earle Kirton and Lane Penn would spend just one season together.

During the Argentinian tour Haden, back in New Zealand, again joined the fray, via the Holmes television programme, saying he knew of discontent among the team over Wyllie's coaching, and that Wyllie needed assistance to find new ideas and tactics.

Add in the frequent suggestions in the *Auckland Star*, in particular, that Wyllie isn't the answer to All Black coaching dreams, and it's easy to draw the conclusion that a man as at ease with the media as Hart might be helping to stir the pot.

Wyllie says he has asked Hart directly about some stories, including quotes from Hart that could be read as undermining Wyllie's position.

"He's denied things I've specifically asked about," says Wyllie.

On the other hand, there has never been any great attempt in public, by anyone other than Wyllie, to explain the plan agreed to by all three selectors after the 1990 tour to France.

At the meeting where the plan for the World Cup was sorted out priorities were set. Nearly 60 players were sent training programmes put together by Jim Blair. It was agreed the top players shouldn't have too much rugby, and that fitness shouldn't peak until after the two tests with the Wallabies. There were risks involved in such a plan. A test, or even two, might be lost. But while Wyllie talked about the plan before the Argentinian tour, before the pressure would go on for Hart to take Lane Penn's position at the World Cup, it was publicly ignored when the All Blacks did lose a test, to the Wallabies in Sydney.

After the Sydney loss the campaign to replace Penn reached new heights, and didn't ease off when the All Blacks won the game at Eden Park. In public Andy Haden hammered the issue of Hart being given a title if he went to the World Cup, and it being pointless for Hart to go without one. The demand seemed bizarre — Hart had always been offered the chance to go to the Cup as part of the All Black squad, so why did he need a title? He'd played a big role in the preparation of the test team for the second test without a title.

Hardly noticed at the time, when most attention was on Wyllie and Hart, was that Hart needed a title if he was to advance in the pecking order ahead of Penn, already officially the assistant-coach. Penn was pushed to step down, held firm, and then squeezed out by the naming of Hart as co-coach, with Wyllie having ultimate responsibility for the team. So Hart's job was at the expense of Penn's.

Penn, rather than attacking anyone over his fate, says that in the whole issue of an assistant-coach, Wyllie wasn't given a fair deal. NZRU chairman Tonks insisted that an assistant had to come from the selection panel.

"John Hart and I were given the chance to select our assistants from outside the panel, but Alex was refused the same right. It wasn't that Alex and I didn't get on well, we did. We lost just one test in the time we were working together, and I get on well with Alex, I find him a good bloke. But there's a difference in attitude between a coach, and an assistant coach. Whether it's John, myself, Earle Kirton, whoever gets to the All Black selection panel, we've got there, and achieved whatever we've achieved by being the principal coach. I firmly believe that doesn't automatically give you the credentials to be a successful assistant-coach. I personally found the assistant's role very difficult. We had similar views on rugby, but everyone has his own way of doing things. I had the right to choose Mark Shaw to work with me. John had the right to choose Graeme Williams and Peter Sloane to work with him. But Alex was never given the same right, and that wasn't fair."

Despite the tensions all three must have felt, especially Penn, Wyllie says the selection of the World Cup squad was free of rancour. There were, he swears, no angry words, no shouting matches. Only the last four or five places had to be discussed at any length, and they were ultimately decided by reason, not by force of personality.

THE LEGEND: *During the 1990 All Black tour of France, Alex Wyllie beat up an Auckland journalist in a hotel after the first test.*

THE REAL STORY: *Wynne Gray, from the New Zealand Herald, had been working in his room on his report of the victory in Nantes. He went to the bar of the hotel, and joined a couple of other journalists for a drink. Later in the evening he was grabbed on the side of his torso by Wyllie, who briefly lifted him off his feet. Then they had a drink together. "It wasn't a fight, or anything like it," says Gray. "That's Grizz, he punches your arm, clips the back of your head. It's not done in anger. I was amazed to find out when I got back to New Zealand that it was supposed to have been some sort of attack."*

Legend

THE AFTERMATH: *Before the vote on the All Black panel for 1991 was taken, Gray was asked by New Zealand Rugby Union officials to give his version of the incident. He confirmed that no offence had been intended, or taken.*

CREDIBILITY RATING (OUT OF 10): *0.*

13

Judging
the group

The chemistry of a successful sports team can never be fully analysed. As coach of the All Blacks Alex Wyllie knows one thing - you can tell when it feels right, and you can tell when it feels wrong.

What's hard is turning wrong into right.

Take the All Blacks in Australia in 1988. It was the first time that Wyllie had the team on tour, and, in the first test in Sydney, the result was something of a dream. The side had won 32-7, scoring 14 points in the first 11 minutes. It was such a total eclipse that Australian coach Bob Dwyer was reduced after the game to complaining that the crowd at the Concord Oval had too many damn Kiwis in it, and the Aussies who were there didn't cheer enough for the Wallabies.

Two weeks later, in Brisbane, everything pointed to a real hiding for the Australians. Their side had several selection changes, and goalkicker Michael Lynagh had to be replaced after he was injured playing for Queensland against the All Blacks the previous weekend. David Campese, whose tackling of John Kirwan in Sydney had the strength and tenacity of tissue paper, was playing at fullback, which promised an open door policy in defence. For the All Blacks there was just one change. Michael Jones, unable to play in the first test because it was on a Sunday, replaced Mike Brewer on the side of the scrum.

So far, so very good. But in the reshuffling of the tour games after the Australian Rugby Union had initially wanted most weekend games to be played on a Sunday, the midweek game, in Townsville, had not been moved back from Wednesday to a Tuesday. And it was a night game.

So the All Blacks drifted into Brisbane late on the Thursday. There would be time for only one training run before the test at Ballymore.

As it happened, it was a cracker. "If we'd played the Wallabies on the Friday, we would have cleaned them right out," says Wyllie. "Everything was on a high, but then, for some reason, it just went dead."

Judging the pre-game feeling is something that can still be difficult, even with Wyllie's experience as a player and coach. "You go around and look at the players in the dressing room, and you wonder, 'Are they there? Are they ready to go? Have they built themselves up?' You can go and yell and scream at them and slap them on the back, but the experts say that only lasts ten minutes. It has to be within them, and the build-up might have started a long way back. You might see someone sitting in a corner looking like he's daydreaming. You might think, 'God, he's not with it,' but that can be the way he is, and he might be ready."

But in Brisbane, the atmosphere was not one that suggested a calm before a storm on the field. So much so that, outside the changing room just before the match, Wyllie would see an injured Warwick Taylor, and the pair could only shake their heads in dismay. "He'd felt it too," says Wyllie.

There were some specifics that could have been blamed for the flatness. Probably not the late arrival, which might have seemed a worry. The Friday run should have put things on track. Perhaps you could blame the feeling among some players that the tour was becoming a bit of a holiday in the sun, or the atmosphere of such boarding school pranks as secret changing of rooms, as wives arrived to see the test and take in Expo '88 at the same time.

"I'm not saying the wives shouldn't be there on tour," says Wyllie, in a tone that hints he's trying to convince himself of that. "But in my experience it's not a great idea, especially just before a test."

Perhaps you could blame the loss of John Gallagher's boots. The man who would switch to league in 1990, had been nervous before the game, and was dry retching in the toilet in his room when the call came for the team meeting before hopping on the bus. In a rush to make sure he wasn't late he'd left his boots behind. They were rushed to the ground while the All Blacks tried to keep the news away from Wyllie.

By the time the All Blacks were in the dressing room there was, says Wyllie, some attempts by players to rev themselves up. "You could tell some players were trying to force themselves, saying, 'I'm ready' and 'I'm going to do this,' and that's a waste of time, because it's too late trying to force things five minutes before the game."

In the first half, all Wyllie's fears came true. On a warm, sunny day, the locals cheered their team to a 16-6 lead. It took a massive effort by the All Blacks to drag themselves back into the game, to the point where Grant Fox had a chance to win the game with a

John Kirwan has scored a record number of test tries for the All Blacks. There's never been one more welcome than this one, that saved the second test against Australia in '88.

conversion of a John Kirwan try. The kick missed, and the All Blacks escaped with a 19-all draw.

Trying to understand what happened has occupied Wyllie often since. He still has no concrete answer. "Anyone who could work out why a group feels good one day, and not the next, would be a multi-millionaire."

But looking for the answers is something that's kept Wyllie in coaching at the top level. His own father says he never fails to be astonished at the way Wyllie can maintain his enthusiasm for the game over so many years.

"I probably could have done with a break after the Ranfurly Shield went," says Wyllie. "But I was probably at a stage where I thought that if I took a break, I might never have got back into it again. There would be many times when I'd felt like getting the hell out of it, and then some challenge comes, perhaps some smart prick in the media says you got this wrong, or didn't do that, and you'd like to stay and prove them wrong.

"The enjoyment can be in the challenges you face. You're always looking at the game, looking for perfection, aiming for the perfect game. You should never feel that you've reached that, because once you do, it's time to get out, you won't be doing the job a coach should anymore."

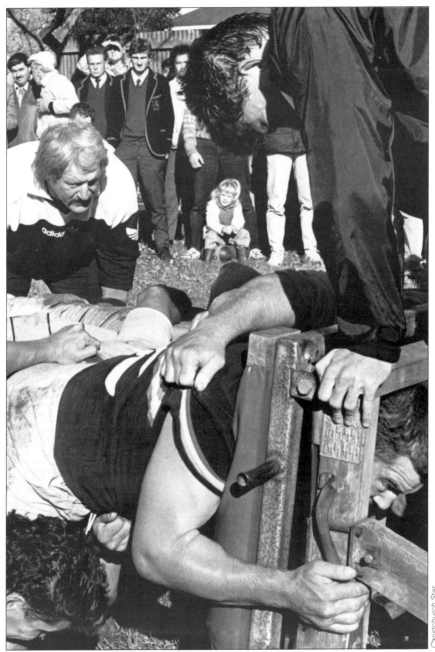

Christchurch Star

Wyllie believes that rugby at the top level is a simple game. As the '88 All Blacks are finding here, he said "simple" not "easy."

One of the most quoted Wyllie statements is that rugby is a simple game. It isn't a throwaway line

"Why I've always said the game is simple is, well, compare what happens in international rugby with club rugby. Now in club rugby, you've got your good players, and some not so good, and you try to fill the spots.

"When you get to the level where you're selecting players for their skills, then it's a simple game. You do the set pieces, but then it's up to the players themselves to show their ability, with whatever skills they have. You may be able to show them a bit, but they have to use their skills, whether it's speed, kicking, jumping or scrummaging abilities.

"It's simple because if you've got the ball the opposition hasn't. So that's the first requirement, to win the ball. After that, as long as you keep control of it, you should win. It's easy to say, but, of course, it isn't as easy to do.

"What I believe is that you don't go out coaching and tell your players what to do in every situation. I've seen some jokers do that, but all it does is turn your players into robots, and that's not achieving anything.

"You should be trying to encourage them to think under pressure, playing their own game, and doing the right things at different times. You put ideas into them, discuss things, give some advice, say when something went right, say where they took a wrong option."

Wyllie the All Black coach maintains a stoney face throughout a game. It's become such a trademark that a Rexona deodorant television commercial's been written around it.

It would be wrong to suggest that the unmoving facade reflects what's happening inside.

"The worst thing about being a coach, after having played, is knowing that you can't do a thing about the game once the players are on the field. You can't go out there on the field. So there's a real build-up of adrenalin, that a player can get rid of on the field. There's nothing much to do about it in the stand. You just have to face that you're a bit old to play now, a bit past it."

Not all coaches contain their nervous energy while in the stand. Wallaby coaches in recent years, Bob Dwyer and Alan Jones, are often in motion, jumping up, yelling, or, in Jones' case, threatening to wrench the collar off his shirt.

Wyllie might feel like jumping up occasionally, but he has several reasons why he won't. "If you're going to get up and yell and yahoo when something goes right, what are you going to do when something goes wrong? At the start of the test with Wales in Cardiff in '89, remember the try Craig Innes scored, coming in from the blind side? We'd worked on that move in training all week. It was something that hadn't been used for a long time. So the move was used, and it worked, and a try was scored, and that was a good start to the game. But hell, there was a long way to go to the end of the match. What if we'd lost it? People would have been turning around, saying, 'Look at that bloody idiot. He was jumping up and down thinking they'd won the game.' You'd end up having to crawl under the seats at the end.

"I just like to sit there and concentrate on the game. I don't applaud our tries, because if you do I think you should applaud the opposition's too. Penalties don't enthuse me much.

"I don't even talk to anyone very much. If you just sit and watch, you can concentrate on what's going on.

"You watch the clock all the time, thinking about what they need to get ahead, or what you need to stay in front or catch-up. At times you can feel you're safe enough, and then they come back in a few minutes. The French did that to us at Lancaster Park in '89 straight after halftime. But that doesn't happen very often. Usually you can reach a point where you feel the game's won, but you're always thinking about the possibilities.

"Of course, when that whistle goes for the team to go on to the field, all you can really do is think, well, I've done all I can now, and go and sit down and see if it works."

The man Wyllie shares his last private moments with before a game starts is a lanky coal miner from the West Coast, whose idea of drinking is an occasional glass of wine with a meal.

John Sturgeon, manager of the All Blacks from the time Wyllie became coach in 1988, is living proof that not every rugby friendship is cemented over a keg, and that not every Coaster was weaned on to beer. "I've had a shandy, but I wouldn't know what spirits taste like. When I left school I had to leave home in Greymouth to serve an apprenticeship, and I finished up with twelve shillings a fortnight after I'd paid my board. When I went home my parents topped my board up, they bought me the tools I needed, they clothed me, and they bought my rugby boots. I wasn't any different to any other apprentice in those days.

"My father worked really hard, he was a miner too. And I worked it out, it'd be pretty bloody poor if he was slogging his guts out, giving me money for me to booze it away. So I didn't drink.

"By the time I was in a situation where I could afford to drink beer, I'd got past that stage where I had to do it to get the courage to do things. I was getting on to twenty-one, I'd been playing senior rugby for three years, and the guys had accepted me as I was. So I sort of got past it, and it's never bothered me since."

Attitude to alcohol isn't the only difference between Wyllie and his manager. "We're totally different people," says Sturgeon, "so it's hard to say why we've worked so smoothly together. What we

Rugby Press

All Black manager John Sturgeon. He's never fully understood why he and Wyllie work so well together.

have in common is that we're both close to the players, and that might be a difference between us and some of the manager-coach combinations we've seen with overseas teams. The first concern for both of us is the players. We look totally different, our football records are totally different. He was a great footballer, and I was a mug club footballer, who enjoyed thirteen years playing as a senior.

"He's a challenge to work with. At times he's pissed me off

something terrible, but I'm still here because, deep down, we've got respect for each other."

The relationship was established very quickly. Sturgeon was appointed manager of the 1987 New Zealand Colts team, to be coached by Wyllie.

There was a fiery settling down period. Both men, in their own ways, have strong opinions on how things should be run. But they soon found they had common goals, and that, above all else, they wanted the team to succeed.

Fierce arguments can still happen. Sturgeon recalls blistering exchanges in France in 1990 when Sturgeon, who had rocketed Wyllie for not letting him know what was going on the previous day, failed to tell Wyllie about drug tests that were coming up. "He really did go at me, and I had to just walk up and apologise. But at the end, this is where the respect comes in. We can have some great rows, but it's only superficial."

In fact, the occasional screaming match between the pair can be a small cabaret turn for the players. When the team assembled at the Poenamo Hotel for the trip to Argentina this year the All Blacks were gathered, signing 100 or so footballs. One of the hotel staff came to the back dining room where the signing session was being held, asking if a few extra footballs, handed in overnight, could be added to the session. Given the okay by Sturgeon the man returned just in time to observe a furious, shouting, swearing, nose to nose "row" between Wyllie and Sturgeon, who managed to keep themselves from laughing until the startled hotel worker had shot back to the safety of his desk, just in time, he must have thought, to avoid being bowled over when Wyllie threw Sturgeon through the nearest available window.

Sturgeon has suffered for Wyllie, and it cost him as well.

On the Colts tour in '87 Sturgeon took a few slightly injured players to a local doctor in Taumarunui. Just before they left Wyllie said casually, "Get me one of those Vicks inhalers, Sturg. I've got a bit of sinus."

After the players had been examined the doctor asked Sturgeon if there was anything else the team needed. Sure, could the doctor fill in a prescription for a Vicks inhaler? Concerned, the doctor asked what the problem was. Sturgeon, foolishly, said that he'd been suffering from a bit of sinus. "I'll have a look at you," said the doctor.

"I've never had sinus in my life," says Sturgeon. "But he whipped this great funnel out, shoved it up my nose, and peered up it with a torch. I thought he was going to ram both his hands up there. 'Ah yes,' he told me, 'I'll be able to give you something stronger for this. I'll give you a course of tablets as well.' It cost me $34 for the tablets and gunk for Wyllie's nose. Of course, when I got back to the hotel and told him it cost that much, he just laughed at me. He could buy the inhaler for $3.50 at a chemist. All the stuff went in the bin. But for a long time afterwards we'd say to each other, 'Keep up the pills and the ointment.'"

For Wyllie, the build-up to a test match, as an All Black coach, begins with the selection, a time when, compared with the club coach, he and his panel have the relative luxury of selecting players whose styles complement each other. "It's no use having a player who's used to running, and then picking a first-five who kicks all the time. So right at the start you have to pick the style of play you want, and get the players who'll fit it."

Being a selector means that Wyllie never goes to a match in New Zealand to relax and enjoy the football. "I think you should always analyse the game, no matter what the level. There could be a player who one day will be good. And you talk to people as well, they mention a player who's been going well, and that might be a help later on. I did go to the Ireland-Wales game in Cardiff in 1990, and people there said to me afterwards, 'Wasn't the rugby awful?' But I was quite happy, because I didn't have to look for the mistakes, though they were there, and tries were being scored."

Most international rugby coaches, and Wyllie is one, would prefer to be judged on what happens on a tour. "When you're touring, the players are virtually in the palm of your hand. The players don't have to go back to their clubs, where they may be

The Magnificent XV, who beat Wales and Ireland on the tour of 1989.

Peter Bush

given different ideas, and the pressure on them may be greater than playing for the All Blacks. There's pressure on the whole team, playing for the All Blacks, but it's not so much individual pressure. If one player is being picked on, one player in an All Black side, it should make it easier for the rest of them. Playing at the top level can be easier than playing at a lower level, because in the All Blacks you only have to be doing your job, they specialise more.

"You take a lock in an All Black side. He has his jobs, pushing in the scrum, jumping in the lineout, getting to rucks and mauls. If he runs with the ball in his hand, that's a bonus. But in club rugby he's getting pushed from every side, he gets knocked around by the opposition, and if he retaliates, he cops it from the referee.

"On tour, you do have to be careful not to try to push the team along too hard, if what you want is bit different from what they've been used to playing. You don't want them falling in between two styles.

"Take the French tour in 1990. We had problems getting quick ball from rucks, and that's something I've always wanted my players to do. I said at the time to the team that I didn't blame them, because two teams in New Zealand, Auckland and Waikato, were playing to their strengths, picking up the ball in the forwards, and forwards hanging off at first-five to run with it. And that was successful for those teams in New Zealand.

"But when we came up against an international side, it wasn't working, and we weren't going as eight forwards. So I said, 'Look, we've got our five tight forwards there to do a job, and they've got to get in there and bloody do it.' Because what was happening, we were getting slow ball, bad ball, and the French were getting in and seizing the opportunities. They could keep putting the pressure on.

"It took a while to get the tight five going, but in the end it did happen, and as a team we were all thinking down the one line. It showed in the first test (won 24-3) and the final test (won 30-12)."

Encouraging players to use their skills, their flair, isn't a case of using pretty words. In Wyllie's mind, it's vital to succeed in international football.

"As the tour went on in France (in 1990) I found that too many moves were being called from second phase, and I think second phase is when it's time for the individual to come out and do his own thing.

"If a move's been called, you don't always overrule it, and young players, especially, don't like to overcall them. But if you just carry on with the move, and this damn big gap opens up, you've missed a chance. Rucked ball, second phase ball, is the time to have a go, to explode, to see what's on. If a gap opens up, you go through it, if it doesn't, give it to the next player, and he may find one. I felt in France the best of some of our players was being nullified by too many calls, so we worked to reduce them."

Home tests have historically been difficult for All Black teams. Wyllie knows why.

"It's very hard in two or three days to get players to change the way they think, especially when you have a large number coming from one provincial team. You're probably silly to try to change it too much, too quickly, because you'll end up with mixed ideas. One player will be trying one way, another player a different way.

"It's hard to convince players from successful provincial teams that you want them to change the way they do things, because they've been winning. So you damn near have to lose a game or two, as we did in France, so they'll know why you want things changed."

Wyllie says he doesn't hammer the players too much with talk of tactics and methods away from training. And when the team's not touring he doesn't spend a lot of time on the phone to the All Blacks. By contrast, when Alan Jones was coaching the Wallabies, some of his players were almost driven crazy by a barrage of letters and phone calls. Constant telephone contact is something some New Zealand coaches seem to crave, too.

"I let them have a breathing space, when we're not directly involved as a team. They're involved with their club or provincial side, too, so you could be putting pressure on them from a second area. If someone's injured I'll call and check on their fitness, but that's all."

Even on tour, he tries to avoid constant rugby brainwashing. "Now and again you'll be having a meal, and the game will come up in conversation. But I think when it's time to relax, you let them relax."

For a home test, the All Blacks assemble on a Tuesday night. International Rugby Board rules used to demand a Wednesday assembly, which made Wyllie's teeth grind, given that England sides work together in camps, then say it's too difficult to take a break before they play an international. The Tuesday assembly gives the All Blacks, especially for the first test in a series, the chance to hand out gear, and go through the housekeeping chores, so the next day is free to concentrate on training.

Wyllie is a one training run a day coach. "Some other coaches have had two runs a day, but I think that it's better to have a hard run, with full commitment, really getting into it, than having them changing in and out of gear. How hard to run on the Wednesday and Thursday depends on how the team's looking, how things are feeling. If the run's constructive, there's no sense in carrying on too long, because that's when people switch off, and things start to go wrong. On the Friday you have a team run, just moves to keep everybody occupied, because there's nothing worse than sitting around doing nothing."

How hard the runs are depends on how much pressure Wyllie feels the players are under. "If we've won the first test easily, you have to worry about whether the players have got too relaxed. If they struggled in the first, there'll be areas to work on. Normally, if you play a three test series, the tests get harder as they go, especially if you've won the first two. If you're touring Britain, and playing the Home Unions, then you have to build up a test at a time, because you're looking at a new team every time.

Wyllie doesn't demand that the team spend all their time away from training together. Nor does he lay down strict rules about diet, or curfews.

"At test match level, it's as much mental as physical, so you don't make the players do something they don't want to do. I was told of a coach in a Ranfurly Shield game who told the players they had to eat a special diet, and what time they had to be in bed by, and they went out and played like mugs.

"You don't put silly pressures on. If some of them want to go to a movie, let them go. If a joker wants to have a couple of beers, let him have a few. He knows how to prepare himself. You don't make him eat something that's going to rumble around or sit in his gut all night. He's better going to bed late, and getting the sleep he wants.

"A group of the current All Blacks are keen on cards, others like watching videos. You let them do their own thing, rather than trying to force something on them to change their attitude to the game or other players.

"You want some relaxation among the team. A pattern is always a calming thing for any player. That's why some get uptight if a meal is very slow in coming, they worry that they don't have time to eat it, they remember the last time they didn't eat properly before a game, and they didn't play well then. There are patterns, and some of them, sitting in the same seat on the bus, in the same seat in the dressing room, can become superstitions."

Wyllie himself, now he's coaching, doesn't like solitude before a big game. "On tour you can have a drink with the dirty dirties (players in the team who are not in the reserves for the match the next day), or some of the media, and fill in time that way. Overseas, if you find you still can't get to sleep, you can fill in time by watching twenty-four hour television. On the day of the game you can get a few phone calls, but usually they just go straight over your head, you're thinking about the game, not anything else. Occasionally some idiot will ring in the early hours of the morning, but usually we get the phones blocked off after about nine o'clock at night."

On the day of the game, forwards go their own way in the morning, backs get together, "anything to keep them occupied," says Wyllie, and then it's off to the ground. Wyllie and Sturgeon exchange their private handshake, and then the test begins.

THE LEGEND: *Alex Wyllie once blew a hole in the wall of the Waipara hotel with a shotgun.*

WHAT REALLY HAPPENED: *Wyllie had bought a new five shot shotgun. He asked Dave Morris, then the publican of the Waipara hotel, to store it for him because he was worried someone might steal it from his Land Rover. The gun, hidden under Morris' bed, was forgotten for some weeks, until pukekos started eating the Wyllies' wheat crop. In the early hours of the morning the gun was brought out for Wyllie to take home. One of the men at the bar emptied all the shells from it. Or believed he had. The gun was handed to Wyllie. "Would you like a demonstration?" he joked. Says Morris:*

Legend

"I'll never forget it. It was like a Texas cowboy movie, blue smoke and plaster, and a big hole in the wall. We had an old bloke in Room 1 across the other side of the bar who'd had a few drinks, and he didn't even wake up." For several years Morris left the hole unrepaired, and covered with a photograph of Alistair Hopkinson selling cattle. When people asked about the story he lifted the photo and showed them.

THE WYLLIE VERSION: *"Did I think it was unloaded?" Small grin. "I may have accidentally on purpose left one in there. I got a surprise about how big the hole in the wall was."*

CREDIBILITY RATING (OUT OF 10): *10.*

14

Buck

A rugby club in Christchurch, and Alex Wyllie is about to field questions from a sell-out audience.

This is hometown stuff. Not a place, surely, where Wyllie would be faced with fish hooks in any of the questions.

Wrong. First up is a young man in the corner, surrounded by his mates, fired up on Canterbury Draught, and ready for some Grizz baiting.

"When are you going to put the best No 8 in New Zealand back in the All Blacks?" The group start chanting "Bring back Buck! Bring back Buck!"

Wyllie meets it head on. "If we decide his form is better than everyone else's, we'll put him back in."

For two tours, and four home series, Shelford and Wyllie seemed, in the public mind, to be the perfect match-up. The image went beyond the usual captain-coach relationship.

Both struck a chord in heartland New Zealand. In public interviews they were blunt to the point of gruffness. Neither played the smooth public relations game, and to a lot of down home followers there was a buzz in seeing Wyllie and Shelford at the top of the tree.

These were men you knew would rather have a beer than a white wine, who played on until they were stretchered from the paddock, and would cuff your ears at the idea of using a mobile phone, or lunching on quiche.

It paid to ignore the fact that Shelford spent some of his working life in supermarkets, encouraging household shoppers to buy Tegel chicken, or that Wyllie was living in a house in Christchurch, and had dagged about as many sheep since he'd been All Black coach as Michael Fay had.

The myths aside, they did see eye to eye on rugby when Wyllie became All Black coach in 1988, and inherited Shelford as captain.

Wyllie, like the rest of the country, was impressed with Shelford's play in the '87 World Cup. The style was similar to the way Dale Atkins had played for Canterbury for Wyllie, and it led to football Wyllie liked.

By driving across the advantage line with the ball, Shelford set up ruck ball for the All Blacks. To Wyllie he was a vital part of the structure that made the All Blacks succeed.

When David Kirk made himself unavailable to tour Japan at the end of '87, the All Black selection panel of Brian Lochore, Wyllie, and John Hart, who would coach the team to Japan, took virtually no time to decide that Shelford would be the new captain. "It was almost an automatic choice," says Wyllie. "He'd captained North Harbour, and captained the Maori team, and he was playing well."

Wyllie didn't consider making any change when he took over as coach in '88. Wales at the start of the year was an easy part. "They weren't a strong team, so there was no pressure on there."

In Australia later in the season, there was never any question of Shelford not being the captain and No 8. Zinzan Brooke, niggled by injury, was no challenge, and Shelford's own form was often inspirational.

During the summer of 1988-89 Shelford went to France, playing in a lower division club. When he returned to New Zealand he was noticeably lighter. The cost of living, especially of red meat, in France had meant he'd fined down. It might have pleased the Heart Foundation, but it wasn't much a help with his rugby.

Wyllie was one person concerned. He passed a few comments to Shelford, but wasn't sure if they'd been taken seriously. Eventually he talked to North Harbour coach Peter Thorburn, saying he thought Shelford's form wasn't good, and he hoped there would soon be an improvement.

Wyllie didn't speak to Shelford directly because to have done so would have, in Wyllie's opinion, amounted to interference with Thorburn's North Harbour side. "I don't believe you can go to players and tell them how to play the game. It mightn't fit in with the pattern of that coach, and you're splitting things up. The joker ends up playing for himself, and it should be a team game."

On tour in Wales and Ireland a bulkier Shelford found his form. By comparison Brooke was only average at the start of the tour, although he did play well in the last few matches, getting on the field against the Barbarians at Twickenham when Shelford had to leave with a neck injury.

Came the 1990 season, and two tests against Scotland.

Wyllie had always said that Scotland would be tough opponents, and they proved to be so.

In Dunedin and in Auckland the All Blacks were harried and pressured by the Scots. The Eden Park test, won 21-18, was the closest the All Blacks had come to being beaten at home for four

*Princess Anne meets Steve McDowell, on the highly successful 1989
tour. Buck Shelford (obscured) was doing the introductions. A year
later and the task would have been undertaken by Gary Whetton.*

seasons. Scotland scored two tries, New Zealand one.

After the game, Shelford was quizzed about the tactics used by
the backline. In the second half the All Blacks had been almost
constantly on attack, but the Scottish backs stood up flat, tackled
hard, and snuffed out the attempts the All Blacks made to move the
ball through the backline.

Why, Shelford was asked, didn't the All Blacks try some grubber
kicks behind Scotland's backline, instead of presenting themselves,
on a slippery surface that prevented tricky moves, as sitting ducks
for the Scottish tacklers? The germ of the Fox v Buck rumours began
that afternoon. He had his head down in the scrum, said Shelford,
so he relied on Fox to be his eyes and ears in the backline, and to pick
the right tactics.

It was an honest answer, although possibly not the most dip-
lomatic one. It was easy for those with malice to read into it that
Shelford had unloaded blame for wrong decisions on to someone
else.

Still, few in rugby were prepared for the bombshell that would
drop 19 days later.

Peter Bush

Wayne Shelford (left) is leading a shadow test team in the 1989 All Black trials. Sean Fitzpatrick and Alex Wyllie consider Shelford's views.

Wyllie had been unhappy with the loose forward display in both tests with Scotland. He had videos of both, and, whenever he had the chance, played through them in Christchurch.

"The team (against Scotland) had been a bit like a car running with a chip in the gearbox. There was a lack of direction somehow."

Studying the videos, Wyllie decided that the problem lay with how quickly Shelford was getting to the ball when play broke down out wide. Mike Brewer was getting to the ball, but the second player there, too often for comfort, was Alan Whetton, not Shelford.

"And we felt there was something not working in the tie-up between the loose forwards and the backline. The team knew how strong Buck had been around the scrum, and perhaps the team was sitting back and waiting for that to happen. Or perhaps he'd lost his drive, because he just wasn't going as far as before. We had to look at somebody else who could do it, or else we were going to have to change our plans in that area."

Wyllie talked with John Hart and Lane Penn, and eventually it was decided Hart and Penn would go to Whangarei to see Shelford play for North Harbour against North Auckland.

Wyllie rang Harbour's coach, Peter Thorburn, to tell him that the match would be critical for Shelford.

It was a call some would criticise, but Wyllie really was in a Catch-22 situation. If he hadn't passed on any message to Shelford it would have been fair comment to say that Shelford, as an unbeaten All Black captain, deserved better treatment from his coach than to be playing a game vital to his future without knowing it. Even the best players can ease down a notch playing a midweek provincial game.

On the other hand, letting Shelford know that he could be dropped unless he played extremely well had to put enormous pressure on him. No matter how you looked at it, trying to do the right thing could be misinterpeted.

Dropping players who have given him good service is something that Wyllie finds extremely hard to do. Canterbury team members recall how Wyllie would always get the manager to read out the playing XV. Says Wayne Smith: "Alex would look away, and look a bit embarrassed. It was the only time you ever saw him like that. Then in '84, a few of us had been in Aussie with the All Blacks, and when we went to Canterbury training, there was this enormous squad. Alex hadn't had the heart to tell anyone not to turn up because we were going to be back on the Wednesday." Warwick Taylor remembers Wyllie struggling to let him know that he wouldn't be in the team to tour Wales and Ireland in 1989. "I didn't feel I'd been badly treated at all," says Taylor, "but it was obviously something Alex hated to do."

While Penn and Hart were at Okara Park, Wyllie had been watching Waikato beat Australia in the opening game of the Wallabies' tour. The trio met in the Koru lounge at Auckland airport that night. When Penn and Hart told Wyllie they thought Shelford hadn't played well at Okara Park, the decision that had to follow still wasn't easy. "You hate doing it," says Wyllie, "but it was one of those decisions that has to be made. There was a lot of discussion, but eventually you have to do what's right for the team. Buck as captain was certainly a good advertisement for the game, but I'm afraid that sometimes our duty is to put the best team on the field."

Wyllie himself wanted to tell Shelford that he wouldn't be in the side to play Australia in the first test in Christchurch.

While the North Harbour team were travelling back from Whangarei, Wyllie tried to get in touch with Shelford. He rang Shelford's home from Auckland airport, and spoke briefly to Shelford's wife, Joanne. He was finally able to get Shelford the next morning. "I told him I was sorry it had happened," says Wyllie. The naming of the All Black team was delayed until Wyllie had spoken to Shelford.

When the team was announced it was stated that Shelford's form had been affected by injury. There were two aspects to that announcement. One was that Wyllie genuinely believed Shelford was injured. "I knew that Buck had been having some treatment for a back injury. When you looked at him on the field he seemed to be having problems bending, which was affecting him when he went to pick the ball up at the base of the scrum. And his body position was too high when he ran with the ball, which could have been the result of a back injury too.

"All players play with injuries at times, but if it affects a player's form, then it affects the team, and then you have to make changes."

Wyllie told Shelford it was planned to say that injury had affected Shelford's form. "Buck told me his leg hadn't been too good lately."

From the moment the team was announced, a hunt for Shelford by the media began. Shelford left his home in Glenfield, after politely declining to do an on-camera interview. On Television New Zealand's 6 o'clock Network News that night an inability to find him during the day was translated as Shelford going into hiding. One of the first calls logged by TVNZ's switchboard after the item was from Shelford, to say he was not in hiding, and would be at his North Shore club's training that night.

Ric Salizzo raced to Devonport, and there, in his first interview after the dropping, Shelford denied he was injured. He'd just been running with his club team. Would an injured man do that?

The divergence over the injury statement was the start of a huge rumour mill that flew without any assistance from either Wyllie or Shelford.

One suggestion was that Wyllie and Shelford had been fighting, either verbally or physically, depending on how enthused the person telling the story was. "Bloody rot," is how Wyllie dismisses that suggestion. "If Buck and I had really had a fight, he could have said that in public. He would have had nothing to lose. Also, we wouldn't have been speaking to each other since, the way we have been."

Another played on the Shelford v Fox theory. Either Fox had told Wyllie he wouldn't play in the same team as Shelford again, or Fox and Shelford had had a fist fight immediately after the test with Scotland at Eden Park. With all due respect to Fox, says Wyllie, a fight with Shelford would have been a terrible thing to watch. The "blackmail" story is just as ludicrous and untrue.

There were no fights, no threats. It was purely a question of form.

The quality of Shelford's captaincy wasn't an issue either. There was never any plan to keep Shelford in the team, but relieve him of his captaincy. "The dissatisfaction was only with his form. Captaincy doesn't have any effect on your speed to the loose ball."

When the All Blacks assembled, without Shelford, for the first test against Australia, Wyllie says the atmosphere was uptight in many ways. "Players were thinking what the hell is going on, because they'd lost their captain, and they were probably wondering if they might be next. There was an intensity there right from the start. Jokers were wanting to know when the next team meeting was, and they were stripped off ready for training long before they had to be. It wasn't the reason Buck had been left out (to ginger up the team), but it did have that effect.

"We worked hard that week. We had another team in to train with, and we worked hard on our scrum, and on our backline defensive patterns, as well as attacking moves. We went into the test in pretty good heart, because the training had gone well. So the win (21-6) wasn't a surprise. I'd felt beforehand everything was right."

The Bring Back Buck movement kept building during the season. On the Wednesday after the second test with the Wallabies, at Eden Park, won 27-17 by the All Blacks, the Australians played North Harbour at the Onewa Domain in Takapuna. On the posters for the game the heading was "Back Buck." The Australians won, 23-12. Shelford was given the man of the match award from the North Harbour supporters' club.

His replacement in the All Blacks, Zinzan Brooke, did nothing to dampen the fires. After the All Blacks lost the third test to Australia, 21-9, at Athletic Park, Brooke fronted up for Auckland for the Ranfurly Shield challenge from North Harbour. Brooke, it was discovered later, had a hairline fracture of the ankle. He played anyway. To Wyllie's mind, Brooke let himself down by playing when he wasn't fully fit.

Wyllie and the selectors were still not convinced that Shelford's form was good enough to justify selection in the team of 30 All Blacks to tour France.

It would not, says Wyllie, need to be a difficulty having Shelford in the team if he was not captain. "It's happened before, with Kirky (Ian Kirkpatrick, who toured to Ireland and Wales in 1974 after being deposed as All Black captain by Andy Leslie). It's up to the player concerned. There are times when you could use the experience of a former captain."

The criteria for getting to France hadn't changed.

"We said if Buck got over his injury, or improved his form, he could be selected again. He denied any injury, so his form had to improve. I didn't think Buck's form was that marvellous in the Shield challenge. To bring back a player of Buck's age, where maybe that age is catching up with him a bit, you have to look ahead a couple of years. The World Cup is a bit different, because that's the most important challenge for a team, an end in itself. But 18 months away from a World Cup, you have to think if his form is that much better than a younger player, who might pass him on the way up."

Early in 1991, Wyllie and Shelford met in Cardiff. It was no high pressure conference. Wyllie was in Wales with the New Zealand members of the cast of the made-for-television movie, "Old Scores." Ian Kirkpatrick, Waka Nathan, and Grahame Thorne, are in the movie too.

Shelford had tried to contact Wyllie in Christchurch, and left a message that he would come to see Wyllie in Cardiff. "Buck wanted to come and see the other fellows anyway. We were all just standing around, having a beer, and Buck and I just drifted away by ourselves. He just asked, straight up: 'How am I placed?' I said we'd be looking at him, the same as everybody else. Everyone's in there with a chance. We've got to pick, in our own minds, what we think is the best for the type of game we want to play, with the best players available, whoever they might be. He understood."

In May, Shelford was named to play opposite Brooke in the late All Black trial in Rotorua. While their styles of play are quite different, there was almost universal agreement that Brooke had the better of the meeting.

Oddly, Shelford, who is in the trial team captained by Gary Whetton, makes no real attempt to run off the back of the scrum.

Wyllie had spoken to all trialists before the matches, but he, too, is surprised at how Shelford, in fact all the No 8s from both trials, don't run with the ball from the base of the scrum.

"I told them all," says Wyllie, "I wanted to see all players given the opportunity to show their own skills, whatever they might be. If one of those skills was picking up the ball and driving from the base of the scrum, I would hope they (the No 8s) would have been able to do it. They certainly weren't told they couldn't."

Shelford doesn't make the All Black team tour to Argentina, but is named as captain of the New Zealand XV to play Romania and Russia. This time there is no public uproar about his omission from the All Blacks.

An opportunity would still be there, says Wyllie, for Shelford to force his way into the World Cup squad. "In the New Zealand XV, as captain, he could virtually play the game exactly the way he wanted to, and he had a chance to show if he was back to his best form."

Shelford played well for the New Zealand XV, but, says Wyllie, it was the firm feeling of the selectors that the Shelford of '91 wasn't the driving force of '87, '88 and '89. "In one TV programme it showed Buck and his form in those years, with the suggestion that form was needed in the All Blacks. What would have been more to the point would have been to show Buck as he was this year."

A last gasp chance for Shelford, says Wyllie, came in the game at Athletic Park where North Harbour played Wellington. The World Cup squad was announced immediately afterwards. "Buck tried to drive on several occasions in that game, and was held up, and pushed back. His main attribute was his driving, being able to drop his shoulder and make ground. Without that his game was gone. He wasn't going to be getting any faster, so his wide game wasn't improving. From what I saw he certainly hadn't come back to the form that was needed to force his way into the World Cup team."

There was a sour end note. Wyllie wasn't impressed when Shelford would say on TV that trading had gone on among the colectors in the naming of the team. "A man who had been through what Buck had been through with the All Blacks should have known what we were like, that it wouldn't happen. That was a pretty bitter pill."

THE LEGEND: As he walked on to the field at halftime in Auckland's successful 1985 Ranfurly Shield challenge, Alex Wyllie backhanded a spectator.

THE REAL STORY: A group of young men, possibly as many as five and at least one woman, made their way into the No 3 stand, and took up a position in a walkway, standing in front of Wyllie and the Canterbury reserves. "Things weren't going too well for Canterbury at that stage," says Wyllie, "and we asked them to get out of the way so we could see what was going on. One of them turned round and swore at us. I told him that if he didn't move we could soon come down and do it. He said, 'Come on, have a go', and wrapped a chain he'd had round his waist around his hand. One of the Auckland reserves said he'd seen another of these guys with a knife. They were moved by the police, but they didn't leave the ground.

"I didn't think much more of it until I was down beside the field, trying to get on to see the team. The crowd had filled up right along the touchline, and I had one hand out in front saying, 'Excuse me, can we get through?' Just as a gap was opening up I was belted with a punch in the side of my back. I half turned and brushed this joker out of the road who'd hit me. The people in front had stepped aside to let Doug (Bruce) and myself through, and that was when the TV camera caught it."

POSTSCRIPT: Thirteen days after the Ranfurly Shield game a gang member walked into the Wooleston Tavern and shot dead a man he didn't know, firing five shots from a shotgun into the victim. The gang member pleaded guilty to murder, and was given an automatic life sentence. Policemen in Christchurch believe the murderer was one of the group in conflict with Wyllie at Lancaster Park, although the murderer was not the man Wyllie hit on the sideline.

It is commonly believed by Christchurch criminals that Wyllie was a target at Lancaster Park for a young man who wanted to make his name in the underworld by sorting out Alex Wyllie. Wyllie was not known personally to any of the men, or the woman, at the ground that day.

CREDIBILITY RATING (OUT OF 10): 1 for the legend, at best. It looked terrible on TV, but Wyllie really was an innocent near-victim.

15

Look at the bloody record

The real measure of success in any field is how a person stands in the eyes of his or her peer group. Each of the seven people asked, in this chapter, to give an opinion on Alex Wyllie, the coach, and coaching in general, has proved him or herself as a coach. Who better to pass judgement on Wyllie's coaching?

F RED ALLEN *(Coach of the Auckland team that set the Ranfurly Shield record of 25 defences in the 1960s equalled by Wyllie's Canterbury team; coach of the All Blacks from 1966 to 1968, when they were undefeated in 14 test matches).*

I think Grizz Wyllie is a great coach, and I always have done.

I'm no great letter writer, but when he was coaching Canterbury I just had to sit down and write to him, to say that I was enthralled with the way his team was going. If you'd ever seen a side playing brilliant 15 man rugby it was that Canterbury side. His record really speaks for itself with Canterbury and the All

Blacks. He gets results. That's what I say when people criticise him, I tell them to have a look at the bloody record.

In some ways I think Grizz's coaching might be a bit like mine. He's not as subtle as some, he's straight, he knows his rugby, and he can build great team spirit, and that's what rugby is all about.

With the All Blacks I get the feeling that he has a few players who have got a bit big headed, they think they know all about the game. Well, you never know the lot in this game, and the day you think you do is the day you've got problems. Even when you're out of it, you look and listen, and you realise just how little you do know about it.

After the Argentinian tour (in 1991) I was talking to Alex, and I told him he should have gone the whole hog, and dropped the two props (Steve McDowell and Richard Loe). I did that with Chris Laidlaw and Kel Tremain, and by gee, the next time they played they were like maniacs, they played the best game I ever had from them.

It's really the only way a coach can deal with players, the old hands, who think they're at a stage where they can take some shortcuts. You just can't allow that to happen.

The best thing I ever did with the Auckland team, when we won the Ranfurly Shield (in 1959), was to call a training run on the West Coast at 6 o'clock in the morning. Some of the old heads, Snow White, Manga Emery, and Albie Pryor, were cutting up a bit, and I had them out on the Greymouth racecourse, freezing cold, and I was in a really bad mood, because I don't like getting up that early either. I can still see one or two of them, hanging on to the rails, throwing up, and moaning and swearing. But we all knew where we stood after it was over.

When you're the All Black coach you get people sniping at you, even people who should know better. I think it's disgraceful some of the things that have been said about Grizz on television. A man like Andy Haden should know better.

The only thing you can do is to ignore it. You're there to do a job, and just to remember that a lot of the criticism is just jealousy.

To my mind Grizz's record is a lot better than John Hart's. I'm not criticising John Hart, he's a great coach too. But so far his record isn't as good as Wyllie's. John will get his turn with the All Blacks, and then we'll see how good he is at that level.

If I had one comment about Grizz's All Black teams, I'd like to see Grizz work on (Graeme) Bachop's pass. Grizz can do it, he knows so much about the game, and I don't believe it would take very long. Bachop doesn't keep his head down when he passes, it's as simple as that. You could get him on the right track in three hours.

But I don't want to take anything away from Grizz. I've been right behind him from the start, and I think he's done a great job.

BRIAN LOCHORE (*All Black coach from 1985 to 1987, and coach of the team that won the first World Cup*).

I was always lucky when I was coaching the All Blacks, living on a farm. I didn't come into contact with the everyday person, who might want to offer you some advice on who should be in the team, or why things were going wrong, or how they could be improved.

In the weekend, at football, I might have to explain what was going on, but most of the time I was able to get away by myself, and do my own thinking in my own time. So I never really felt much public pressure, which some coaches must feel.

The only time I ever felt any pressure from the media was when the tour to South Africa in 1985 was called off. With the sports reporters I didn't have any concerns. Most of them knew me, and they respected what I was trying to do, so I didn't have any worries about being misquoted. But during the period of the cancellation of the tour I was dealing with news reporters, and that was more stressful.

The sort of media attacks that Grizz is facing, the suggestions that John Hart should be the coach and not him, must be very hard to take. He knows that John challenged for the job, and it must have some effect, undermining your confidence in your own coaching.

I'm only surmising, but I would assume that with so many Aucklanders in the team that some of them are Hart supporters, so possibly it's more difficult for Alex to wade in and lay down the law than it might otherwise be. I don't know if that's actually happening, but you can see how it might.

In 1987, when Alex and John were on the panel with me, there was never a moment that was ever a problem between them. We all got on really well. We were totally frank with each other, and very open about saying what we were trying to do in terms of game plan and selection.

We all believed in the same type of rugby that we wanted to see being played, and with the selection of players, we agreed so easily on that we only spent 10 minutes picking the final squad for the World Cup. There was only discussion on one position, whether we should pick Brent Anderson or Albert Anderson at lock.

It was very funny actually. We stayed in the room at the Grand Hotel in Whangarei after the team was picked, just to make the selection look more important and serious.

John Hart had a crook back, so he was on the floor and we were trying to manipulate it to fix it up. I remember saying: "If only the media could see us now."

I felt that both Alex and John wouldn't be happy if they were only used to help select the team, so I used them both over the campaign to help with the coaching. Whoever was with me would always run the backline, or the forwards, at the start of the session, and then I'd get the whole team together to finish off the run. There was never any doubt in the players' minds who was carrying the can at the end.

I'd rate Grizz very highly as a coach. He's got a very good tactical appreciation of the game at provincial and international level. Because he was a forward, he's probably more comfortable coaching forwards. I'm not saying he's no good with backs, but he's generally coached at more depth with the forwards than with the backs. He had Doug Bruce working with him in Canterbury, and it seems to have been forgotten that Lane Penn has been working with the All Black backs. I think the contribution that Lane makes to the All Blacks is overlooked too often.

PETER THORBURN (*North Harbour coach from the inception of the union in 1985 to 1991, coach of the New Zealand seven a side team*).

He's got a lot more understanding of the game than people in the northern area might give him credit for. Some of the things he did with Canterbury with young players coming through who would listen, he did some innovative, and very exciting things with the backline, and brought some very interesting players through who became All Blacks.

In the last couple of years, he's had trouble with the dominance of the northern style in the backline. To my view, in the first test against Australia (in 1991), they went on the field with a game plan, which I knew from players in the team, and from what they did in training against us on the Tuesday night before they went over.

They went on the field playing the expansive game, moving the ball wide to give JK (John Kirwan) and John Timu a chance to run the ball at weak defensive wings, and an average defensive fullback for the Australians. They put up a bomb, good for variation, scored from it, and then the on-field decisions were changed to stick with the ball in the first-five's hands all the time. Second phase ball went to first-five all the time, and they became restricted with the ability to use the ball wide.

My own strong belief is that for a year or two Grizz has, not deliberately, been undermined, so he hasn't had the chance to do the job fully that he's proved in the past he can do.

I'm not saying for a moment the undermining has been deliberate.

To name names, Grant Fox has been a major influence in how the game is played in the backline. Look at the Auckland backline. It's become predictable, and they've lost the ability to move the ball through their backline, and score regularly against good opposition. Yet the basis of what the All Blacks are trying to do in the World Cup is an expansive game, with the same players.

I know they've tried inside-outside centre, that in the early games in Argentina they missed first-five a lot, and they scored a lot of tries out on the wings. As soon as they got to a test match it went into the first-five's hands all the time.

I'm not saying that everything that Fox does is bad. He's got a lot of ability, and made a lot out of what he's got. But he's like so many of us as we all get older - and I know because I was a captain and a No 8 - you have a reluctance to let the ball get away from you because you lose control. It's happened in every era, it happened in '71, it happened with Murray Mexted. I believe it's not even a conscious thing. It just happens.

At this stage when the ball goes through Fox's hands, it's so easy to defend against, because you don't have to stay and watch the guy. When John Schuster was playing second-five, even though he was quiet, he had the presence to make the play, but Walter Little's a very quiet Fijian boy who won't just go ahead and do what he wants to.

I'm not blaming Fox for all the All Blacks' woes, but he has to be held responsible for the tactical decisions being made by the All Blacks on the field. Grizz and his senior players set the game plans before the match, but it depends on the captain or the leader, the person who calls the shots, as to when and how it's changed. If a mistake is made on the field with decisions over the game plan, you've got problems. The coach is in the on-field leader's hands in an international game especially. The coach can't even go on at halftime in an international game.

Training is about supplying the decision makers on the field with options. But on the field only they can decide to change the pattern, not the coach. On the field in the All Blacks, I think some of those decision makers have been found wanting.

I don't know how many people could handle the All Black coaching job. I think the pressure gets to Grizz Wyllie sometimes. Mind you, we don't know whether Harty could handle it, he's never been in that pressure situation. If he got the job he could have a couple of selectors who were after his job as soon as they could get it, have to put up with all the sniping in the world, and he'll find the sychophantic media up here will boost him along until he has a couple of things go wrong, and then they'll be into him. Sometimes I feel sorry for Grizz, but I guess if you're in the kitchen you have to take the heat.

Grizz gets on well with players. His gruff exterior is just that. He's got charisma that very few people have, he's got mana. It's different, and it obviously doesn't appeal to everybody.

As a country, with the economy bad, and all the news gloomy, people look to the All Blacks and when they're not going so well they blame them. We all do it. And Grizz is the brunt of that, as the head man. It's far more than it ever was in the past with so many more radio and television stations, and people look for a whipping boy.

I think Alex has handled that burden brilliantly. I've always had time for him, because there's one thing about the guy, you know where you stand. And that's really pleasant in life, because there are so many people where you don't know where you stand.

GRAHAM LOWE *(New Zealand, Wigan, Manly and Queensland rugby league coach).*

I don't know Grizz extremely well, but I'm proud to call him a friend.

If I was trying to sum him up I'd say he's a real good bloke, a very strong willed, very loyal coach, who is totally loyal to his game, rugby union.

To my mind, there isn't a magic formula that makes a successful coach.

The most important thing is that you stick to your principles. If you start to let outside influences compromise your principles, you've got trouble, in fact you might as well get out of it.

I get the impression that Grizz is a very strong minded person, and that's important. As a coach, you must also be open-minded enough to be flexible in your thinking when you have to be. It sounds like a contradiction, but you can be strong willed and open minded at the same time.

What are the basic principles to stick to? Fairness and honesty. Really that doesn't change, whether it's in life in general, league, rugby, netball, soccer, tiddliwinks or moonwalking.

There are many different types of coaches, the authoritarian kind, the good guy, the casual one, the play it by the book type, to name a few.

If I had to describe myself, while it's difficult to analyse yourself, I'd say one of the main things I work on is discipline. When I took over Wigan, for example, the main thing I worked on was discipline, in training, and in following the game plan on the field.

However, you do have to be prepared to take different approaches at times, but you must stick with what you believe.

I'm a good friend of John Hart's. I probably know him better than I know Grizz. But I can't see any point in people in New Zealand comparing them all the time.

That's the whole point about a coach. Each one has to be true to his own style.

In Grizz's case, I think he's from the old school, the school of hard knocks. He perhaps doesn't go for that one-on-one motivational thing, which is more in vogue these days.

It appears to me that Grizz has an enormous amount of pride in the job, and in the All Blacks. Some coaches are more flamboyant, he's more the get out there and do the job type.

He's been very successful, and every coach's style is an extension of his own personality. While Grizz has got the job, he does it his way. If other people don't like that, then it's tough shit. He's been given the job because he's Grizz Wyllie, not anybody else. If you buy an apple, you don't turn around then and try to turn it into an orange.

As part of the coaches' "union" I feel sad when I see Grizz being criticised, usually by frustrated coaches. When he's the coach he should be given support. If it doesn't work, then, like all of us, he'll be replaced.

Anybody who says he isn't affected by criticism isn't breathing either. All successful coaches will have times when they get a lot of praise, but as well as praise they have to be prepared to cop some bagging as well.

I've had stages, luckily for a couple of months rather than years, when I've been very bitterly criticised. In Wigan at one stage we had to have police protection. But most coaches are pretty hard-nosed, which is what I'd say Grizz is, and dig their heels in over what they believe in. I can be real pig-headed when I feel I'm right.

As the coach of the All Blacks, the coach of the best rugby playing country in the world, Grizz is in a position that will automatically carry heaps of pressure. Everybody else thinks they could do it better.

Grizz can take that. He's a guy that isn't prepared to compromise, he just wants to win.

He's very loyal to players, which is a special quality, although if I had one question over him as a coach it's whether he's ruthless enough. At times a coach has to be absolutely ruthless, and if he doesn't have that ruthless streak, players can take advantage of him. I get the feeling that once the guys take the field, not every All Black sticks to Grizz's game plan. As I see it, that's when the ruthless streak should really come out. It has got to be the coach, or the player.

But the baseline for me is this: Grizz is a good coach, a successful coach, he's his own man. And he'll go down as part of New Zealand history. He's a legendary personality.

BOB DWYER *(Wallabies coach since Alex Wyllie became the All Black coach in 1988).*

It's a strange thing being an international rugby coach. During a home series you don't actually get to coach the team much, because the side only assembles on a Tuesday, and, like New Zealand, we don't have get togethers the way some other nations do. We don't have squad training weekends.

So as a coach, your ability to influence a player's approach to a game, when it's a home series, is limited.

Your role is largely an organisational one. You can influence the style being played by an individual player marginally, but unfortunately, under pressure, they tend to revert back to what they were doing the week before.

To my mind, the main job for a test coach is organisational and tactical. If you can give the team the confidence that there's someone there pulling the strings, then they, hopefully, can concentrate on their own position.

An example of organising for a test would be taking the forwards, and getting the scrum organised, and the lineouts structured. On a tour, of course, it's different, you can get guys and get them working inside the team plan, understanding why something they do will have an impact on someone else.

My observations of Grizz have been from a distance, but whether it's him on his own, or him working with the senior players in his team, the ability of the All Blacks to analyse the weaknesses of the opposition, to attack those weaknesses, and to gain pluses for the All Blacks, has been enormous.

I said before the (1991) test in Sydney that the difficult thing about playing the All Blacks is that you don't know how they're going to play until after you come off the field. They vary their play so much. Some countries don't. You know when you go on the field how the opposing team will play. That's not the case with the All Blacks.

In 1988, and again in 1990, we were confronted by teams that changed their approach so much, which makes it pretty difficult to counter them.

Do I keep in constant contact with my test players, phoning them all the time, that sort of thing? No, I don't. To be frank I think that's bullshit.

For a start I work for a living, and I've got other things to do. Secondly, I think it can be a bit insincere. For example, what can I say to a player who's going to be dropped? I usually explain that face to face, and I don't think there's any good way to break bad news.

I'm astounded at the way Grizz gets rubbished by some critics in New Zealand.

His attackers don't know what he does with the team, and what other forces there are that might impair that influence.

My impression of Grizz is that he isn't too much of an extrovert. He doesn't go round shouting out what he's doing, so it must be doubly difficult for his critics to know what he's really doing.

Personally, I find it very offensive what they do to him. We've worked extremely hard to manage to have two wins and a draw with New Zealand. It's a much better record than any other team in the world has had against them in recent years. So I reckon it's a bit insulting when these so-called experts suggest the All Blacks lost because they played badly. Maybe the other team played well.

We're not close in any shape or form, but I think his critics should shut up and let him get on with the job.

Public attacks in the media can be damaging. A coach could get so demoralised and despondent he loses focus, or he could take no notice at all. That is difficult to do. The saying that no man is an island does ring very true. Or the third alternative is to produce some resolve, and to get even more determined to show the critics that they don't know what they're talking about. By the look of his chin, I'd guess that Grizz would be in the third group.

I was talking briefly to Grizz at Lancaster Park earlier this year, I think it was after a Queensland-Canterbury game, and I said how I envied the fact that they didn't change their All Black side very much. I think Grizz took exception to it, but I really wasn't being critical.

In Australia we have to change our team so much, either through older players being unavailable for tours, or losing players to league.

To me the All Blacks are a bit like the Australian cricket team. They say here that it's harder to get out of the cricket team than it is to get into it. I believe that's not a weakness, it's a great strength.

ARTHUR LYDIARD (*New Zealand's greatest athletics coach. The man whose programmes took Peter Snell and Murray Halberg to Olympic gold medals*).

I'm like every other New Zealander, I have an opinion about the All Blacks and about how they've been going.

I think the All Blacks this year (1991) have got a bit stale. They have a lot of pressure on them from every direction. Look at how many Aucklanders there are in the side. They have the pressure of playing Ranfurly Shield rugby, then they go to Argentina, then to Australia, and they're hardly off the plane before they're being criticised in the media.

Then there's the physical work they do, with a lot of anaerobic work (training that puts players into oxygen debt). Staleness, as we call it, is a psychological reaction to a physical condition. When you have too much anaerobic effort, it affects your central nervous system, so you get tired, you get bitchy, and it can affect your health.

I don't want to criticise Jim Blair, but I think the All Blacks are doing too much gymnasium work, which is developing an imbalance in their muscles. Their quads are too strong, which is leading to the injuries to hamstrings and achilles tendons.

With my athletes, I never had any hamstring injuries. There's no need for them. If you do some hill work, springing up hills during your conditioning stages, you develop a balance in the muscle groups, and you don't get injuries.

I've never met Alex Wyllie, but Dick Tayler (the 1974 Commonwealth Games 10,000 metres gold medal winner) knows him well and says he's a fine type of person.

So I don't want to be critical, but I think it's very important that players are not put under pressure by a coach.

Let me give you an example. In 1964, in Tokyo, I sat down with Snell and (John) Davies, two days before the 1500 metres final, and we sorted out our tactics, how the race would be approached. Then I said to them: "Now go away, and don't talk about running with anyone. As much as you can, put it out of your head." They didn't need reminding what they had to do. If they couldn't keep the plan in their heads for two days, couldn't remember it, we were in big trouble anyway. (Snell won the 1500 metres, and Davies finished third).

When you go into a big competition you need to be fresh and sharp. Your mind needs to be clear.

So the last thing you need as a coach is to be putting pressure on players. We used to ease off the anaerobic work 10 days before a big competition. If we did any it was very short and sharp.

It's like a racehorse, you don't give it a hard race on a Thursday if you want it to run well on the Saturday. If things aren't right physically three or four days before a big event, it's too late to change things with hard training then.

I get the feeling some of the current All Black team may be a year or two past their best. Perhaps we should have given some more young guys a go after the '87 World Cup.

But as well as the coach not putting any pressure on a team, I think we (the public) should be fair to them too. The All Blacks should feel we're with them, not against them.

The players will do their best to get it out of their minds, but it makes it hard for them when they're constantly being criticised.

LOIS MUIR (*New Zealand netball coach for 16 years, and coach of the 1987 world championship team*).

It can be very difficult for a coach in New Zealand, especially the coach of the All Blacks, with rugby being the national religion.

The country feels it owns you, and it must be very hard for Alex just to go into a pub. That's something that a woman doesn't have to worry about thankfully.

I think Alex handles pressure quite well. He seems to manage to create some space for himself by looking gruff, which I would imagine doesn't encourage people to approach him if they don't know him. Sometimes, if I really want to concentrate, I'll hold up a newspaper or a magazine, or won't look up, which makes a bit of a barrier. Usually I don't really mind talking to people, and for me it's often a dear old lady saying how thrilled she was the team went well. But it's not so enjoyable when people want to tell you which team you should put on.

Alex is really such a public figure the poor man must find it difficult to even scratch his nose in public without everyone knowing. When I started coaching the New Zealand team I used to be a bit cunning, and put the team bench on the side where the television cameras were. In those days they were a lot less mobile than they are now, so you were pretty private during a game.

I horrified a television director in England once by refusing to let him extend the length of the halftime break so they could fit their commercials into it. I said, "Is that England and New Zealand playing out there? No, we won't change the halftime break." In the commentary in the second half they said I was a tough, aggressive lady.

I gave a speech for the Canterbury rugby supporters' group, and the MC said after I'd spoken that he'd hate to think what sort of children Grizz and I would have. They'd run through anything. I didn't think I was being that stern! I just talked about commitment and determination.

If you look at Grizz, the media put him under a lot of pressure by implying there's a division between him and John Hart. For all we know the information is flowing between them, but that's not usually how it's presented.

What do I think are the most important things for international coaches?

In a team sport I am a great believer in attitude. Now, how do you motivate a team, considering that all of us have so many different reasons for doing things? For me, that's where the fun was, getting all of the players linked together and thinking as one in a game.

That's what makes a champion team, players who are not just concerned with their own individual performance. If you don't have that attitude, you won't take on other responsibilities. It's covering for other people, maybe delaying the pass a little, moving into a gap, making someone else look better. That's the way you win an international level.

I looked at John Kirwan (in the 1991 test with Australia in Sydney) when he was under the high ball, and there didn't seem to be anyone else nearby. If he'd had other people with him he wouldn't have been under the pressure he was.

It's always back to attitude. You can always improve your skills, as a player or a coach, if you've got an open mind, but at international level the key thing is mental.

You need purpose and drive. Of course, for a New Zealand side, in any sport, there's nothing worse than losing to the Australians. Their attitude after a game is a bit loud mouthed. New Zealanders tend to feel good about things, feel a bit of warmth, but we're a bit humble with it. You don't need much motivation against an Australian side.

Coaching – and the word according to Wyllie.

Legend

THE LEGEND: *Early in a club game at the Glenmark ground, one of the Glenmark props clashes heads with an opponent, and rips the top of his ear. Alex Wyllie calls on a Zambuk, wraps sticking plaster around the prop's head, and tells him he'll be fine. But the ear is bleeding so much, the plaster keeps slipping, and the ear tears more. At halftime the prop has had enough. "I'm going to Amberley to get this stitched up. My ear's just about falling off." Wyllie tells him: "Alright then, bugger off, and we'll get someone on who **wants** to play.*

THE SOURCES: *A Glenmark player, and an opposing coach. On the other hand, several Glenmark players from the Wyllie era can't name a prop it could have happened to.*

THE WYLLIE VERSION: *He counters with another story, about the time winger Jimmy Brown complained his leg was injured, and Wyllie, thinking it's just a bruise, demanded he stay on the field. "It turned out when the leg was X-rayed that it had been broken. No wonder it was a bit sore."*

CREDIBILITY RATING (OUT OF 10): *6 (1 point added because, even if the ear story isn't true, it should be).*

16

The best farmhands Glenmark never had

NZPA, CHRISTCHURCH. - An unusual experiment in farm labour pools is being carried out by the Glenmark branch of Federated Farmers in North Canterbury.

They have appointed a local man, Alex Wyllie, to set out on a hiring campaign for farmhands for the district.

A spokesman for Glenmark Federated Farmers says anybody hired must be a "handy sort of footballer," who could be of some assistance in the continuing success of the local rugby club. "Federated Farmers and the rugby club are the same thing up here," says the spokesman.

There is a tradition in the area of good rugby players working on farms. Wyllie himself has had Bruce Deans and Craig Green working for him, All Black midfielder Andy Jefferd worked for the Thompsons, and All Black lock Graeme Higginson for Jack Reid.

Wyllie, as well as acting as an employment agent for Federated Farmers, will be coach, captain, referee, linesman, and "anything else he likes" in the new group, says the federation official.

In an exclusive interview, Wyllie says current Glenmark players have nothing to fear from the move. "The local boys who are in the team now get first choice. The farmhands I'll be looking for are strictly backups."

Wyllie was prepared to reveal some of the men he had on his shortlist.

"I'd have to look at Fergie McCormick at fullback, because he'd be handy on a farm. He used to work at the freezing works, so he could kill the odd bit of mutton for you. He's a qualified plasterer, which could be handy, and he can stir a lot of other things as well. He's got a bit of land himself now, so he's probably more of a country fellow now in lots of ways than a townie.

"John Gallagher being a Pom wouldn't really be a problem. We've had the odd Dutchman, and a few Poms working around the area. He is a bit forgetful. If he can leave his boots behind before a test, you might find he leaves too many gates open, and mixes the sheep.

"On the wing Craig (Green) played for Glenmark when he was out there, so as long as you could get him out of bed in the morning he'd be quite handy. He's been in Italy for a fair while, and there's no Italian takeaways or anything like that in the district. He might have to start up his own shop. I think it'd suit him out there.

"John Kirwan wouldn't be any use unless it was doing the night shift. He's a great man for his sleep. We'd consider Terry Wright. Possibly build him a little office, and he could do the accounts, it's what he does when he's in Auckland.

"Bryan Williams in his prime would be fine, and Grant Batty was pretty tough. Batts came home once when we were going to Australia to play in an invitation game. He gave us a hand to shift some grain, but he found it hard work, because the bags were about as big as he was.

"If we got Joe Karam down, he and Batts would soon have things organised at the pub, playing cards, taking over the pool table, running the sweeps."

Tony Steel (All Black in the 1960s while playing for Canterbury, and a former headmaster of Hamilton Boys' High School) is now a Member of Parliament, and, in Wyllie's view, could put a few facts forward in Wellington for the local area, politicians having wiped all subsidies for farming.

"Bill Birtwistle (a lean Canterbury and All Black wing in the 1960s) was a banker, which could keep him busy if there was any money to bank. These days in farming he'd have bugger all to do.

"At centre, well, Andy Jefferd played for us, he was a cocky, so he should be able to whistle the dogs around. Elsewhere, you'd have to look at Bruce Robertson, he could be handy. He could even help take the training for the club, with the work he does in Auckland as a coaching coordinator. He's a fairly slightly built bloke, but he was a schoolteacher, so he could go there and look after the kids."

What about Victor Simpson? "The work might be too hard for Vic now, after his sales job for Honda. If you'd got him a couple or three years ago he could have been okay. You'd put him down the back of the farm with an axe, or to grub the nasella tussock, just let go. Victor being Victor, if you told him to harrow the paddock, he'd probably end up ploughing it.

"Joe Stanley drives a truck, which could come in handy, and there are a few large cottages around the district so he and the family would have enough room to fit in. We used to have quite a few large families in the area.

"Warwick Taylor would settle in well in the country. He'd get on

Derek Arnold (left), would keep the social functions humming, while Grant Fox would find plenty of dirt to use to tee up the ball.

with anyone. He comes from Matamata, so he's used to smallish country places.

"Craig Innes and Walter Little are young guys with long careers ahead of them. I think it's best they don't get mixed up with some of the forwards we may have joining us. Likewise Inga Tuigamala would be very welcome, because as well as his football he can play the guitar, and play the piano, but I think he's a bit young to be around some of these forwards. It's the same reason why we wouldn't chase Michael Jones. I don't think someone like him should be on a bus with some of the blokes we're thinking about.

"At second-five Derek Arnold (a livewire second-five for the All Blacks in the 1960s) was a pretty mean sort of footballer, at his best. He used to sell stock too, so you could always look at that side of it. He used to play the tea chest bass pretty well, so he'd keep things going for the odd social function.

"Ian MacRae (the big All Black centre and second-five from 1963 to 1970) was a forestry worker on the West Coast once, and he had family connections with Loburn, in Canterbury. Possibly they'd be a bit upset if we got him playing for us.

"Doug Bruce used to teach in the country, but we're starting to get a hell of a lot of teachers, which is a bit of a worry. Just shows they've got a hell of a lot of time to devote to their sport. Doug's knocked off smoking now, so you wouldn't have the worry with him round a haystack or a barn you might have had once.

"When I started with Canterbury Bruce Watt was the first-five. You wouldn't ever have to worry about him shooting through on you. He hated flying, had to have a few gins before he got on a plane. Being a banker he's another one who could look after money for you. We'd just have to make sure we kept Bruce and Derek Arnold apart, or they'd be likely to have a few.

"It would depend what sort of game we wanted to play. Bruce and Doug wouldn't be doing much running now. We might have to look at somebody like Wayne Smith to really get things going.

"I don't know whether Foxy would like it. He'd probably get too upset with the animals, if they wouldn't do what they were told. He'd have to get used to teeing up the ball for his kicks with dirt instead of sand. We've got plenty of dirt up there though.

"Sid Going could come down. He'd be good at driving the bus after the game, because he doesn't drink. We've got some glasshouses down the road, so Lyn Davis would work out fine, because he's been a tomato grower. Not too good carting hay, the bales might get the better of him, they're bigger."

Wyllie says he would have a firm policy of not hiring school teachers for the forwards. "We've probably got too many in the backs already. Next thing we'll be hiring varsity students!"

For his fellow loose forwards Wyllie would look to Ian Kirkpatrick, who worked in North Canterbury, and now farms in Poverty Bay. "Being a North Island farmer you'd have to stir him up, and make sure he was getting out round the sheep. North Island farmers don't seem to work as hard as South Island ones.

"Stu Cron (a long serving Canterbury player who toured Argentina with the 1976 All Blacks) used to play out our way, but like Dale Atkins, he couldn't be considered because he's a teacher.

"Buck Shelford's under consideration, but we're a bit concerned that with his Navy background he could be overseas when we had vital jobs on, like crutching, or lambing."

The current Canterbury coach, John Phillips, wasn't considered suitable by some Glenmark farmers, who said they worried Phillips might lose gumboots that lodged in the side of other people's faces.

"Mike Brewer could be okay for us. He could work the horses. He certainly takes a tremendous interest in them from the point of view of investing on them. He's in a pub in Dunedin at the moment, and he might find a part-time job at the local pub. Could be a bit

Christchurch Star

Don Hayes, careful with the Ranfurly Shield, and patient with the sheep.

more lively for him if the tussock gangs came back into the district.

"Then there's Jock Hobbs and Don Hayes. Don's a cocky any-way, so I'm sure we could find a bit of dirt for him to work on. He says himself that he's a very slow tractor driver, but he's very patient, so he could be good with the sheep. He wouldn't lose patience with them if they get in the wrong race, or go out the wrong gate. Jock's selling football boots now, he was a lawyer, and it's worth having one of them around the place.

"AJ Whetton being an Aucklander wouldn't be a problem at all, but because he's so easy going, so casual, we'd keep an eye on him. When he was driving his truck, we'd make sure he was always pointed in the right direction."

Kel Tremain, who captained the Hawkes Bay side when Canterbury won the Ranfurly Shield in '69, attended Lincoln College as a teenage farm cadet, but it's his travel agent's business in Napier today that attracted Glenmark's attention. Explains Wyllie: "We've often had trips with the club, sometimes up to Blenheim, and they take a fair bit of organising. We've found in the past it can take up to a week to get up there and back. And with some of the front row forwards we're considering, the trips could take at least that long in the future."

It would also, Wyllie believes, in the light of the forwards, and some of the backs being considered for the scheme, be vitally important to have a man in the group with good connections with the breweries. "Not many players work for the breweries because too many are such good customers. But Waka Nathan would be very helpful indeed, with the swap-a-crate deals. He was with Lion for many years, so I'd say he was a vital member of the squad. When we were making the movie 'Old Scores' Waka had his own personal physiotherapist, and in this outfit he wouldn't be the only one. You'd almost need a team of physios and doctors.

"Andy Earl's got his own farm up the road, but if we could get him back to the club (he's a former Glenmark man), not only would he be familiar with the work on a farm, we also know we wouldn't lose any time with him wanting to rush off to the hairdresser. Just give him a curry comb and he'd be away laughing.

"Andy can cover several positions on the field, and so could Tony Thorpe (who played in Wyllie's 1980s Ranfurly Shield team). Tony worked on a farm as well, so that's a bonus.

"Graeme Higginson is an old Glenmark man, and he can do saddlery work. But I know from past experience you'd have to keep an eye on him. He's the sort of bloke who might be tempted to get a few of the others and bugger off to the pub. He could be a worry in that area.

"You'd have to look at the Tree, Pinetree Meads. He'd be a useful sort of footballer, and when you were fencing he could carry the fenceposts for you. He enjoys a couple of pints at the local.

"Sam Strahan (All Black lock from 1967 to 1973) is another farmer. He probably wouldn't want to leave where he is, up in the Manawatu, though. They used to call it millionaire's row, where his farm was. Tree mightn't want to leave the King Country either.

"Mind you, you might be able to negotiate with Tree. It'd be a new thing for him. They didn't have a lot of it in his day. Jokers tended to play for one club and not chop and change.

"We'd find an orchard for Pole Whiting (the towering All Black lock from 1971 to 1976) to work in. It'd be a big saving on ladders when the trees needed pruning. He's in the diamond importing business now, so he should keep all the women happy, getting them diamonds at a good price.

"I'm not sure that Andy Haden would go down too well. He'd be on the radio and television all the time, and we're not too keen on that stuff down here.

"I don't know whether Gary Whetton would fit into the farm life too well, although with the mobile phone, if he was rounding up sheep, he could always ring back and tell us if he got lost. And with his work at Panasonic, with the tie-ups to Fisher and Paykel, he could be a big connection for the housewives wanting cheaper household appliances.

"Then there's Hamish Macdonald, and now this group is starting to worry me a bit, because if you went very far, there wouldn't be many pubs left with any beer by the time you came back. Hamish would be there, but you'd hope he'd quietened down a bit, because he'd have a lot of mates in this outfit."

Which brings Wyllie to Alistair Hopkinson, who even played a couple of times for Glenmark in friendly end of season games. Wyllie says he isn't sure if the legendary Canterbury and All Black prop would want to make himself available again.

"When we played they were nor-west days, pretty hot, and Hoppy found it a bit tiring. He talks a fair bit, I suppose he could bluff his way through a lot.

"How seriously would he take it? He does make a joke out of most things, but I think there are enough serious minded players to keep him on the straight and narrow. Hoppy's a stock agent, which is good in one way, but there could be some problems with him and Bluey Arnold arguing. I don't know how they'd get on.

"Getting Hoppy home would be a worry too. We might have to leave Sid with him, but then we'd need somebody to drive the bus. We might have to look at a few more teetotallers like Michael Jones to balance things up.

"John Ashworth used to be in the area, and he'd be good. There were times when you could find you'd have trouble getting the Wish home too, I would think. It's that front rowers' club.

"Then there's the likes of Thimbo (Neil Thimbleby), you could always consider him. If you had any trouble loading sheep at the wharf, he could negotiate for you, having been a watersider. Of course he's off the wharf now, I think he made so much money when he was on it, but I'm sure he'd still have the contacts.

"Jazz (Brian Muller) would be a big help, because he could mow the lawns and mow the hedges at the same time, so you'd be saving on buying hedge clippers. He'd just take the lawn mower and carry on. If the mower was powerful enough he could prune trees with it too.

"Keith Murdoch would have to be there, because if you have any trouble with flat batteries he could just hook up a tow-rope to the tractor, or the truck, and he could just pull it to get it started.

"Chris Earl is in the area, and Murray Davie works at the freezing works, and Richard Loe could always go back to his family farm, but Stuart, Richard's cousin, could be a bit young to be mixed up with some of these older jokers like Hoppy. They could easily lead him astray.

"Steve McDowell works for the breweries, so he could always work at the local, but I'd hate to think what would happen if some of the other front rowers wanted to get behind the bar too. There's Kerry Tanner, who could run the pub for you, but he'd be a worry to you as well.

"Jules Le Leivre had a farm up in Culverden, but I wonder whether he'd want to work for anybody else, having been his own boss. Jules would certainly be handy, because he'd probably be a bit more sensible than some of these others, and keep them under control. Mind you, I've seen Jules play up a bit too. There are not many props that don't.

"With the front rowers we're looking at, Bruce McLeod would have to be in there somewhere. They'd be lost without him. He's looked after them many times.

"Tane Norton and Lyn Davis could always pair up, and work together, instead of arguing with each other about prices every time they meet. Lyn's retired now, because he's made enough.

"Andy Dalton would be able to make the speeches afterwards, because he's a good speaker, and I would say he should be able to give us all a very good price on farm bikes.

"In the current side, Sean Fitzpatrick used to be a carpenter, and now I think he's in a duty free firm. Either one could be useful. He could do a few repairs with the hammer and nails, and we could possibly send him overseas to make a few sales, especially in Japan, which is an important market for us. Gary (Whetton) would be good too, with his Panasonic connections, arranging some good prices in Japan.

"On the field, Fitzy could double as a winger, because he's covered that position before. In fact he's actually played there a few times, not officially, but he's been out there a few times."

From the days when Wyllie was coaching Canterbury, one hooker, John Mills, is automatically disqualified because he's a school teacher, while John Buchan, a solicitor, is farming in Ashley, south of Christchurch, so Wyllie doubted if he would be interested in moving from his own farm, even though his legal skills could be of some use.

Finding a manager for the team is something Wyllie says leads him to wonder if he really wants to be involved with it himself.

John Sturgeon, the current All Black manager, could, in Wyllie's opinion, almost lead to a walkout. "He'd be trying to keep them off the booze, and there'd be an uproar." Sturgeon sits easily with the current All Black team, who are very moderate in their social activities, but the Glenmark group under consideration might not be.

"We might have to consider several managers," says Wyllie, "or perhaps a flying squad that would follow us around each weekend."

Former Prime Minister, Sir Robert Muldoon, could make a good manager, Wyllie believes, as might Police Minister John Banks, if it wasn't for the fact Banks has always been involved with rugby league. "I think Muldoon might even join in the after-match functions."

Wyllie is not deeply concerned about the fact that not every player on his list of possibilities would be in peak physical condition. "We've got enough of them scattered around the district to only make it necessary for some of them to play every two or three weeks, which wouldn't be too bad. In the past in Glenmark we have usually taken the attitude that you shouldn't have a big medical team at the ground. If you needed a doctor, then you should be in hospital."

One official who could be invited is former Wellington coach and All Black selector, Earle Kirton, a dentist , who could attend not only to broken teeth, but might also be of vital importance as a taster now that vineyards are being established in the Glenmark area. "In winter he might be able to loan a few spectators a spare scarf or two," says Wyllie, "and you could always put some of the scarves out to flap around in the paddocks, frightening the birds away from the crops."

For social occasions, to ensure that the women of the district didn't feel neglected, Glenmark plan to approach former All Black, television frontman, and current Member of Parliament, Grahame Thorne. "Thorney would be in his element. He could talk about hairstyles and cooking," says Wyllie. "And JK (John Kirwan) could come into it too, discussing fashion with the ladies. He dresses up in very modern style, like a clown really."

Locally Glenmark would look to Barry Corbett, Ken Anderson and John Dunn to provide some publicity. Nationally, Paul Holmes might be approached, although some officials are concerned that Holmes might not be noticed if there was a rush to the bar, and could be trampled underfoot, or hit in the eye by a knee.

In summing up prospects for the scheme, Wyllie himself is thinking of a change of emphasis.

"When I think about having Hoppy, Hamish Macdonald, Higgy, Kerry Tanner, John Ashworth, and some of these other guys in one group, I think I'd look very hard at trying to get involved in running the local pub."

Footnote: Wyllie says that, in fact, it's impossible to try to narrow down all the players he'd been associated with over the years into a first XV, or anything remotely like it. "For a start you can't really compare the players of one era with the players of another."

But, if farmers ever got decent wool prices again, the players named in this chapter would at least begin a list of some farmworkers who might also prove handy on the football field.

THE LEGEND: *Alex Wyllie and Victor Simpson had a fist fight after disagreements over where Simpson should play in the Canterbury team.*

WHAT REALLY HAPPENED: *They wrestled. Simpson, who called himself "The Man of Steel", always believed he could throw Wyllie to the ground. Finally, after a training run, Wyllie was persuaded to join in the Canterbury team's version of World Wrestling Federation.*

THE WYLLIE VERSION: *"It didn't last very long."*

CREDIBILITY RATING (OUT OF 10): *0. They didn't have a real fight at any time.*

Legend

17

Two weeks
in the life

FRIDAY, AUGUST 9, 1991

Alex Wyllie, in the black and white Canterbury International company's All Black track suit, sits in the second to front seat of a large diesel bus, carrying him and the All Blacks across the Sydney Harbour Bridge on their way to training at the Sydney Football Stadium.

They'd woken that morning to another superb Sydney day. From his room in the front section of the Manly Park Royal Hotel Wyllie could pull back the curtains from the mock Spanish windows, and look out at the sun glinting on the water curving into the Manly foreshore. He thought about the rain and sleet at home, and understood why so many New Zealanders chose to live in Australia.

But there were more important things to think about than the exodus of Kiwis across the Tasman. The All Blacks had arrived on Wednesday, and, so far, everything had gone smoothly for the test on the Saturday.

It had been a very early start at the Poenamo Hotel on Auckland's North Shore on Wednesday morning. On the bus at 5.45am for the 8am Air New Zealand flight to Sydney. With the two hour time difference the team arrived at their hotel in time for an early lunch, and then had trained at an Army base at North Head, not far away.

That run had been good. Australian observers were amused to hear Wyllie comment, after the All Black backs had smacked into tackle bags held by the reserves: "You guys are pansies." Terry Wright had to cry off the run early. The Auckland accountant had some sort of infection, or slight poisoning, which had left him with a red rash on his leg, and a splitting headache that made him feel dizzy. He had recovered quickly, and was with the team heading for the football stadium.

Wyllie had been to just one game at the stadium in the past, the 1990 first test between the Wallabies and France. Most of the All

Blacks had never been there. On the '88 tour of Australia the matches in Sydney were all played at the Concord Oval. The All Blacks liked the Football Stadium a lot more than Concord Oval, where the playing surface was like a farm paddock. "The surface at the stadium is very good," says Wyllie, "and the dead ball areas are reasonably deep."

There's a maul of media people, who have to be cleared away before the All Blacks can get to work. The previous day the team had trained at North Head, in what was billed as a secret session. "It doesn't worry me a lot whether we have a private run or not," says Wyllie. "If you do things properly, it doesn't matter if the opposition know or not. But it was offered, it was easy to close the Army barracks off, so I thought, why not? We didn't do anything special. We just looked at the defensive patterns we wanted to use. The Australians used a lot of moves off the scrum that were really copied from us. They'd stated in the papers that they'd studied videos of our play. So we had to make sure that we stopped those moves around the scrum."

On the day before a test match, the run is not heavy, or leg deadening. A quirk of the stadium's design is quickly revealed to all. The tiers that make up the beautiful looking stadium leave a gap that the wind can whistle through, and a westerly that earlier in the week was very strong is still blowing. To make it more comfortable for spectators, canvas has been stretched across the gaps, but the canvas can't keep all the wind out.

Greg Cooper, the reserve fullback, and Grant Fox, had slipped into the stadium late on Thursday afternoon to check out their goalkicking. Fox had landed 20 out of 20. Cooper says to Wyllie: "From about six feet to ten or twelve feet there's a fair sort of wind blowing. But when you kick the ball above that height, the wind must disappear, because the ball doesn't move at all." So for 20 minutes Wyllie and the team prowl the field. Fullback Wright tries some kicks for touch. Halfback Graeme Bachop kicks the ball high, the way he might over a scrum or ruck. Then the players all stretch, do some quick grid work, and then have a brief run as a 15. It all feels good, so Wyllie calls the session off.

Down in Wollongong, at the North Beach hotel, the Australians have been relaxing all day, playing lawn bowls, and getting ready for a 24 hour media ban. Captain Nick Farr-Jones says he hopes people will understand why calls are not being connected after 2pm. "I just feel we've had a lot of media attention this week, which has been great. But we need to make sure everybody's feet are firmly on the ground, and guys are allowed to concentrate on the task ahead."

The All Blacks take the bus back to Manly, and then they have free time until a team meeting at 6.15pm. The forwards meet for a few lineout drills at 5 o'clock anyway. Some of the backs go into the city on the Manly fastcat, others drift in and out of rooms. If they read that night's Telegraph Mirror they find that scalpers are offering $35 seats for the test for $150, and getting the cash. "It's the most sought after test we've ever had," says an Australian Rugby Union official. A Brisbane bookmaker is offering official, legal, odds on the All Blacks at 10 to 9, and on the Australians at 5 to 4.

Wyllie is due to meet a friend from Lion Breweries, Max Travers, at 8 o'clock, but in the New Zealand social whirl that engulfs the central city Travers can't get to Manly, so Wyllie joins a few of the New Zealand media contingent at the hotel for a quiet meal. He's in bed at about 11.30pm. Even as a player, on the night before a test he didn't like trying to get to bed extremely early, and then not being able to sleep.

SATURDAY, AUGUST 10

The first phone call of the day for Wyllie comes from Paraparaumu, from a private radio station, 2XX. On the Saturday morning sports show run by Aaron Cardie and Wally Blackburn, Kapiti Coast listeners are the first people in New Zealand to hear Wyllie speculate on what he says will be a tough test for the All Blacks. That interview is over by 7.50am, Australian time, but the telephone calls, most of them from journalists, don't stop, including the regular Wyllie discussion on 3ZB.

As on most test match mornings, there is little chatter amongst the players, or with Wyllie. The players go through their rituals, Wyllie goes through his cigarettes.

Today, when the team boards the bus for the Sydney Football Stadium, there are two policemen on motorbikes to lead the way, holstered guns slapping on their hips. But Sydney cops don't take the point role with the flamboyance that the French, or even the British, do. The traffic in the central city is very heavy, down to a crawl as they near the stadium, and the All Blacks arrive at 2 o'clock, right on the deadline they'd want for a 3 o'clock kickoff.

Down the ramp into the changing room, and Wyllie finds immediately that, while the stadium looks superb, there are many strange design quirks. The biggest is the fact that when it rains almost all the spectators in the plastic bucket seats get drenched. The rain swirls around the stadium in a way that Sydney reports have compared to the effect of a washing machine.

There's a wall in the changing room, that actually splits the team into two groups as they strip, change and stretch. The previous day, Wyllie had envisioned the reserves changing on one side, the 15 starters on the other. It doesn't quite work out that way, but they cram in for a final word before the referee, Ray Megson, blows the whistle to call the teams into the tunnel. Gary Whetton leads the side down the blue vinyl of the tunnel, and they run on to the stadium turf, as 41,565 people roar loudly enough to drown out the brass band.

Anthems are played, with Michael Jones, Zinzan Brooke, and Grant Fox clutching the silver fern on their chests. Andy Earl's body language spells aggression, as he stands with clenched fists on his hips, a tough guy in town looking for trouble. Steve McDowell leads the haka, and then Fox kicks off.

In the first 20 minutes, things mostly go the All Blacks' way. Wallaby coach, Bob Dwyer, will say later that weathering the early storm was a vital part of the Australian game plan. "You don't need to be a genius to work out that the All Blacks will put on early pressure."

For Wyllie, the start is better than he might have hoped for. The ball goes through the All Black backline twice. That's the plan, to move the ball wide, to test the defence of David Campese and Rob Egerton. And the early stress is on the Wallabies, which is more important to Wyllie than many, probably including Dwyer, might realise. "Something that's always worried me about this All Black side was that we'd never had a lot of pressure put on us before. It's a bit the same with Auckland, they never have a lot of pressure on them, and we have so many Aucklanders in the team. So a worry at the back of my mind has always been what we'd do under pressure. What if some team took it to us? Are we in a position to withstand it?"

Those doubts don't need to surface for much of the first half. After 17 minutes Fox kicks a high punt to the Australian right wing, and Campese, playing his last test for the Wallabies in Australia, knocks the ball down into his own in-goal area. Ian Jones is following up quickly, and dives on the ball for the try. Fox converts from the touchline, and it's 6-0.

Three minutes later the Wallabies equalise. A missed touchfinder by Fox from the Wallabies kickoff lets the Australian captain, Nick Farr-Jones, punch the ball back to within two metres of the All Blacks line. From the lineout there is a patently obvious Australian knock-on, but referee Megson awards the try to Tim Gavin. Michael Lynagh converts, and it's 6-all. Megson an Edinburgh solicitor, grew up in Sydney, his family returning to Scotland when he was 12. That night he will tell Wyllie he realised later the try should not have been awarded. Wyllie will reply: "I'm not blaming you for that. We all make mistakes - players, coaches, referees."

As halftime approaches, with Lynagh and Fox swapping penalty goals to make it 9-all, Wyllie is pleased with the way the All Blacks have gone. They've withstood the challenge of an Australian team running hot, with the fans, and the news media right in their corner. It hasn't led to arrogance in the Australian camp either. On the morning of this test Simon Poidevin, playing his 19th test against the All Blacks today, says "for any rugby player worth his salt, playing against the All Blacks represents the ultimate test of skill and courage. To an Australian rugby player it has the added dimension of a trans-Tasman contest where, traditionally, Australians have been regarded as the low life, the poor cousins."

The poor cousins start to do better after halftime. Richard Loe is penalised for wrenching the ball out of a maul, and Lynagh kicks the penalty. Australia ahead 12-9. At 22 minutes comes a vital break for the Wallabies. Megson penalises the All Blacks for pulling down a scrum. Sean Fitzpatrick is outraged at the ruling. "I think it was the only scrum all day that collapsed like that, and we certainly didn't pull it down. It simply caved in."

Wyllie is just as adamant. "It wasn't as if the Wallabies were going for a pushover try. They were twenty yards out from our line. He pinged us for it straight away, but later on scrums collapsed and he didn't do anything. That night he told me he'd seen our fellows pull it down. I said that was fair enough, but it was the one thing that really upset them. They said they definitely didn't pull it down." On the field the anguish is compounded when Lynagh kicks the penalty, and the Australians go out to 15-9.

Four minutes later the game is sealed. A Lynagh kicks pitches on the point of the ball as it lands, and John Kirwan is left stranded as Egerton flies away for a try converted by Lynagh. Australia ahead 21-9. Fox kicks another penalty with eight minutes to go, so the test is won by Australia, 21-12.

The Australians lap the stadium, and throw their changing room open to media and friends. The All Blacks, as always, run a tighter ship, but when Wyllie, Whetton, and manager John Sturgeon, face the media in a first floor room of the Sydney Cricket Ground, next door to the stadium, there is no whining or excuses. The trio sit under a sign advertising Australian Airlines, Driza-Bone oilskin coats, and XXXX beer, some of the sponsors of Australian rugby. Wyllie manages a smile when asked if he thinks the Australians have played All Black tactics in the test, after studying videos of previous All Black games. "Perhaps they liked what they saw," says Wyllie.

Had Wyllie's confidence been shaken for the World Cup? "Not at all, I've said before that if you play Australia three times a year, beating them three times hasn't been done many times before. How much better they can get, who knows? We know very well we can play better."

Any special things, asks a Sydney journalist, about the Australian side that impressed him? "This is one of the most complete sides Australia have had. They're very strong in the lineouts. We knew it was going to be hard to win the ball on their throw-in. They can use their backs, they're a very complete side."

Two weeks to repair the damage. Is that enough time? "Yeah. I believe it is. We have to cut down on the mistakes we made. We'll work on that."

Dwyer and Farr-Jones arrive. They don't crow. Dwyer is asked how he rates the win. "I don't think it was awful pretty, but it was very powerful and determined and effective. I suppose last year when we beat the All Blacks we might have taken them a little bit by surprise, maybe, because they'd won the two previous ones, and maybe there wasn't so much riding on it for them. In this one they would have been concerned about the publicity the Australian team were getting, and also, they would have well remembered Wellington. So we can probably draw more pride from today's win. People have been saying beware the wounded All Black and I think that was the case. So it makes it a pretty good win. Probably the best win I've had."

Had Dwyer heard suggestions that the Bring Back Buck campaign had been superseded by the Bring Back Willy O campaign? "We've got him, we're going to keep him. It was a bad mistake to let him go - by Tonga."

Farr-Jones sits turned almost to one side, looking like a man who thinks saying too much could incite the All Blacks in the next test.

"It's difficult to analyse a game when you're out there playing it. There were a lot of mistakes made. But I think that's an indication of how good both teams are, because they put a lot of pressure on each other. The defence is very good from both teams. A lot of things didn't go as we planned today. It's just the nature of the opposition. They're so much better, they put a lot of pressure on you. I think the All Blacks were playing a very good Australian team, so don't bucket the New Zealanders."

What was the atmosphere in the changing room? Did the thought of Eden Park in a fortnight inhibit celebrations? "No, it's jubilation. You don't beat the world champions week in, week out. The guys were absolutely delighted to have beaten New Zealand before we go to Auckland, and then the World Cup. But that's the third game of what we hope will be ten this year, so it's important you keep your feet on the ground."

Farr-Jones notes that the game will lift the image of rugby, against league in Australia, and says he could hear, on the field, the cheer from the crowd when it's announced that the crowd is a record. "It was like, 'There you go leaguies, we beat you.'"

Can Farr-Jones single anybody out from the team? "I don't like to, but Michael Lynagh kicked brilliantly in general play. People don't realise what a terrific bonus that is to the team. It's just so important you get those extra ten metres. In the forwards, the guy who played nineteen tests against the All Blacks (Simon Poidevin),

I find it astonishing that he's managed that."

Farr-Jones gets really animated when asked who he smiled at in the stands while the anthems were being played. His wife Angela, and their new baby, Jessica, had been there, and he'd been able to pick them out. A huge smile spreads over his face. "I don't want to get sentimental about it, but, yeah, it was nice. Puts a smile on your face."

He only digs into New Zealand once. He's disappointed that the Bledisloe Cup isn't being played on a one-off basis. The Australian executive should have put more pressure on New Zealand, then most of his team could have experienced the thrill of winning the Bledisloe Cup. As it is now, if the All Blacks win in Auckland, the series is tied, and the Cup stays in New Zealand. "It should have been a one-off test."

The conference is closed down. The All Black and Australian teams return to Manly, for a low key dinner at the Park Royal, where Wyllie gets into an unusual conversation with test referee Megson.

"You won't believe this," says Megson, "but the people back home won't believe the way I refereed this game today."

Wyllie is set back on his heels a little. He asks Megson to explain what he means.

"They just won't believe it at home. Normally I would have blown that game just about off the field. Ask my wife Kim. Isn't that right, Kim?" Kim Megson agrees. Wyllie says he can't believe what he's hearing.

"You wait and see what happens with the next referee (from Scotland), who'll take the test in Auckland. He blows up things a lot more than I do."

Wyllie says: "Hell, if you're going to keep doing this to the game, you'll stuff it within two or three years. One of the problems we've got at the moment is too many stoppages. Look at what happened when (Roger) Quittenton and (Clive) Norling came out for the last World Cup. They thought they were the top refs, and they went home with their tails between their legs because they weren't kept for the final games. Norling realised the mistake they'd made. He became number one, but number thirty-one on the field. He got into the game, and made it a game. He spoke to the players, they had confidence in him and knew where they stood. If you won't do that, you'll stuff the game."

Megson sticks to his guns. "The rules are there, and we play to the rules."

Well, says Wyllie, that's the attitude that'll ruin the game for everyone.

There's not much else to be said. The dinner winds down early, at about 10.30, and the Aussies are soon gone. Wyllie, like most of the All Blacks, doesn't leave the hotel. On the night of a test loss, the

All Blacks don't wreck hotels or start scraps.

SUNDAY, AUGUST 11

The day starts at 6.20am with a wake up call, and the team shuffle quietly on to the bus at 6.45. The bus meanders out to Kingsford Smith airport. The All Blacks are flying home economy class, on an Air New Zealand flight loaded with supporters, some of them in much worse shape than anybody in the team. To France the previous year, and to the World Cup, the All Blacks enjoy business class. The change isn't some sort of punishment for a poor performance. "Three and a half hours (from Australia) in economy is easy enough to handle," says Wyllie.

He is back at his Ilam Rd home in Christchurch after 6pm. He manages a few hours there, and then he drives back to the Russley Hotel, near the airport, to see John Hart, who has coached the New Zealand Colts to a 61-7 victory over the Australian Colts. Hart describes the New Zealand team as the best motivated side he has seen since the 1985 Auckland team who won the Ranfurly Shield (which Hart also coached). The two discuss the Colts game and the test.

MONDAY, AUGUST 12

The phone rings almost constantly through the morning at Wyllie's home, but at lunchtime he is able to get enough clear space to drive his dark blue Toyota Celica into the city, to the old library chambers on the corner of Cambridge Terrace and Hereford St. On the first floor, across the landing from New Zealand Cricket's headquarters, is Herbert and Company, also the office of Margin Release Ltd, the promotions and marketing company that Wyllie works for when he's not coaching (he is not paid for coaching the All Blacks).

Wyllie is there to sit down and run through his diary with Chris Herbert, a man whose aversion to publicity could be compared with Keryn Wyllie's. In a city where reserve is a way of life, Herbert plays things so close to the chest even close friends are confused about where he fits into the scheme of things with Wyllie. On the wall of Herbert's office there is a photograph of the club cricket team Herbert plays for. Look closer and you'll see Wyllie there too, as well as Victor Simpson, Brian McKechnie, Doug Bruce, Scott Cartwright, Richard Wilson, Joe Leota and former New Zealand cricketer Brian Andrews.

The connections between Wyllie and Herbert go well beyond a shared enthusiasm for cricket. In 1970 Herbert was a teenager, back at his parents' home in Wanganui after a year working on a station in the Ruahine ranges. His parents knew some shorthorn cattle breeders who knew Wyllie's parents. On the rural grapevine it was passed around that Wyllie needed a good keen boy in case he was selected for the South African tour. Young Chris seemed to fit the bill, so one Sunday afternoon he glanced out the lounge window to see Wyllie striding up the drive. Herbert would have packed up that day.

He worked on the farm at Glenmark for just over a year, living in a farmworker's hut behind the house, then occupied by Alex and Keryn, which now houses Joe and Jean. Herbert played on the side of the scrum for Glenmark that season, the first time, as Wyllie enjoys reminding him, for about a decade that Glenmark didn't win the championship.

By the time Herbert moves back into the city to attend Lincoln College he is going out with Adrienne Sloss, Wyllie's first cousin on his mother's side of the family. Herbert finishes a Diploma of Agriculture, and then he and Adrienne marry in 1973. They strike out overseas, and, after three years in England, Herbert can't settle to the pattern most men of his background do, either working for the Ministry of Agriculture, or a stock firm.

He humps empty beer bottles for 12 months, and then stumbles, almost by accident, into real estate. He's an employee for six years, and then sets up his own business in 1983, which he runs to this day.

There is a streak of the entrepreneur in Herbert, sparked during his time out of New Zealand. He plays a game of indoor cricket, senses the potential in the sport, and develops two of the country's first modern stadiums. After a couple of years he sells out.

During all this time he wonders how Wyllie manages to make a living. Farming, Herbert knows, is making no money, and Wyllie is spending an increasing amount of time embroiled in rugby. Herbert even talks to Bernie Brown, the former 3ZB sales manager, in Auckland, suggesting Brown might be able to discuss promotional work with Wyllie.

Brown and Wyllie talk, and Wyllie turns up one day in Herbert's office. Typically, Wyllie is blunt. "Okay, what are we doing?"

Herbert studies the amateur regulations, talks at length with Jock Hobbs, the former All Black captain, and a lawyer, about amateur regulations, and sets up Margin Release.

His first task for Wyllie is a Cooper and Lybrand television advertisement. The ad, for the large accountancy firm, is set up by a former Auckland rugby player Kevin Ramsey, now the advertising man behind the 1991 television commercials for the Auckland team. Ramsey puts Wyllie in what purports to be a training run, in which one of the players is also Wyllie's accountant. That player isn't spared some cutting remarks from Wyllie. There is humour in some rugby circles at what sounds like Wyllie berating "Harty". Sadly for that story the scripted name is "Harding."

As with all Alex Wyllie's TV commercials, Herbert negotiates the deal. "I could establish Alex's worth. If he'd been approached directly he might have taken a fraction of the fee finally agreed to." Herbert also goes through the contracts and scripts.

With the contracts he hunts for clauses that might see Wyllie tied up for several years, with no ability to renegotiate. That's not an uncommon occurrence in celebrity advertising. At the start of the World Cup campaign Herbert refused to sign one major contract until he was satisfied the finished commercial didn't have the potential to overexpose Wyllie in the market.

There is also the issue of doing the right thing by Wyllie as far as his image and rugby coaching goes. The Cooper and Lybrand ad probably strained the fabric as far as the New Zealand Rugby Union went. Nothing was ever said, but Herbert picked up clear hints that too many more showing Wyllie so closely associated with coaching wouldn't be appreciated.

On the other hand, Herbert was in a frenzy of indecision over the ad Wyllie did for Rexona deodorants. That's the one where Wyllie's expression doesn't change as sub-titles announce that he's worried, nervous, and, finally, overjoyed.

"Rexona had used top sports people in the past," says Herbert, "like Ivan Lendl and Susan Devoy. I didn't want Alex standing there in a bathroom putting on deodorant. But the name of the product, dry solid in a black pack, fitted okay."

At the Lintas agency in Wellington the concept of using the public image of Wyllie as an intensely stone-faced rugby watcher was developed. Says Herbert: "I thought it'd work, but I really hesitated about using something so very personal to Alex to hawk a product. It isn't an act when he sits in a stand poker-faced. I felt very awkward about commercialising that image."

The first night the ad ran it was a matter of moments before the telephone rang at Herbert's home.

On the line was a prominent Christchurch businessman.

"You've denigrated the guy," he told Herbert.

By the time the painful conversation had finished Herbert's spirits were down to zero. Thankfully a series of calls over the rest of the night told a different story. Others had been amused, and unoffended, by the commercial.

There were no self doubts for Herbert about the Mitre 10 commercial in which Wyllie and a rugged group of rugby mates are picked up in a limousine by Welsh actor Windsor Davies. Says Herbert: "I've seen Alex a hundred times round the farm in a t-shirt like that. The production was good too. That's been something we've always looked at with the ads. The key to TV advertising is quality. If it's a cheap production, we don't go near it."

Not that all the work Wyllie does for Margin Release is in front of cameras. There are several long term, thriving business associations that, to date, haven't involved television.

An association with Toyota began back in the Canterbury Ranfurly Shield days, when Wyllie, as the coach, was provided with a car. There were cartoons and satirical columns galore when the Shield went. Who would get the car back from Wyllie?

As it happens, no one. Wyllie still drives a late model Toyota, and he frequently talks at Toyota sales meetings. There is a close relationship with Jack Wills, Toyota's marketing manager in Wellington, and in Christchurch Gary Donnethorne, and in Auckland Andrew McKenzie at Giltrap Toyota, men quick to help Wyllie in many ways.

Wyllie is one of the most frequent travellers in New Zealand. Darrell Park, now Air New Zealand's commercial manager for the south, often smoothes the way for Wyllie, who picks up air tickets around the country the way most people buy a bus pass. "One of the great things with Alex is that he isn't a taker," says Herbert. "Nine times out of ten any business relationship he develops is a lasting one."

New Zealand Breweries is another organisation that Wyllie, through Margin Release, has a flourishing relationship with. You can see Wyllie in many South Island bottle stores, looming in cardboard effigy over trays of Canterbury Draught beer. The contract with New Zealand Breweries means that when Wyllie speaks at a rugby club, the club isn't footing the bill.

The relationship with New Zealand Breweries was formalised two years ago, and, after a slow start, is now thriving. "Everybody knows where they are now," says Herbert, "and it's working brilliantly. Our main contact is Stu Burt, and he's very organised. He does a good job."

Without the commercial tie-ins, Wyllie wouldn't be able to make the rounds of so many small New Zealand rugby clubs. "It's great," says Herbert. "With the structure in place, people in Gore and Nightcaps and Cromwell and Napier get to see and meet the All Black coach."

Once the deals are set up, Herbert doesn't hover at Wyllie's shoulder, which is one of the reasons Herbert recoils when he's called Wyllie's manager. "I don't enjoy being around Alex when he's coaching the All Blacks, and I suppose I've only heard him speak at a function a couple of times, no more than that. I like to keep my profile low, although now I'm looking after Chris Harris (the Canterbury and New Zealand cricket player) I suppose I'll have to be more public."

On this August Monday, Wyllie and Herbert are comparing diaries, an essential task with Wyllie so committed. Just once in three years has Herbert been twitchy about Wyllie fulfilling an engagement. Wyllie was in Auckland during the day, seeing several people. Herbert, trying to double check, was, on the telephone, always one place behind him. At 5 o'clock Herbert got a phone call. "I'm here," said Wyllie. He had just arrived at Christchurch airport.

The diaries are a mass of appointments. There had been rugby clubs to speak at in Invercargill, Dunedin, Fairlie, Ashburton, and three in Christchurch in the fortnight before the All Blacks went to Australia for the test in Sydney, as well as three provincial matches, and a New Zealand Rugby Union meeting in Wellington. In that fortnight Wyllie had spent one free day at home, on Sunday, August 4.

They look at the lists for the rest of August and September. They are just as busy. Herbert has the video of the test in Sydney, cued to the try awarded to Tim Gavin. The replay clearly shows the Australian knock-on.

Wyllie drives back home. He changes into work clothes, goes to the back of the section, and doesn't finish chainsawing branches and tree stumps until it's too dark to see. As the sideline experts gather to condemn there's something satisfying about the bite of the saw's teeth into wood.

TUESDAY, AUGUST 13

Wyllie is up early, and driving through lingering mist to the farm at Glenmark by 7am. He goes around the paddocks with his son, Craig, looking at how the grass is freshening up, and checking on the ewes and early lambs. Across the road at his parents' place his father has a fire going in the paddock near the house. Wyllie gets behind the wheel of the tractor, and uses the blade at the front to push a few logs into the blaze.

He's back in town in the late afternoon, checks out a few more points with Herbert, and then heads for a Marist rugby club function in the city. He's joined by former All Black wing Stu Wilson, and the Kiwi league team's manager, Frank Endacott. There are plenty of questions after the speeches, and Wyllie is not heading home until about midnight.

WEDNESDAY, AUGUST 14

The 9.30am Air New Zealand flight out of Christchurch to Auckland leaves on time, and Wyllie is checking into the Airport Travelodge by 11am. He arranges a conference room for himself, John Hart and Lane Penn to gather in after the Counties-Otago game that afternoon. They are scheduled to pick the All Blacks for the second test on the 24th.

As soon as the door closes on the room he'll stay in that night, Wyllie is on the phone. He rings Hart, to confirm that Hart will pick up Wyllie and Penn on the way to the provincial game in Pukekohe. Then he rings physiotherapist Dave Abercrombie. Michael Jones has been to see Abercrombie, and a minor leg injury is clearing up. Kieran Crowley, on the other hand, cannot be considered for the test, says Abercrombie. His calf muscle needs more time to heal. Penn arrives at 12.30, Hart not much later. The trio travel to Pukekohe.

Counties win, 24-22, with the 20-year-old Counties lock, Mark Cooksley, dominating the lineouts. But he won't be a shock selection in the All Blacks that night. In fact, there will be no selections in the All Blacks that night. With Hart in New Zealand with the Colts, and Wyllie and Penn in Argentina and then in Australia, the three men have never had the chance to sit down together and compare notes on how the various candidates are shaping up. It's agreed they'll delay naming the side until the following Saturday morning.

THURSDAY, AUGUST 15

In the morning Wyllie fields media calls about the delays. "I suppose some people might have thought we'd had disagreements over the team," says Wyllie, "but that wasn't the case at all. In fact we had a hell of a good discussion, and we probably could have picked a team last night. But there were still a few players with injury worries, and we all wanted to have another look at the video of the Sydney test, so we delayed it until next Sunday. I didn't see any need for picking the team in a hurry. If there were any surprise selections I think the players wouldn't have had any trouble getting the week off for the test."

Wyllie flies back to Christchurch in the early afternoon, and that night, along with Stu Wilson, who has been in the city doing some public speaking, he goes to Rangiora to talk with a Canterbury sub-unions netball team. The All Black coach, and the former All Black captain, talk about preparation, the approach to playing the game, and training. Wyllie wonders aloud why the netballers train for two hours when their matches last one hour.

FRIDAY, AUGUST 16

There's an early flight to Wellington, for a meeting with the New Zealand Rugby Union, going over plans for the World Cup. Wyllie also talks with New Zealand Breweries executives, discussing future work with them.

SATURDAY, AUGUST 17

Wyllie flies to Auckland to see the final of the Auckland club championship between Marist and Ponsonby. John Kirwan, Terry Wright, Zinzan Brooke and Bernie McCahill are turning out for Marist, Craig Innes, Va'aiga Tuigamala, Joe Stanley and Olo Brown for Ponsonby.

The game has been moved from Eden Park to Western Springs, a speedway stadium, which has one of the best drained football fields in Auckland in the centre of the cinder track. After one of the wettest winters in history in Auckland, the Springs offers a good surface, but only average viewing facilities for rugby. Wyllie watches the curtainraiser, between University and Pakuranga, in an old wooden commentary box, which at least gives him the height to observe the game clearly. He stretches his legs before the main game begins, and finds, when he returns, that Andy Haden is sitting next to Wyllie's spot. Haden has a big set of headphones clamped to his ears, and exchanges not a word with Wyllie during the main game. Haden, who has been dismissing the efforts of the All Blacks in general, and Wyllie in particular, is someone Wyllie says he'd like to have a heart-to-heart talk to. "It amazes me how Andy can bag some guys that he says are his mates."

Marist win the game, 13-9, with Ponsonby rarely in the hunt. Wyllie doesn't linger for aftermatch socialising. He joins Stu Burt, from New Zealand Breweries, to race to Napier, where, months before, he was committed to speak at a dinner for the top supporters of the clubs in the Hawkes Bay. The date had been set when, in theory, the All Black team would have been long since named. There is no flight from Auckland to Napier in the late afternoon, so Wyllie and Burt face a hectic four-and-a-half hour drive to Napier. They're barely out of Auckland when they hear Murray Deaker, on 1ZB, slamming Wyllie's decision to make the speech. It would seem, Deaker tells his listeners, that the All Black coach thinks it's more important to make money than to select the national team. Wyllie, whose whole upbringing is geared to keeping promises, no matter how inconvenient, is outraged. Not only is he not being paid for the speech he makes in Napier, but he wonders if Deaker realises the time that rugby demands of people like himself during the winter. Says Wyllie: "I can't say what I think of Deaker."

SUNDAY, AUGUST 18

At 6.45am Wyllie is on the telephone. He talks through the team selection with John Hart and Lane Penn. Wyllie is booked for a 9am flight that will get him back to Christchurch that morning. His daughter Kirstin is having a family 21st at home. By the time Wyllie is able to get a flight through Palmerston North to Christchurch it's getting towards 3pm before he is home.

The All Black team sees just two changes. Aucklander Bernie McCahill replaces North Harbour's Walter Little, and Andy Earl, the blindside flanker in Sydney, is replaced by the Auckland openside flanker Mark Carter, with Michael Jones going to the blindside in the scrums, and No 6 in the lineouts.

In Auckland Deaker is talking on 1ZB with Hart. It's difficult not to read between lines in many of Hart's responses.

Deaker asks if we have no better tight forwards than the group he says were outplayed by the Wallabies in Sydney. Hart says: "The fact of life is that at the moment the tight five are probably the best that offers in New Zealand. We were very disappointed with their performance in Sydney. I think they might have been disappointed too. It's no use changing players for the sake of changing. I think we need to get better focus. Need to get our motivation right. Need to get our organisation right. And I have no doubt that if the tight five are focused, motivated and organised, they have the ability to not only equal the Australian tight five, who are very good, but to beat them. If we're not able to do that, with our best players, then the All Blacks have got problems."

Deaker: "John, you know, you take the implication out of that that they weren't focused for the first test."

Hart: "Well, I think in a way, you know, the tight five got very loose. Maybe we played the game...the way we played the game early...led to that. Whilst a lot of people say we played exceptionally well in the first twenty minutes, I'd question that. Whilst we looked a little bit fizzy, and we moved the ball around, we didn't take any prisoners, we didn't put any pressure on the Australians, and in the end, we might have taken the tight five out of the game. I think we've got to get our focus right to get the tight five into the game, and get back to some good old-fashioned forward play."

Deaker: "I couldn't see a game plan last week, John."

Hart: "No, well, I don't disagree with that. We'd have to have some concerns about the way that game developed, so maybe we didn't get it all right in terms of our preparation for it, although everyone says our preparation was very good. In the end, you've got to have the right game plan, and you've got to go out and play it. I think there's been a misnomer about playing the wide game, Murray. I mean, playing the wide game is a word that everyone seems to be using. What we've got to do is play a fifteen man game and play it in the right areas of the ground, and promote all players."

Hart talks of several players. Graeme Bachop was "light years" ahead of every other halfback earlier in the season, but no halfback would have had a happy time behind the All Black forwards in Sydney. Buck Shelford remained very much in the selectors' total approach to the World Cup. The selectors didn't share the view that Zinzan Brooke had a bad game in Sydney. AJ Whetton and Mike Brewer were not considered because of injury. "We do nothing for them, or the All Blacks, by playing them when they're not fit."

Walter Little has not been sacrificed, says Hart. He's unlucky, and Hart feels sorry for him. "We've gone for a little more experience in the midfield."

Deaker: "John, a lot of people have been asking me in talkback this question, are you, John Hart, going to get involved in the coaching of this team this week?"

Hart: "I certainly enjoyed working with the Colts last week, Murray, and I guess, if I'm needed, and there's a role for me, I'm available."

Row back on some of the Hart statements, and you see why he and Wyllie could have an uneasy relationship. "I think we need to get better focus. Need to get our motivation right. Need to get our organisation right." Who was most responsible for focus, motivation and organisation with the team in Sydney? Wyllie. "Whilst a lot of people say we played the game exceptionally well in the first 20 minutes, I'd question that." Who was one of the people who thought the All Blacks had played well early in the game? Wyllie. "I don't disagree with that (there being no game plan for Sydney)." Who was most responsible for there being a game plan in Sydney? Wyllie.

Hart is not a man who makes unconsidered public statements. Perhaps on this occasion three unguarded comments slipped through in as many minutes.

MONDAY, AUGUST 19

There's another trip to the farm, and a function to attend in the evening. While Wyllie is in the Omihi Valley, wheels are spinning in rugby. Pressure has been going on Lane Penn to step down from his position as assistant-coach at the World Cup. Lobbying in New Zealand rugby doesn't involve a lot of people, but it can be intense for all that. New Zealand Rugby Union chairman Eddie Tonks has been championing the cause of John Hart as assistant-coach since 1989, and Malcolm Dick, manager with Hart on the tour to Japan in 1987, when Wyllie was Hart's assistant, is another strong backroom booster of Hart's. Dick says privately that he's concerned about Andy Haden's public campaign for Hart, which may have become counterproductive.

Wyllie attends a rugby function in Christchurch in the evening. He'll be leaving early for Wellington.

TUESDAY, AUGUST 20

Wyllie, Hart and Lane Penn meet with Eddie Tonks and Malcolm Dick in Wellington, and while most people are finishing breakfast, or on the bus to work, the issue of who'll coach the team in Auckland, and, on to the World Cup is discussed. The meeting isn't publicised, and it isn't reported at the time. Eventually it's agreed all three selectors will be involved with the training of the team in Auckland. What role each will play will emerge once the All Blacks begin their preparation.

The All Blacks assemble in the late afternoon at the Poenamo Hotel, and the players are told the training run the next day will be at the Naval Base in Devonport. Everybody in the squad drives a few kilometres down the road to Devonport that evening for a meal at Porterhouse Blue, a popular non-vegetarian restaurant named after a biting British novel by Tom Sharpe, in which a Porterhouse Blue is the name given to a stroke suffered after over-eating.

WEDNESDAY, AUGUST 21

The All Blacks wake to the sound of rain splashing into the pool that the Poenamo's rooms surround. It's the sound Aucklanders have become familiar with in recent weeks. And when the team squelch on to the rugby field at the Devonport Naval Base, the heavens are beginning to open. Great sheets of rain sweep over the players.

Hart is taking a much bigger role in the training than Lane Penn, which will lead to cruel jibes, most notably by Andy Haden on *Boots 'n' All*, about assistant-coaches being at training to prop up goalposts. Wyllie has decided to give Hart a full role in the training, so the effects of Hart's input can be fully measured.

At night the whole team goes to the trots at Alexandra Park. A small school strike a quinella worth more than $1000, but in most cases the hottest tips go cold on the crushed seashell track.

THURSDAY, AUGUST 22

By tradition this is the day of the key training run for a test team. The All Blacks will spend the day at Whenuapai, an Air Force base 20 minutes' drive from the All Blacks' hotel, past semi-rural blocks of land, gradually being swallowed up by urban sprawl.

There's a watery sky at 10.05am, as the Newmans cruiseliner carrying the All Blacks rolls past the immaculate lawns that border the roads inside the air base.

At the main rugby ground the blue and white goalposts are topped with red and black streamers, attached overnight by a fiercely loyal Cantabrian who works at the base. The ground is in good condition, unlike Eden Park, where they are still considering ways of removing surface water.

Wyllie, John Hart and Lane Penn, all in black and white All Black tracksuits, stroll on to the ground together. They'll be watched closely through the session, after the amount of publicity given Hart's role in the Devonport run. Jim Blair, the fitness expert, is there as well, in a blue Adidas suit. He'll run the early part of the session.

At 10.10 the first All Blacks arrive, and go through their stretching rituals. In 1961 a French forward stunned New Zealanders at the first training run in the country by relieving himself against a goalpost. There won't be anything so startling here. The All Blacks use these goalposts for nothing more dramatic than keeping their balance while they stretch their hamstrings and calf muscles. Zinzan Brooke amuses himself by taking 15 or 16 footballs out of a gear bag one by one, and seeing if he can gently punt them down the field so that all end in one group about 20 metres away.

Blair starts a basic warm-up exercise, the players darting and weaving through a confined area, flicking a ball from man to man. Hart calls to the players to "communicate, keep communicating, use your names, use your names." The players run, not too quickly, darting out of each other's way. Blair stops the first exercise, and then it gets busier. The players are in groups of three. When Blair yells "down" the ball goes down on the ground. One man dives on the ball, and then flicks it up to restart the game.

The game gets livelier. Craig Innes doesn't want to stop. He takes the chance to tackle John Timu to the ground. Hart is yelling at the players to keep the passes to the pit of the stomach, not at chest level. Wyllie joins in, urging the team to rip the ball free. Blair starts calling names. When a name's called that player has to race from the group to slam into one of four tackle bags being held outside the exercise area. Timu hits a bag that hard it slides five metres across the slightly muddy surface.

Hart winds the game up more. When a name is called the group of three around the man must all fly out and hit a bag. "You're not exploding quick enough." Wyllie isn't as loud, but he's talking to the players too. "Concentrate. Think about what you're doing."

There's more urgency still. "How many tackles will you have to make on Saturday?" asks Hart. "Everyone's going to count." By now there's mud smeared over all the players. Michael Jones bowls one tackle bag, then, called to switch, races across diagonally and smacks another. Sean Fitzpatrick grunts like a professional wrestler as he slams a bag. Wyllie tells the team to "communicate, make the calls, listen for the calls." Hart says: "This time the bloody names are going to be called quick." Players are bumping into each other. Innes bumps Timu over. Gary Whetton drives into a tackle bag. And then Jim Blair says "stop".

It's 10.30, and now they're all warmed up Blair calls them into the middle of the field, where they jog on the spot in two lines, flipping footballs between them. The training so far has been much like a full rugby game, with brief periods of intense activity. The difference here is that when the bursts stop the players go to ground and stretch some more.

Dave Abercrombie, the physiotherapist, has already worked on Walter Little's back, and is now helping Steve McDowell with hip extensions, bending McDowell's thigh over to loosen the hip joint. McDowell is a great believer that flexibility is one of the key elements for a prop forward.

After five minutes of loosening and stretching, Blair moves the team down to the ingoal area for the traditional grid games. Now the players are divided up into groups of three. Andy Earl, John Kirwan and Richard Loe are together, Graeme Bachop, John Timu and Gary Whetton together, the backs' heads coming to the middle of Whetton's chest.

At 10.38 the grids change pattern again. "Drag a bit more out of yourself," says Wyllie. "Give us your guts, you'll need it on Saturday." Now there are four footballs going. Imagine a square, with players at each corner, running to a centre point where footballs are passed. The potential for collision is enormous. Blair keeps reminding the players to take the ball at pace. Wyllie urges the players to "keep your timing and communicate."

Three minutes into the grids Walter Little goes down, clutching at his calf muscle. He's taken to the sideline by Abercrombie and Dr John Mayhew. They take off Little's right boot, and examine his calf muscle. It doesn't look promising. He's taken away by Mayhew and manager John Sturgeon, swinging off their shoulders, with his feet off the ground. (Little will drop out of the squad and be replaced by Joe Stanley).

At 10.45 the grid pattern gets even more difficult. The players in the middle, instead of taking the pass and moving on in a straight line, turn 90 degrees and run to the corner to their right. McDowell pushes a short pass to Kirwan that looks as if it'll drive the winger's ribs back.

Five minutes later the grids stop, and the team splits into backs and forwards. Hart and Penn move to the centre of the field with the backs, Wyllie heads towards an old wooden scrum machine, weighted down with petrol tins filled with sand, with the forwards. The backs swing quickly into action, Hart yelling "Score the try, score the try" as Timu skids over the tryline, unopposed. Jon Preston feeds the ball into the All Black scrum. Wyllie needs no artificial aid to whistle the team up. The whistle through the teeth that works for sheepdogs works for All Blacks.

Wyllie, Whetton, Loe and McDowell discuss the scrum formation. Wyllie once propped a couple of scrums in an international, against Scotland's Mighty Mouse, Ian McLauchlan, who, it was reported at the time, said that Wyllie was the best scrummaging prop in the All Blacks. Wyllie spends some time with Loe, the tighthead, examining the stance, the bend of the knees. The forwards grunt into the machine, weighed down more by reserves sitting on top of it. In the fourth scrum Wyllie demands that the forwards don't ease off. When they develop a second heave that bounces the machine back, he whistles them to stand up. After six scrums with the machine, a live pack is stitched together.

The All Black forward reserves are joined by New Zealand B lock Robin Brooke, and Waitemata club players Darrell Wells, Willie Lose and Adam Martin, with team doctor Mayhew at No.8.

"Get in there and push," says Wyllie. The scrums rattle on. While the forwards are working, Hart drills the backs. They should be very familiar with each other, Bernie McCahill having played outside Fox for Auckland for four seasons.

At 11.30 the team joins together, working at kick-offs. Hart, acting as one of the opposition, is tackled to the ground by Michael Jones. "Beautiful tackle," says Hart, as he climbs to his feet. Moments later Andy Earl drives Hart back as well.

After ten minutes of kick-offs the backs are almost ready to quit the field. Sean Fitzpatrick keeps throwing the ball in. Fox tries a few up and unders to Terry Wright, who almost bowls a straying toddler as he concentrates on a high ball.

By now Wyllie and Hart are together with the forwards. In turn they tell the players to concentrate, not to leave any gaps. The drills are working quickly, Bachop at halfback, Jon Preston at first-five, to catch the ball and flick it back for another lineout. It's now clear where the players will be in the lineouts on Saturday. McDowell at the front, then Whetton, Loe, Ian Jones, Brooke, Michael Jones and Mark Carter at the tail.

At noon the session is over. Whetton sits beside the northern goalposts to allow a better eyeline with a woman reporter from England's ITV, whose crew is shooting a documentary.

Wyllie drifts across to a group of radio and print journalists. Loe wanders past, and is asked by an Auckland journalist if he'll pause for an interview. "No thanks," he says quite cheerfully. "I've been jerked enough by journalists lately." (Loe has been suspended from his Waikato team, after published statements his coach, Glenn Ross, considers an insult to the rest of the team).

Wyllie agrees that the training ground surface has been good, but notes that conditions at Eden Park may not be so ideal. "So perhaps it might not have been so good training in conditions we won't strike in the game."

Will he go back to the mud at Devonport on Friday?

Wyllie chuckles. No, possibly not.

What they will do the next day is possibly go to Eden Park, have a look, see what it's like.

Wyllie's asked what he thinks about the No 4 referee in Scotland having charge of an All Black-Australia test. You might, he says, have possibly thought the World Cup referees would have been sent out for the Bledisloe Cup games. The impromptu conference becomes less like a quiz, and more like a discussion British journalist, Terry O'Connor, says it's a bit cock-eyed, but because the Scottish referees didn't make the World Cup panel, they were given the tests in Australasia. You would never guess from the mood of the gathering that Wyllie has sometimes been presented as a difficult man for the media to deal with.

A major job, says Wyllie, has been to lift the players up, after they were brought down by criticism during the week. Can they lift themselves enough to win? "It's a matter of going out there and proving they've got the ability to do it. I'm still confident we can match them. In the first 20 minutes in Sydney we had pressure on them, but we didn't break them and score points. We've got to do that now."

What will his final message to the team be, asks John McBeth, from Radio New Zealand. Wyllie smiles. "I mightn't be able to say that over the radio, John." Says McBeth: "Well, cut out the swear words." Wyllie says, "It's just a matter of putting together what we've talked about, what we've trained for. Time spent over the years, just don't let ourselves down now."

The group breaks up, Wyllie wanders over to a mini van, being driven by the liaison man for the All Blacks, old Christchurch friend, Kevin Gimblett. The All Blacks, the journalists, and the 100 or so rugby fans disperse. By 12.30 the only reminders of the training run are the red and black streamers fluttering from the goalposts.

It's decided that Little's ankle is too tender to be risked on the Saturday, even as a reserve, so Joe Stanley is called in to join the team. For the afternoon and evening the team are free, but most stay at the hotel. For so many sportsmen, and the All Blacks are no exception, a lot of time between events and training is spent watching reruns of old movies on TV.

FRIDAY, AUGUST 23

The morning call is for a short run, which is held straight across the road from the hotel, at the Onewa Domain, home of the North Harbour provincial team, and the Takapuna club side. There wouldn't be anything to remember about it, except that Grant Fox bumps his ribs, and, although it isn't announced at the time, there is an immediate fear he may not be able to play in the test.

For the rest of the squad there's time to let off steam at the Takapuna indoor bowling centre. Some of the players are dynamite, Craig Innes bowling like he tackles. Richard Loe almost creates a sensation by winding up so hard that his bowling ball flies off his hand behind him, scattering fellow All Blacks the way Loe had hoped it would scatter 10 pins.

A phone call is made to Simon Mannix in Wellington, and the young first-five is booked on the early morning plane to Auckland. On the eve of such a vital test, a new first-five may be on the books for the team.

SATURDAY, AUGUST 24

Simon Mannix takes the 7am flight from Wellington to join an All Black camp that some are saying is the least supported of any team in living memory. On a radio talkback show in Auckland on the Thursday night, Nick Farr-Jones and Peter FitzSimons, the big Sydney journalist who has just missed out on selection for the Australian World Cup squad, are astounded when people, who say they are New Zealanders, urge them to defeat the All Blacks.

When the All Blacks' bus pulls into Reimers Ave, on the northern side of Eden Park, it becomes obvious to the players that a few disgruntled callers to talkback radio are not the real voice of the people. There have been waves, toots from cars, and numerous thumbs up signs before they even leave the bus. There are more expressions of goodwill as the team stride into the North Stand. And when Gary Whetton and the team clatter down the concrete ramp to follow the Wallabies on to Eden Park the roar from the crowd is as loud as the famous ground has ever heard. A loss in Sydney, Whetton muses later, might have been behind the "fantastic" support.

Very early in the game it becomes obvious to the 30 players and 43,000 spectators that there's something strange going on with the Adidas ball, the one that'll be used at the World Cup. Grant Fox and Michael Lynagh, the two best goalkickers in test rugby, are struggling to kick the ball between the posts. Two of the balls, Fox notes, are patently out of shape. Later it will be discovered that both balls had been grossly over-inflated. By Murphy's Law it's the distended balls that are most often in play when the kickers are shooting for goal.

There's an urgency about the All Black forwards that wasn't there in Sydney. Nick Farr-Jones could recall getting just one ball delivered cleanly enough to him from a ruck in the first half at Eden Park to be of use in attack. And Farr-Jones' flyhalf, Michael Lynagh, is being boxed off by the All Black loose forwards. In one vital moment in the first spell Lynagh runs, because Michael Jones is covering the man outside Lynagh. Staying two or three metres inside Jones is Mark Carter. Carter will say later: "Our (the loose forwards) main goal was to disrupt Lynagh, which I think we did. He's the pivot of their backline the way Foxy is to ours. That time he (Lynagh) ran, Jonesy was on the second-five. I just couldn't believe my luck. He was just there, waiting to be hit." Carter's tackle on Lynagh is fair, but teeth-rattling. Carter would say: "Once we got Lynagh that first time, their backline didn't look threatening."

At 16 minutes Fox bombed the ball from near halfway, and, as it drifted down near the Wallabies' 22, Zinzan Brooke, whose first half, especially, would draw praise from a tough critic, former All Black captain, John Graham, springs into the air to win possession.

The Australians are penalised for killing the ball in the subsequent ruck, and Fox is finally able to kick a goal. The All Blacks take the 3-0 lead to the halftime break.

It isn't the lead the team might have expected from the effort that's gone in, although just two minutes into the second half, after John Kirwan is brought to ground 30 metres from the Australian line, Fox gets a kick at goal with one of the correctly inflated balls, and makes it 6-0 to the All Blacks.

There are mixed feelings about the second half. At the ground the closeness of the score, and the run across the field during an injury break by two topless Australian women, whose exotic dance routine at the Poenamo's nightclub later that week reveals them to be known professionally as the "Cheeky Chicks", keeps most of the crowd engrossed. But the referee, a 39-year-old fire officer from Scotland, Ken McCartney, is playing an increasing role in the match. McCartney, ranked No 4 in Scotland, is, like his countryman Brian Megson who refereed in Sydney, not considered good enough to take a World Cup match. The only conclusion that can be reached is that he and Megson have got the Bledisloe Cup games as consolation prizes for missing the World Cup. Farr-Jones describes McCartney's appointment as "very strange. Perhaps they (the Scottish appointment board) don't regard the Bledisloe Cup as very important. But it's very important to us."

Over the whole match McCartney awards 18 penalties to the Wallabies and 15 to the All Blacks. He rarely plays advantage, and, while he is technically correct when he resets every scrum in which players slip over, on the greasy Eden Park surface playing the spirit, rather than the letter, of the law about collapsed scrums, would have made more sense. With 11 minutes to go Lynagh kicks his first penalty goal. He had volunteered to step down and let fullback Marty Roebuck kick (remember that during the game the goalkickers didn't know for sure which ball was over-inflated), but Farr-Jones asked him to bash on. Lynagh was hitting the ball sweetly enough, Farr-Jones believed, but something was happening to it in flight. There was something happening in flight, and it wasn't anything a change of kicker would correct, just a few seconds of deflation.

At 6-3 into the last minutes, captain Whetton begs his team to avoid giving away penalties. But tension will do strange things in a big game. Farr-Jones, universally recognised as the best halfback in the world, is chastised by coach Bob Dwyer for bobbing the ball in the air from the base of a ruck, while falling backwards as he lost his footing. A tough, physical player, Farr-Jones would normally have set up another, more stable, ruck. Dwyer is also critical of an attempted dropped goal by Tim Horan two minutes from time. "That's trying to fluke a win (in the series), not earn it, which is not good enough."

In the last 60 seconds, the Wallabies have a chance to draw the game. McCartney awards his second to last penalty, for All Black forwards killing the ball in a ruck. Lynagh has the agony of seeing yet another of his kicks swing wide. Fom the dropout David Campese launches into a run and a kick ahead. When he slaps the ball forward he's penalised. Fox kicks the ball to touch, and throws his hands up in pleasure as McCartney blows for the end of the game.

Moments after the final whistle Farr-Jones is interviewed by Brendon Telfer, an experienced and capable Television New Zealand sports reporter. On this occasion, Telfer badly misreads Farr-Jones' mood. Farr-Jones, disappointment etched into his face, notes that he had thought, when Lynagh kicked his last penalty, that the ball was on target. "One last question I'd love to ask you," says Telfer, "did your concentration go when those streakers appeared on Eden Park?" Farr-Jones is heading for the changing room as he snaps, "Nah."

The disappointment is still very clear to see 40 minutes later at a print and radio conference in a long, narrow, varnished wood-panelled room jammed with Australian, New Zealand and Japanese photographers, and about 40 journalists. It has been apparent in Sydney, and is even more apparent in Auckland, that the Bledisloe Cup means a lot more emotionally to the Australians than it does to the New Zealanders. The result at Eden Park means that the All Blacks, since rugby tests between the countries have begun, have scored 64 victories to the Wallabies' 23. So, just as a Kiwi league win over Australia is a cause for near hysteria in New Zealand, the Wallabies want the Bledisloe Cup so badly you can just about taste it.

Farr-Jones is subdued, and honest. "We're not real happy. I guess our biggest disappointment is that we haven't got the Cup. Campo's now played 55 tests and won it once."

What had changed since Sydney? "We weren't so good. They were a lot better in the first half than they were in the first test. We're disappointed with our own performance."

Were the Wallabies complacent? "I don't think so. I don't think we thought before this game that we'd climbed Everest. But...I understand the All Blacks watched the first test on tape over and over again. They really analysed it. We were a bit jovial when we looked at the tape. We'd won, we were happy. I don't believe we really analysed it. We'll sit back and look at our performance in this test, and think, 'hang on, we've got to go better in these areas.'

"Perhaps in November we'll look back and be glad about what happened today. You wouldn't be real happy if you played stunning rugby for your first eight tests, and then lost in Dublin."

Dublin? The possible semi-final of the World Cup. "If things go according to favouritism we should meet New Zealand there. I think New Zealand will probably have a tough job on October 3 (against England at Twickenham). If we're as good as we think we are, we should get through our pool and the quarter-final."

Farr-Jones goes when coach Dwyer arrives. Dwyer is a man with a great turn of phrase, who doesn't hold back on what he thinks about rugby.

The test? "It was a pretty ordinary game really, which was a shame. I thought it was a race to see who was the worst, and we won. (Pause). Just by a little bit."

Could the Wallabies have won? "With some patience and composure in the last minutes we could have won it. We didn't have the composure to do it. That's our fault, and nobody else's. The good news is that we'll talk long and hard about it, and learn. It's a bitter lesson, but if we don't learn it we're not good enough to go through for the World Cup."

Dwyer says he rates the Bledisloe Cup, because of the two teams involved, as on a par with a World Cup final, and reveals the Australian camp's feelings going into the second test. "How often do you get where you're 100 per cent certain you could win a Bledisloe Cup...and not win it? It's extremely disappointing."

By contrast the All Black leaders, Whetton and Wyllie, are happy, but far from exultant. Whetton jokes about the stitches he's just had in his head. "I don't know how many there were, I couldn't see." It was, he says, a game the All Blacks had wanted very badly. "The crowd support really made us proud to be representing our country."

Wyllie says the whole All Black team had played well. The first test had been a learning experience. Now the tight five had picked their game up, which gave the loose forwards a better shot at their game. The forwards as an eight playing better gave the backs a better chance.

"So, overall, today was an improvement in Sydney. A lot of work has gone in this week. A lot of thought by the players, and we worked as a selection panel with the team."

Now the aim was, as it had been from the start of the season, to have the squad at peak fitness for the World Cup. "If we don't win the World Cup, everything else will be forgotten."

Footnote: On Friday, September 6, after the World Cup squad of 26 is named, it's announced that John Hart will be co-coach of New Zealand at the Cup. Wyllie, says New Zealand Rugby Union chairman Eddie Tonks, will have "ultimate responsibility" for the team.

ALEX WYLLIE FIRST
CLASS CARREER

PLAYING

	M	W	L	D	T	C	PG
Canterbury/Canterbury SU	214	153	55	6	42	10	7
New Zealand	40	31	6	3	12	-	-
Trials	13	6	6	1	2	-	-
South Island	8	2	6	-	-	-	-
Scottish President's XV	1	-	1	-	-	-	-
Ian Kirkpatrick's XV	1	1	-	-	1	-	-
Centurions	1	-	-	1	-	-	-
President's XV	1	-	1	-	-	-	-
	279	**193**	**75**	**11**	**57**	**10**	**7**

CAPTAINCY

	M	W	L	D
Canterbury	108	78	28	2
New Zealand	3	2	-	1
Trials	4	2	2	-
South Island	3	1	2	-
	118	**83**	**32**	**3**

COACHING

		M	W	L	D
Canterbury	1982	17	12	4	1
	1983	19	18	1	-
	1984	18	16	1	1
	1985	19	15	3	1
	1986	19	15	3	1
		92	**76**	**12**	**4**
NZ Colts	1987	4	3	1	-
New Zealand	1988	15	14	-	1
	1989	19	19	-	-
	1990	13	10	3	-
	1991	11	10	1	-
	Tests	23	20	2	1
	Other	35	33	2	-
		58	**53**	**4**	**1**